NEWPORT HIGH SCHOOL FOR GIRLS

Form	Name	
R3	Georgia Bishton	10 co 1

GCSE for AQA

COMPUTER SCIENCE
Student Book

David Waller

Course consultant: Ann Weidmann

CAMBRIDGE
UNIVERSITY PRESS

University Printing House, Cambridge CB2 8BS, United Kingdom

Cambridge University Press is part of the University of Cambridge.

It furthers the University's mission by disseminating knowledge in the pursuit of education, learning and research at the highest international levels of excellence.

www.cambridge.org

Information on this title:
www.cambridge.org/9781316504048 (Paperback)
www.cambridge.org/9781316504079 (2 Year Online Subscription)
www.cambridge.org/9781316609989 (Site Licence Online Subscription)
www.cambridge.org/9781316504017 (Paperback + 2 Year Online Subscription)

© Cambridge University Press 2016

First published 2016

Printed in the United Kingdom by Latimer Trend

A catalogue record for this publication is available from the British Library

ISBN 978-1-316-50404-8 Paperback
ISBN 978-1-316-50407-9 2 Year Online Subscription
ISBN 978-1-316-60998-9 Site Licence Online Subscription
ISBN 978-1-316-50401-7 Paperback + 2 Year Online Subscription

Additional resources for this publication at www.cambridge.org/education

Approval message from AQA

This textbook has been approved by AQA for use with our qualification. This means that we have checked that it broadly covers the specification and we are satisfied with the overall quality. Full details of our approval process can be found on our website.

We approve textbooks because we know how important it is for teachers and students to have the right resources to support their teaching and learning. However, the publisher is ultimately responsible for the editorial control and quality of this book.

Please note that when teaching the GCSE Computer Science (8520) course, you must refer to AQA's specification as your definitive source of information. While this book has been written to match the specification, it cannot provide complete coverage of every aspect of the course.

A wide range of other useful resources can be found on the relevant subject pages of our website: www.aqa.org.uk

Contents

Introduction

Computers and our lives

There isn't any area of our lives that isn't dependent on computers. There was probably a computer involved when you were born and most likely there will be when you die. And in between, computers will have an impact on every single aspect of your life. It's easy to think computers are in control of so much of our lives. But of course they aren't. It's the people who control the computers who are in charge. Controlling the computers is what this GCSE is all about.

Why learn Computer Science?

Learning about computers and how to use them is important. But that is not a good enough reason for you to study computer science. You could just as well say that you need to learn how cars are made before you drive one, or learn how to build a house before you live in one. Obviously learning how to use and do things is important but education is about much more than that.

Computational thinking

You should study computer science because it affects your brain and the way you think. Computer science is all about formulating, tackling and solving problems in a particular and unique way. A computer scientist coined the term 'computational thinking' for the way in which problems are analysed and solutions are created and tested. And the solutions must be explained clearly and unambiguously because they are going to be carried out by a computer – a mindless machine. If it can't understand an instruction it doesn't pause and try to work it out. It just stops and refuses to budge!

So studying computer science will develop your **problem-solving abilities** – which will be useful in whatever you choose to do after your GCSEs. It will help your **clarity of communication**. And it will also develop your **creativity** – anyone can paint any old picture, but creating a masterpiece takes skill, creativity and work. In the same way, producing a creative solution to a problem in an elegant, efficient way needs these same skills.

How to use the book

The book is divided into 15 chapters which cover all of the content listed in the specification.

At the start of each chapter are the expected **learning outcomes** – what you should understand and be able to do by the time you reach the end of the chapter.

Throughout the text there are **activities** for you to complete. These will help you to see if you understand the ideas covered in the text and are able to apply the concepts to solve problems.

Each chapter contains a **challenge**. This is where you can use computational thinking, creativity and your coding skills to produce solutions for larger, real-life problems.

There are **real-life examples** at the start of each chapter and throughout, to help you understand how computer science is important to everyday life.

There are features throughout the book to help you build knowledge and improve your skills:

Tip

Tip boxes provide helpful hints.

Maths skills

Maths skills boxes highlight the key mathematical skills that you'll need for computer science.

Key term

Important computer science terms are written in **orange**. You can find what they mean in the **Key term** boxes and also in the **Glossary** at the back of the book.

Remember

These appear near the end of each section to help your understanding. Look back at these useful summaries to **remember** for your revision and before completing the final challenge in each chapter.

⚑ Watch out

Watch out boxes help you to avoid making common mistakes.

WORKED EXAMPLE

Worked examples guide you through sample answers to help you understand methods of answering questions.

📝 Practice questions

Practice questions give you a taste of how your knowledge and skills will be assessed.

Working on Cambridge Elevate

Cambridge Elevate is the platform which hosts a digital version of this student book. If you have access to this digital version you can annotate different parts of the book, send and receive messages to and from your teacher and insert weblinks, among other things.

As you work through the student book, you will find links to Cambridge Elevate. You can use these to watch animations explaining concepts from the book, complete interactive activities and download worksheets to help you reinforce your learning.

🎥 **Watch the bubble sort algorithm animation on Cambridge Elevate**

⬇ **Download Worksheet 1.1 from Cambridge Elevate**

💼 **Complete Interactive Activity 1a on Cambridge Elevate**

IMPORTANT NOTE:

AQA has not approved any Cambridge Elevate content.

1 Algorithms

Learning outcomes

By the end of this chapter you should be able to:

- explain what an algorithm is and create algorithms to solve specific problems
- use sequence, selection and iteration in algorithms
- use input, processing and output in algorithms
- express algorithms using flowcharts and pseudo-code
- analyse, assess and compare different algorithms
- create, name and use suitable variables
- use arithmetic, relational and Boolean operators
- use conditional statements.

⭐ **Challenge: create an algorithm to help a taxi company calculate fares**

- By the end of this chapter, you should have a thorough knowledge of how algorithms can be used to solve complex problems and how they can be displayed using flowcharts and pseudo-code.
- An algorithm is a step-by-step procedure for solving a problem. It can be followed by humans and computers.
- Your challenge is to create an algorithm to help a taxi company calculate fares.

Why algorithms?

Algorithms run our world! In every area algorithms are used to decide what action should be taken in a particular circumstance. As computers can consider all the possibilities far more quickly than a human brain, they are becoming more important to the running of the world. Here are just a few examples:

- In a game of chess, when each player has made three moves, there are over 9 million possible moves available; after four moves there are over 288 billion. Computers have the ability to consider all these possible moves far more quickly than humans. That is why no chess grandmaster has beaten a top computer chess algorithm since 2005.
- Algorithms are used by financial organisations to trade shares on the stock market. A computer following an algorithm can decide which deal to make far more quickly than a human and a split second difference can be worth millions of pounds.
- Closely guarded algorithms are used for internet searches to make them quicker and the results more relevant to the user. They will even auto-complete the search terms based on previous searches.

Algorithms are used to control automatic-pilot systems in airplanes. If you have flown in an aeroplane, you have probably been piloted by an algorithm!

What is an algorithm?

An algorithm is a step-by-step procedure for solving problems. It is a set of instructions that can be followed by humans and computers.

We use algorithms to carry out everyday tasks often without thinking about them. For example, an algorithm to solve the problem of getting ready for school might be:

Get out of bed.

Shower.

Get dressed.

Turn on kettle.

Put bread in toaster and turn on.

Wait for kettle to boil and make tea.

Wait for bread to toast, butter it and add marmalade.

Drink tea and eat toast.

Gather school books and put in bag.

Put on shoes and coat.

Leave the house.

Watch out

In an algorithm, the order in which the tasks are carried out is very important to its success or failure. For example, this algorithm would not be very successful if 'shower' was placed after 'get dressed'. The sequence is very important.

Key terms

sequence: the order in which tasks are carried out
sub-tasks: small steps making up a larger task

The algorithm shows the sequence of tasks. Different people will design different algorithms, as they will do things in a different order, meaning there can be many solutions to the same problem. Some of these tasks could be further divided into sub-tasks as they might be made up of smaller steps.

For example, 'showering' could involve many different steps including turning on the shower and setting the correct temperature. If all the possible sub-tasks were included, the complete algorithm would get very large and complicated.

ACTIVITY 1.1

Create an algorithm for someone who has never made a cup of tea before to follow, in order to make a cup of tea successfully.

Compare it with other members of your group. There will probably be differences, for example some may include the addition of sugar.

Download Worksheet 1.1 from Cambridge Elevate

This example seems pretty easy. However, like a typical algorithm, it is simply a list of steps. Here is part of another algorithm which is the start of a recipe to make a perfect meringue.

1. Tip 4 large egg whites into a large clean mixing bowl (not plastic). — **SEQUENCE**
2. Beat them on medium speed with an electric hand whisk. — **SEQUENCE**
3. Keep beating until the mixture resembles a fluffy cloud and stands up in stiff peaks when the blades are lifted. — **ITERATION** **SELECTION**
4. Now turn the speed up and start to add 115 g caster sugar, a dessertspoonful at a time until there is none left. — **ITERATION** **SELECTION**
5. Continue beating for 3–4 seconds between each addition. — **SEQUENCE**

In addition to sequence, this algorithm has two new elements: iteration and selection.

Iteration means doing things over and over again. The cooks have to beat the mixture and then stop and ask themselves if it resembles a fluffy cloud. If it does not, they have to beat again, check again, beat again and check again until they are convinced they have made a fluffy cloud. There is also repetition when adding the sugar. It has to be added a spoonful at a time until there is none left.

Selection means making decisions. As well as doing things over and over again, the cooks have to make a decision. Does it resemble a fluffy cloud?

Key terms

iteration: a procedure or a set of statements or commands is repeated either for a set number of times or until there is a desired outcome

selection: a question is asked, and depending on the answer, the algorithm takes one of two courses of action

Complete Interactive Activity 1a on Cambridge Elevate

ACTIVITY 1.2

Using sequence, selection and iteration write an algorithm that a person (who has never done this before) could follow in order to successfully prepare a bath with the water at the correct temperature. Annotate the algorithm to indicate sequence, selection and iteration.

You could set it out as shown in the table below where the first four tasks have been done for you.

`Put plug in the bath.`	Sequence
`Turn on hot tap.`	Sequence
`Is the water at the correct temperature?`	Selection
`Turn cold tap until water is at the correct temperature.`	Iteration

What makes a successful algorithm?

The two most important criteria are:

- **Correctness**: it successfully solves the problem

- **Efficiency**: it solves the problem in the least possible time.

List A is the 'getting up' algorithm we looked at earlier. List B is similar but with the sequence slightly altered.

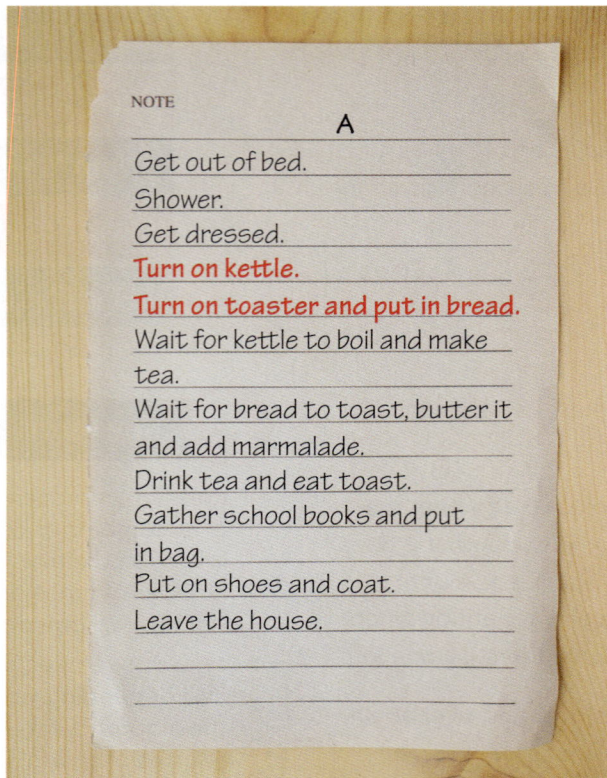

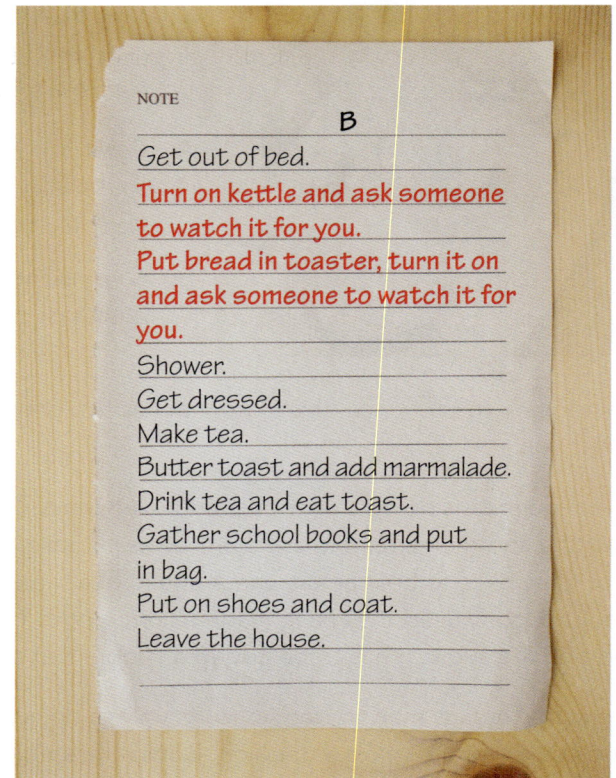

NOTE

A

Get out of bed.

Shower.

Get dressed.

Turn on kettle.

Turn on toaster and put in bread.

Wait for kettle to boil and make tea.

Wait for bread to toast, butter it and add marmalade.

Drink tea and eat toast.

Gather school books and put in bag.

Put on shoes and coat.

Leave the house.

NOTE

B

Get out of bed.

Turn on kettle and ask someone to watch it for you.

Put bread in toaster, turn it on and ask someone to watch it for you.

Shower.

Get dressed.

Make tea.

Butter toast and add marmalade.

Drink tea and eat toast.

Gather school books and put in bag.

Put on shoes and coat.

Leave the house.

Watch out

The algorithm is now more efficient and also safer; it would not have been safe to leave the kettle and toaster unattended. Computer scientists must consider health and safety issues when designing real-life solutions.

List B is more efficient as it could be implemented in less time. The kettle and the toaster are turned on before taking a shower and so the water will boil while the person is showering. There will be no waiting time.

An algorithm for a computer

Now let's look at a simple algorithm that we could create for a computer to follow, instead of a human. Computers are ideal for obeying orders and carrying out actions over and over again. In fact, that is their main function.

It is important for the temperature in a shopping mall to be kept at a set value. It will keep the shoppers comfortable and it will help to prevent condensation on glass shop windows and slippery floor surfaces. Here is an algorithm intended to be used to control the temperature in a shopping mall and maintain a temperature of 20 °C.

1. Check the temperature.

2. If the temperature is greater than 20 °C, then turn off the heaters and open the ventilators.

3. If the temperature is less than 20 °C, then turn on the heaters and close the ventilators.

4. Go back to instruction 1.

This is a simple algorithm but it includes the basic building blocks:

*   *Sequence*: there is a list of instructions in the correct order.

*   *Selection*: the 'if' statements in instructions 2 and 3 allow a decision to be made and an action to be taken.

*   *Iteration*: instruction 4 tells the computer to go back to instruction 1 and so the sequence will run over and over again indefinitely.

> ### Remember
>
> 1. An algorithm is a step-by-step procedure for solving a problem in a finite number of steps.
> 2. The basic building blocks of algorithms are sequence, selection and iteration.
> 3. The criteria for a successful algorithm are correctness and efficiency.
> 4. An algorithm must be translated into a programming language before it can be executed by a computer.

Flowcharts

Flowcharts can be used to represent algorithms visually.

They use symbols connected by arrows to show the flow of the algorithm.

The symbols used are:

This represents the start or end point of the flowchart. You always start and finish your flowchart with this symbol.	
You use this to represent data input or data output. For example it could be a number or name entered by a user.	
You use this where a decision has to be made. It is also called selection. It will contain a question, for example: 'Is the temperature greater than 20 °C?' If it is, then an arrow will point to a task to be carried out and if it is not, then an arrow will point to a different action.	
You use this to represent a process that must be carried out by the algorithm. In this example it is used as a result of one of the questions that has been asked, e.g. 'Turn on the heaters' or 'Turn off the heaters'.	

Watch the flowcharts animation on Cambridge Elevate

WORKED EXAMPLE

Here is the flowchart of an algorithm to calculate the area of a rectangle:

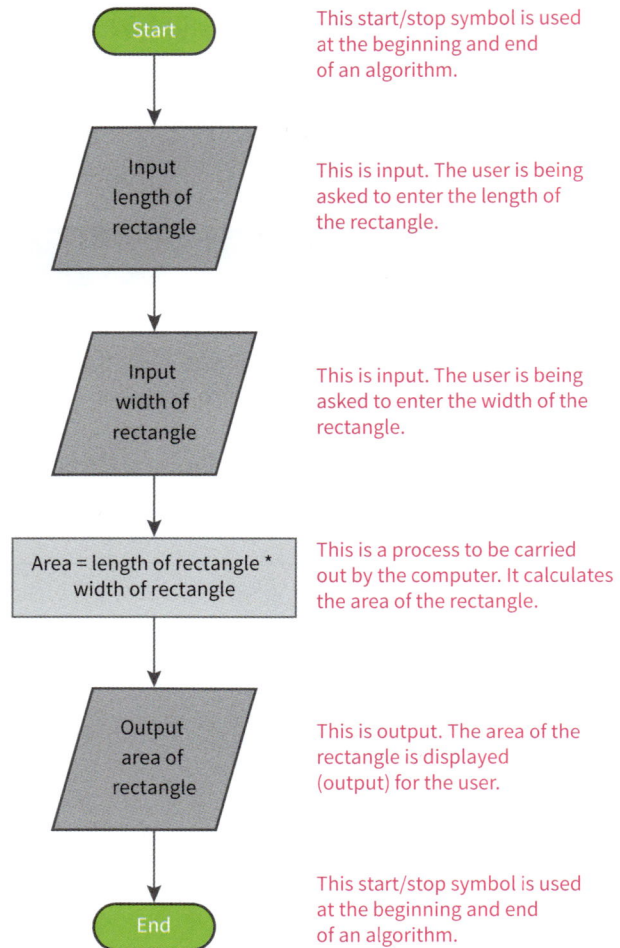

Start	This start/stop symbol is used at the beginning and end of an algorithm.
Input length of rectangle	This is input. The user is being asked to enter the length of the rectangle.
Input width of rectangle	This is input. The user is being asked to enter the width of the rectangle.
Area = length of rectangle * width of rectangle	This is a process to be carried out by the computer. It calculates the area of the rectangle.
Output area of rectangle	This is output. The area of the rectangle is displayed (output) for the user.
End	This start/stop symbol is used at the beginning and end of an algorithm.

There are two inputs of the dimensions of the rectangle, a process to calculate the area and an output of the area.

In this example, there is just sequence: a list of tasks to be performed.

Complete Interactive Activity 1b on Cambridge Elevate

ACTIVITY 1.3

At the end of each day, an ice cream seller calculates how much money he has collected. Assuming that the ice creams all cost the same amount, draw a flowchart of an algorithm that would output the total amount collected during the day.

WORKED EXAMPLE

Here is a flowchart of an algorithm to identify a vertebrate animal. It includes sequence and selection.

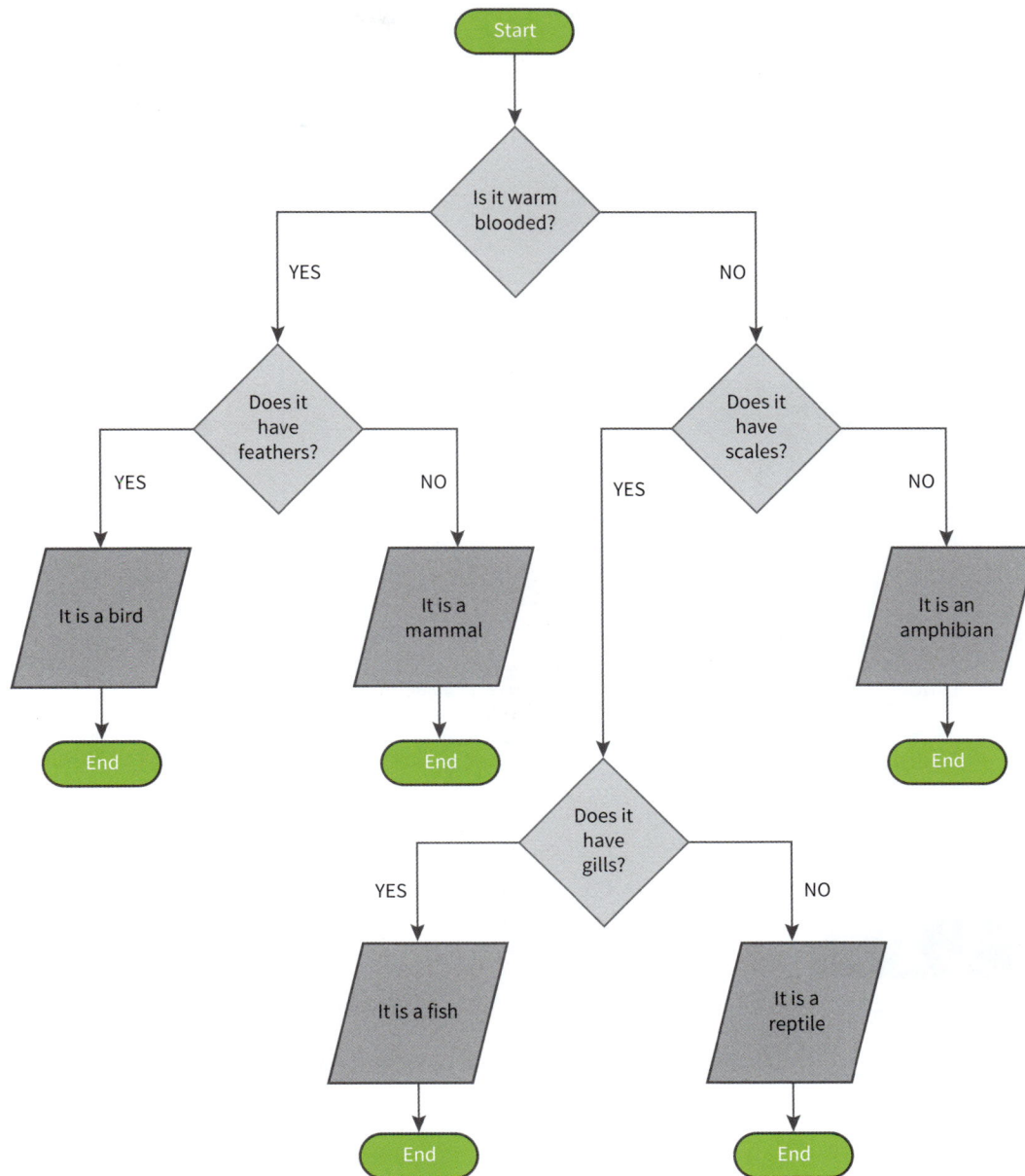

Complete Interactive Activity 1c on Cambridge Elevate

ACTIVITY 1.4

A teacher is marking his students' test papers on a computer. If they achieve over 50 per cent, he would like the message 'Well done!' displayed. If they achieve over 90 per cent, they should also receive a second message stating 'This is an excellent result.' If they score 50 per cent or lower, the message will be 'You must try harder next time.'

Draw a flowchart of an algorithm that would output these messages.

WORKED EXAMPLE

A flowchart to represent the algorithm to control the temperature of the shopping mall that we mentioned earlier would look like this. It contains sequence, selection and iteration.

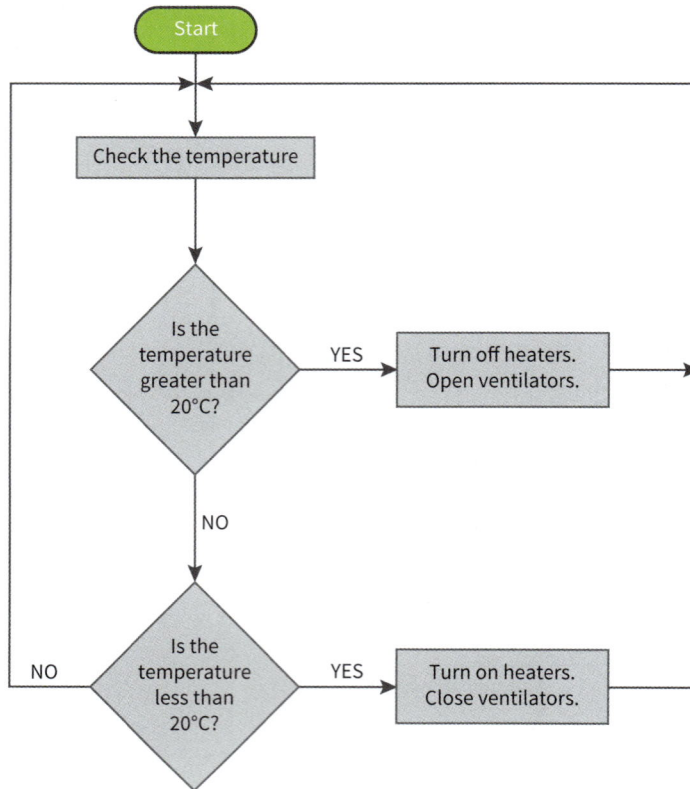

There are three **processes**: one to check the temperature in the mall and two to either turn off the heaters and open the ventilators, or turn them on and close the ventilators.

There are two **decisions**: is the temperature greater or is it less than 20°C? Both are needed as the temperature could in fact be equal to 20°C.

There are only two possible answers for each decision question: *yes* or *no*, and the arrows show the relevant action to be taken depending on the answer.

Iteration is shown in the flow diagram as the arrows always lead the flow back to the first process. So the algorithm will repeat over and over again indefinitely.

As the algorithm repeats forever, no end symbol is required.

Tip

Look back at your answers for Activity 1.1.

ACTIVITY 1.5

Draw a flowchart to illustrate an algorithm for making a cup of tea.

It should include sequence, selection and iteration.

Input and output

In some of the previous examples, user input was required and information was output to the user.

Key terms

decision: when a question is asked (as in selection) the answer will lead to one or more varied alternative actions

process: an activity that a computer program is performing

A common request for user input is to enter a password.

WORKED EXAMPLE

Here is a flowchart of an algorithm to authenticate a password.

When a user enters a password, it has to be confirmed that it is true; it has to be authenticated.

Key term

authenticate: confirm that a user's password has been entered correctly

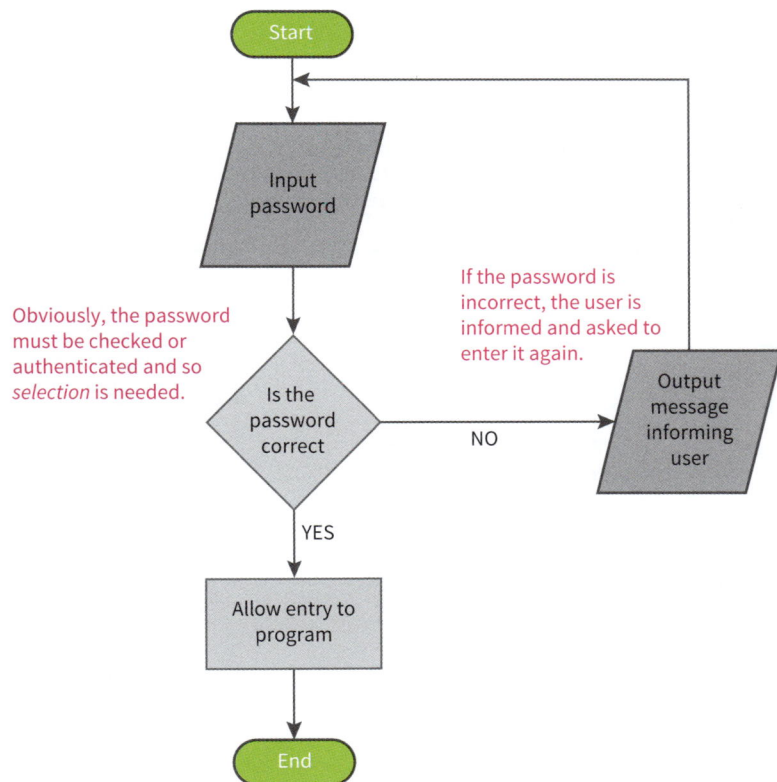

Obviously, the password must be checked or authenticated and so *selection* is needed.

If the password is incorrect, the user is informed and asked to enter it again.

```
Start
  ↓
Input
password
  ↓
Is the
password
correct  --NO--> Output message informing user
  ↓ YES
Allow entry to
program
  ↓
End
```

In this flowchart there is iteration. If the password is incorrect, then in this particular algorithm, the user is asked to enter it again, and again, and again, forever or until it is correct.

Download Worksheet 1.2 from Cambridge Elevate

Now assume that the user is given three attempts and then the account is locked.

Information: HandiTax 2015

Too many failed login attempts, account LOCKED

Ok

WORKED EXAMPLE

Here is a flowchart to authenticate a password and lock the account after three incorrect attempts.

The algorithm will have to keep a count of the number of attempts that have been made.

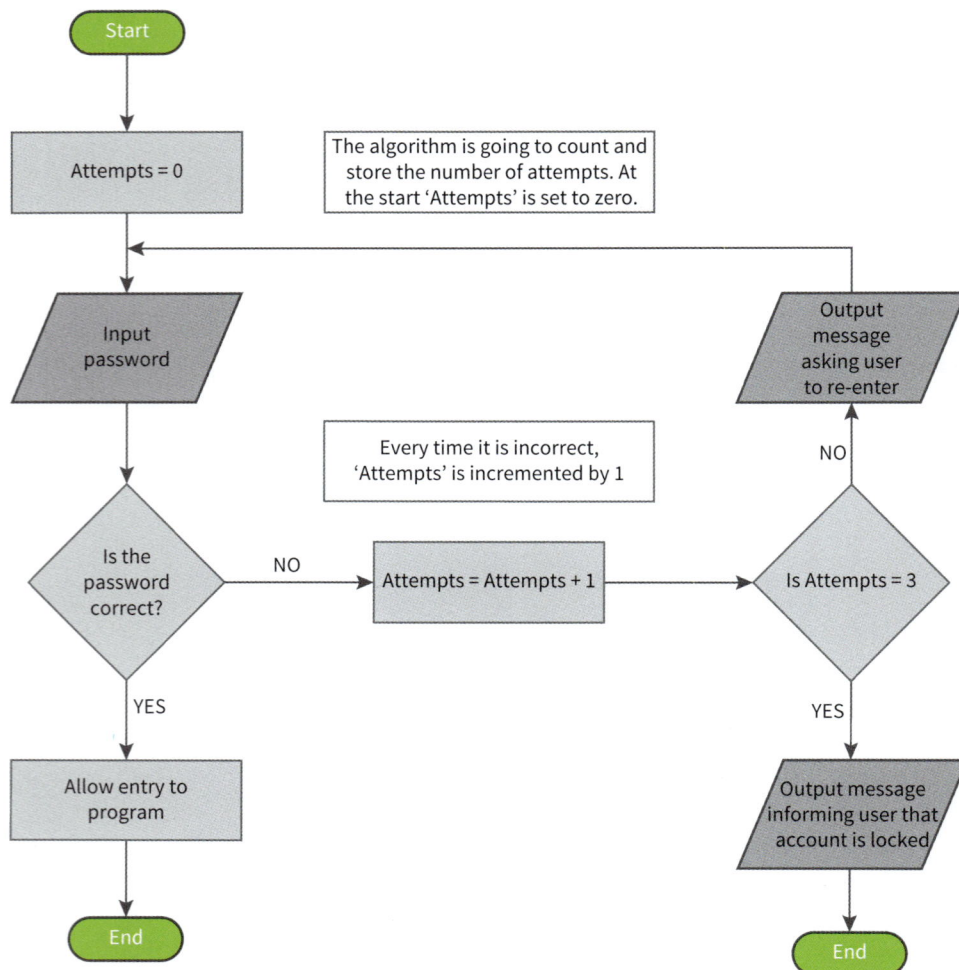

In this algorithm, we have used a container called 'attempts' to keep a count of the number of attempts that have been made.

When incorrect attempts are made, the value of 'attempts' changes. It does not keep the same value throughout the algorithm, but it can change because it is a variable.

On the first attempt, it is changed to 1, on the second attempt it is changed to 2, and on the third attempt it is changed to 3.

If three attempts are made, then the container 'attempts' equals 3 and if there is still no correct password, then the account is locked.

Containers like 'attempts' are used in algorithms to store values that can change as the algorithm is running. As the values they contain can change, they are called variables.

Key term

variable: a container which is used to store values such as an 'attempts' counter

Download Worksheet 1.3 from Cambridge Elevate

ACTIVITY 1.6

The following flowchart shows the algorithm used to create usernames for a school network.

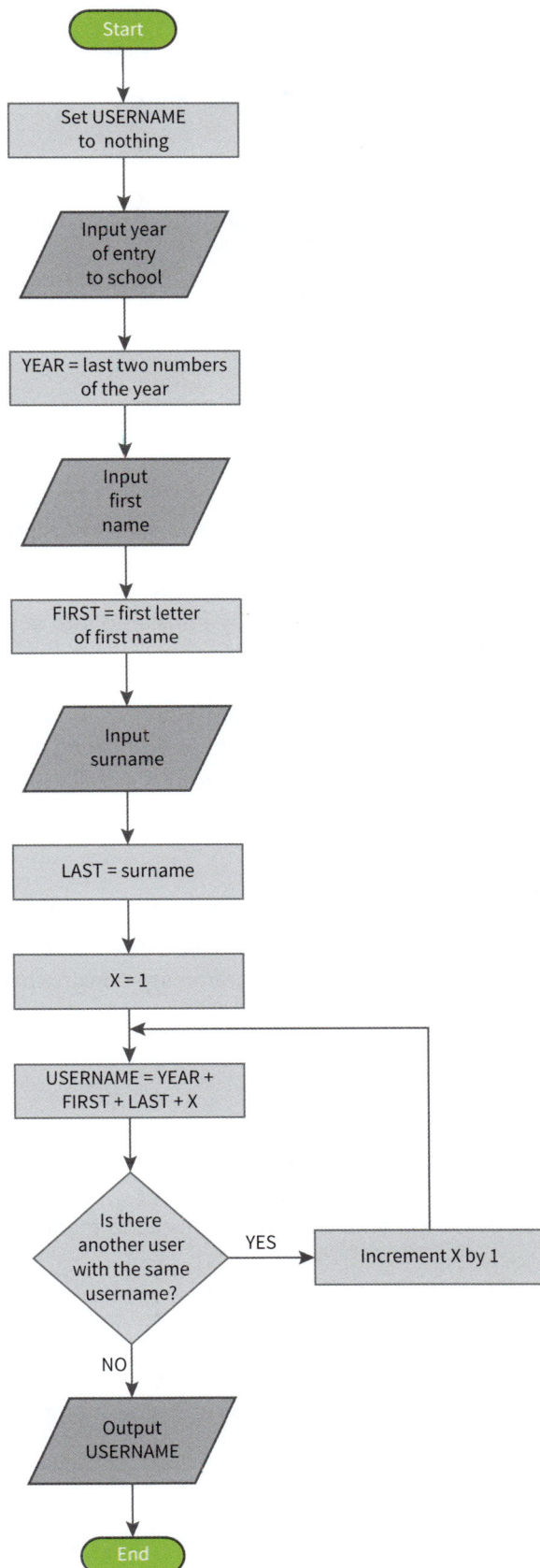

Follow the algorithm shown in the flowchart and then answer the following questions.

1. Identify, and list the variables that have been used in this algorithm.

2. State the usernames that the flowchart will give to the following students (assume that there are no other students with the same username):

    i.   Catherine Jones who joined the school in 2005.

    ii. Fred Green who joined the school in 2006.

3. A student has been given the username of 03SSmith13. State four facts that you can work out from this username.

Pseudo-code

As we have seen, flowcharts make algorithms easy for people to understand. However, computers cannot understand flowcharts, they can only understand programming languages.

In addition to flowcharts, algorithms can also be expressed using **pseudo-code**.

Pseudo-code is a form of structured English for describing algorithms. It is a generic, code-like language that can be easily translated into any programming language.

Writing in pseudo-code helps you to concentrate on the logic (the process) and **efficiency** of your algorithm before you have to start thinking about the code that you will be using. It is important to check that you have included all the stages in your process as it is easier to spot anything missing at this stage before you carefully translate it into code!

There are many different varieties of pseudo-code; some programming teams or organisations have their own versions of pseudo-code. However, all pseudo-code must be able to express the basic programming constructs that we will be looking at.

Variables

Before we look at examples of algorithms expressed in pseudo-code, we should look at variables in more detail.

As we mentioned above, a variable can be changed and manipulated as an algorithm is running.

So that programmers can keep track of variables, they are given names or **identifiers**.

An algorithm might contain many variables, so it is important to give them meaningful identifiers.

If you were creating an algorithm that stores people's ages, it would be sensible to name or identify that variable as 'age' and not something like 'X' or 'Y'.

Key term

pseudo-code: a language that is similar to a real programming language, but is easier for humans to use and understand when they are developing algorithms. Although it doesn't actually run on a computer it can easily be converted to a regular programming language.

Tip

Have a look through the *AQA Pseudo-code Guide* to familiarise yourself with the commands and keywords that are needed.

Key term

identifier: the 'name' given to a variable

Choosing variable identifiers

Variable identifiers should be as descriptive as possible so that anyone reading the code will be able to see what they represent. For example, look at these identifiers:

Code
```
X ← 10
```
and
```
distanceToSchool ← 10
```

Anyone reading the code would know immediately what the value '10' represented in the second example.

1. Shorter identifiers are easier to type and spell. A longer identifier could easily be misspelt.

2. Longer identifiers may be used if they are more descriptive of the data they represent.

3. Some identifiers may be reserved words used by the programming language and cannot be used, for example: 'print'.

4. In many programming languages, identifiers cannot begin with a number.

Naming conventions

Again, it is important for all variables to be written in a similar way throughout an algorithm. This makes the program consistent and easy to understand. This is even more important when a team of programmers is working on the same project.

- A commonly used convention is to use **camel case** (or CamelCase) for compound words.

   For example:

   FirstName, LastName,

   Often the first word of a compound word is given a lower case initial, for example 'f' for 'first' and 'l' for 'last':

   firstName, lastName.

An alternative is to use an underscore. This method is often called **snake case**. For example:

Code
```
first_name, last_name
```

Assigning values to variables

All variables have to be given or assigned a value. This is done in **assignment statements**. It is done differently in different varieties of pseudo-code.

Tip

Study the *AQA Pseudo-code Guide* to see how assignment is made in the variety of pseudo-code that you will be using.

Tip

People have variables! We all have a variable that is our age. The identifier 'Age' stores the length of time we have been alive. It changes every second but is celebrated when it changes on the anniversary of our birth. So you could say 'Happy variable change!'

Our pulse rate, blood pressure and temperature are also our variables.

The school stores variable data about you in variables identified as 'Year' and 'Tutor Group'. Their values change each school year.

Key term

assigning: giving a variable a value

Here are two examples, one that assigns a number and the other that assigns text.

Code
```
myAge ← 21
myName ← "David"
```

Several variables can be assigned in the same statement:

Code
```
myAge ← 21, myName ← "David"
```

Constants

A **constant** is a value that cannot be altered by the program during normal execution: the value stays the same.

For example, a constant could be used to hold the number of hours in a day or rate of value added tax (VAT).

In pseudo-code these could be declared as:

Code
```
numberOfHoursInDay ← 24
vatRate ← 20
```

These can then be used in code such as:

Code
```
OUTPUT "Please enter the net cost of the item."
netCost ← USERINPUT
fullCost ← netCost + (netCost/100*vatRate)
```

The use of the identifier makes the code far more understandable than multiplying by 20.

If there is a later change to the VAT rate then instead of having to search through the code for every occurrence of the VAT rate all that needs to be done is to change the value of the constant identifier 'vatRate' at the one place in the program.

Different programming languages use different key words for declaring constants.

In C++, 'vatRate' would be declared using 'const' and the data type:

Code
```
const int vatRate = 20
```

In Java the numberOfHoursInDay could be declared using 'final':

Code
```
final int numberOfHoursInDay = 24
```

Error messages will be generated if any attempt is made to change the values of these constants while the program is running.

Key term

constant: a value that does not change while the program is running

Tip

Constants are also given identifiers.

Remember

1. A variable is a value that can change while a program is running.
2. Variables are given names, called identifiers.
3. Variable identifiers should be descriptive of the data they are storing, for example age or firstName, not identifiers such as X or Y.
4. Variables should be written in a consistent way, e.g. they should all be camel case or all snake case and not a mixture of the two.
5. Variables are assigned a value using the ← symbol.
6. Constants are values that cannot be altered as a program is running.

Complete Interactive Activity 1d on Cambridge Elevate

WORKED EXAMPLE

The first flowchart we looked at illustrated an algorithm to find the area of a rectangle. Here it is expressed in pseudo-code. It asks a user for the width and the length of a rectangle. It then calculates the area and prints it on screen.

Where variables are first assigned a value, they are shown in red.

Code	Explanation

`OUTPUT "Please enter the length."`
 	
`length ← USERINPUT`
	This is how the pseudo-code allows users to input data. Note how the prompt text is enclosed in speech marks.
	The variable 'length' will be assigned the value entered by the user.

`OUTPUT "Please enter the width."`
 	
`width ← USERINPUT`
	The variable 'width' will be assigned the value entered by the user.

`area ← length * width`	The variable 'area' will be assigned the value of the variable 'length' multiplied by the variable 'width'.
`OUTPUT area`	The value stored in the variable 'area' is printed on the screen.

Adding comments

When writing pseudo-code it is a good idea to add comments to explain to others, and often to remind yourself, what the code is intended to do.

To separate these comments from the actual code, the hash sign # is used.

The pseudo-code example used above could have been commented in the following way.

Code

```
OUTPUT "Please enter the        # Ask the user for the length
length."                        of the rectangle

length ← USERINPUT

OUTPUT "Please enter the        # Ask the user for the width
width."                         of the rectangle

width ← USERINPUT

area ← length * width           # Find the area by multiplying
                                the length by the width

OUTPUT area                     # output the area
```

Tip

Check the commands and keywords used in the *AQA Pseudo-code Guide*.

Tip

The printed message could have been made more user-friendly by including some text rather than just the area value. To do this, the text would need to be in speech marks to show that it is **literal** text and not a variable name. It would need to be joined to the variable 'area'.

```
OUTPUT "The area is" +
area
```

The literal text 'The area is' and then the value for the variable 'area' have been joined together (concatenated) using the '+' symbol.

Key term

comment: a piece of information for the programmer. It does not form part of the program and is not executed by the computer. It is for information only

ACTIVITY 1.7

Write the pseudo-code to ask a user to enter their name and their age. It should then print the following message:

```
Hello (name entered). You
are (age entered) years of
age.
```

You should add comments to your pseudo-code.

Keywords

If you look through the pseudo-code guide you will see words like 'OUTPUT', 'FOR', 'ENDFOR', 'IF' and 'ENDIF' that are used in commands. They are **reserved** or **keywords** as they have specific meanings for the language and therefore cannot be used as variable identifiers.

Operators

The algorithm you wrote in Activity 1.7 just printed out the data a user had input. Often you want the computer to do something with that data, usually a calculation.

In the worked example, the values of two variables were multiplied together to find the area.

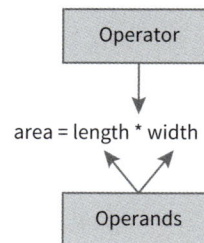

area = length * width

Key term

operator: the symbol that tells the computer what to do

An operator is a symbol that tells the computer to perform a specific action on the data and manipulate it in a particular way. The data on which it performs the action is called the operand.

Watch the arithmetic, relational and Boolean operators animation on Cambridge Elevate

Arithmetic operators

These are operators we have been using all our mathematical lives.

The following list shows the most common arithmetic operators:

Operator	Function	Example
+	**Addition:** add the values together.	3 + 6 = 9 firstResult + secondResult
-	**Subtraction:** subtract the second value from the first.	6 - 3 = 3 dailyProfit - dailyCosts
*	**Multiplication:** multiply the values together.	3 * 6 = 18 length * width
/	**Real division:** divide the first value by the second number and return the result including decimal places.	13/3 = 4.333 totalSweets/totalChildren
DIV	**Quotient:** like division, but it only returns the whole number or *integer*.	13 DIV 3 = 4 totalSweets\totalChildren
MOD	**Modulus:** this will return the remainder of a division.	13/3 = 4 remainder 1. Therefore: 13 MOD 3 = 1
^	**Exponentiation:** this is for 'powers of'.	3^3 = 27. It is the same as writing 3^3.

Order of operations

In computer programming, the order of precedence (the order in which you do each calculation) is the same as in mathematics and science.

To change the order of operations parentheses are used.

Therefore:

$$13 \times (3 + 6) = 13 \times 9 = 117$$

Multiplication and division are carried out before addition and subtraction. Brackets (parentheses) are calculated before multiplication and division.

ACTIVITY 1.8

Using pseudo-code, create an algorithm that will ask a user to input the diameter of a wheel.

It should then calculate the area (assume Pi is 3.142) and output the result.

Complete Interactive Activity 1e on Cambridge Elevate

Relational operators

Let's look again at the temperature control in the shopping mall.

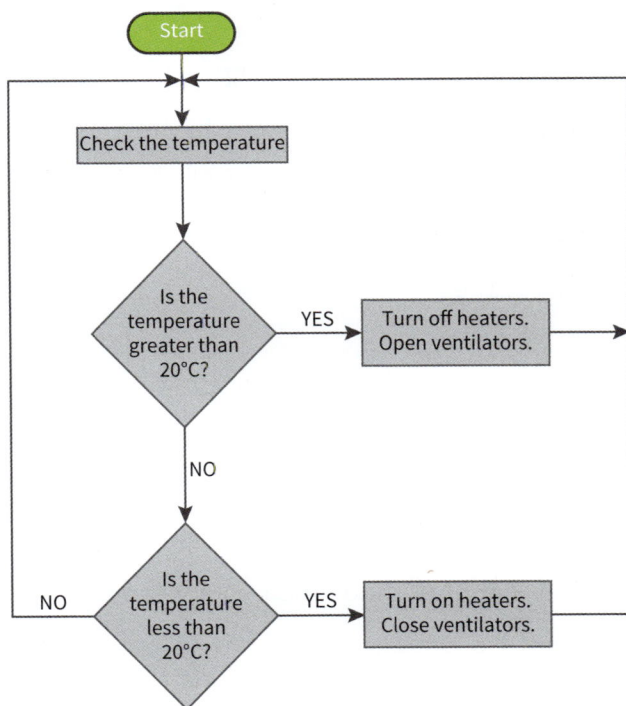

Key term

parentheses: brackets

Tip

In a division such as 13/3 the '13' is called the **dividend** and the '3' is called the **divisor**.

The **quotient** is the number of times the divisor divides into the dividend: in this case four times.

The DIV operator returns just the quotient and so in some pseudo-code dialects it is called **integer division** and the symbol used is a backslash \.

Maths skills

Remember BIDMAS!

This is how the following would be evaluated: $3^3 \times 6 + (16 - 7)$

Brackets $3^3 \times 6 + (9)$

Indices $9 \times 6 + (9)$

Division

Multiplication $54 + (9)$

Addition   63

Subtraction

Therefore:

$$13 \times 3 + 6 = 45$$

Maths skills

The area of a circle can be found by the formula $Pi \times r^2$ where r equals the radius.

In this flowchart, two questions are being asked:

'Is the temperature greater than 20°C?'

and

'Is the temperature less than 20°C?'

We used two different relational operators: greater than and less than. Relational operators test the relationship between two values. As they compare the values they are sometimes called **comparison operators**.

Key term

relational operator: an operator which compares two items of data, for example <, >, =

Operator	Function
=	**Equal to** checks if two values are equal, for example: length = width
≠	**Not equal to** checks to see if two values are not equal, for example: temperature ≠ 20
<	**Less than** checks to see if one value is less than another, for example: temperature < 20
>	**Greater than** checks to see if one value is greater than another, for example: temperature > 20
≤	**Less than or equal to** checks to see if one value is less than or equal to another, for example: temperature ≤ 20
≥	**Greater than or equal to** checks to see if one value is greater than or equal to another, for example: temperature ≥ 20

Complete Interactive Activity 1f on Cambridge Elevate

As mentioned above, we used two of these operators in the flowchart for the algorithm to control the temperature of a shopping mall.

If the temperature is greater than 20°C, then one course of action is carried out and if it is not, then something else is done.

We can rewrite this using the 'IF', 'THEN' and 'ELSE' statements in the pseudo-code.

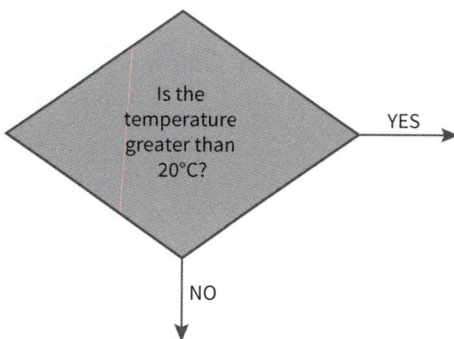

Code

```
IF the temperature is greater than 20°C
THEN turn off the heaters and open the ventilators.
ELSE do something else.
ENDIF
```

If we put both of the selections together we could write:

Code

```
IF the temperature is greater than 20°C
THEN turn off the heaters and open the ventilators.
check the temperature again
ENDIF
IF the temperature is less than 20°C
THEN turn on the heater and close the ventilators.
check the temperature again.
ENDIF
```

When the computer is running a program coded from these 'IF' statements, it will run both of them. But if the first one is true, it does not need to run the second one as the temperature cannot be greater than and less than 20 °C at the same time!

The computer will be wasting time. The algorithm is inefficient!

Therefore another term, 'ELSE IF' can be used.

In this example, x is actually equal to 2.

Inefficient algorithm	Efficient algorithm
IF x = 1 do this	IF x = 1 do this
IF x = 2 do this	ELSE IF x = 2 do this
IF x = 3 do this	ELSE IF x = 3 do this
IF x = 4 do this	ELSE IF x = 4 do this
IF x = 5 do this	ELSE IF x = 5 do this
IF x = 6 do this	ELSE IF x = 6 do this
ELSE do this	ELSE do this
ENDIF	ENDIF

In this example, it will not make much difference as there were only six 'if' statements but in large programs there might be hundreds or thousands of 'IF' statements and going through them all would waste a significant amount of time.

> **Tip**
>
> When 'IF' statements are used, each one will be checked even when the correct condition has been found. However, 'ELSE IF' statements will not be checked after the correct condition has been found.

> **Tip**
>
> If you study the pseudo-code guide, you will see that 'IF', 'THEN' and 'ELSE' are written in upper case.
>
> You should also notice that after the statements are used the checking is stopped using the 'ENDIF' statement.

WORKED EXAMPLE

A teacher would like a program that allows her to enter three test results and calculate the average.

If the average is 50 or above, the program should output the message 'Pass' and if it is below 50, it should output the message 'Fail'.

```
OUTPUT "Please enter first test result."
test1 ← USERINPUT
OUTPUT "Please enter the second test result."
test2 ← USERINPUT
OUTPUT "Please enter the third test result."
test3 ← USERINPUT
```

The user is asked to input the three test results which are stored in the variables test 1, test 2 and test 3.

```
average ← (test1 + test2 + test3)/3
```

The average is calculated and stored in the variable 'average'. Notice how the additions are in brackets to ensure that they are done first.

```
IF average ≥ 50 THEN
     OUTPUT "Pass"
```

This 'IF' statement checks to see if the average is equal to or greater than 50. If it is, the message 'Pass' is output.

```
ELSE
     OUTPUT "Fail"
```

There is no need for another 'IF' statement as if the average is not 50 or above it must be less than 50. Therefore an 'ELSE' statement is used.

```
ENDIF
```

In the pseudo-code dialect that we are using, an 'ENDIF' statement must be placed at the end of the selection block of code.

Tip

The instructions that follow 'IF' statements (and are executed as a result of the 'IF' statements) should be indented. Look at the examples to see how this is done.

Complete Interactive Activity 1g on Cambridge Elevate

Indentation

It is considered good practice to indent statements that occur within an 'IF' statement.

Some programming languages demand it, but most will accept it if you do not indent these statements. Indentation helps to show the logic in your algorithm.

The statements above should be set out in the following way:

Code

```
IF average ≥ 50 THEN

        OUTPUT "Pass"        This is indented as it is dependent
                             on the 'IF' statement.

ELSE

        OUTPUT "Fail"        This is indented as it is dependent
                             on the 'ELSE' statement.

ENDIF
```

ACTIVITY 1.9

Create an algorithm, expressed as pseudo-code, which asks a user to enter a number between 1 and 10.

If the number is five or less, the message: (the number input) 'is a low number.' is output to the screen. If the number is over five, the message: (the number input) 'is a high number.' is output.

ACTIVITY 1.10

A teacher created an algorithm to automatically generate one comment for a student's test result based on the score out of ten.

```
OUTPUT "Please enter the test result."

score ← USERINPUT

IF  score < 5 THEN

        OUTPUT "You must try harder next time."

ELSE IF score >= 5 THEN

        OUTPUT "You have gained half marks."

ELSE IF score > 7

        OUTPUT "This is a good result."

ELSE IF  score > 8

        OUTPUT "This is an excellent result."

ENDIF
```

The teacher input a score of nine and expected the message 'This is an excellent result.' to be printed. However, the comment produced was not as expected. What would have been generated? Explain why this was the case.

Boolean operators

These operators are named after George Boole, a 19th century English mathematician who formulated an algebraic system of logic.

They are sometimes referred to as logical operators.

Look at this Venn diagram that shows the number of rainy and sunny days in a fortnight.

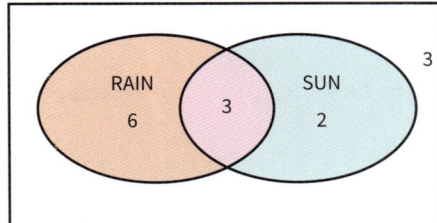

There were three days where there was RAIN **AND** SUN.

There were six days where there was RAIN **AND NOT** SUN.

There were two days where there was SUN **AND NOT** RAIN.

There were 11 days where there was SUN **OR** RAIN: six days with RAIN only, two days with SUN only and three days where there were both.

The words in bold are all Boolean operators.

> **Key term**
>
> logical operator: operators such as 'AND', 'OR' and 'NOT' that perform a Boolean operation on some inputs

> **Complete Interactive Activity 1h on Cambridge Elevate**

Operator	Function	Example

AND	**Logical AND operator**
	If all of the operands are true, then the condition becomes true.
		```IF length > 6 AND width > 3 THEN```
		
		`        area ← length * width`
		
		`ELSE`
		
		`        OUTPUT "Rectangle is not large enough."`
		
		`ENDIF`
		
		In this example, the length must be greater than 6 AND the width must be greater than 3 to work out the area.

OR	**Logical OR operator**
	If any of the operands are true, then the condition becomes true.
		`IF score < 0 OR score > 100 THEN`
		
		`        OUTPUT "The score is invalid."`
		
		`ENDIF`
		
		In this example if the score entered is less than 0 OR if it is greater than 100, it will not be accepted.

NOT	**Logical NOT operator**
	Used to reverse the logical state of the operand.
		`IF NOT (length > 6 AND width > 3) THEN`
		
		`        OUTPUT "Rectangle is not large enough."`
		
		`ELSE`
		
		`        area ← length * width`
		
		`ENDIF`
		
		This produces the same result as the first example.

Remember to indent all of the statements which follow an 'IF' statement as they are only executed because of it.

WORKED EXAMPLE

A student would like to select a suitable T-shirt from local shops. The colour could be red, blue or white, the size needs to be medium and the shop must be no more than 10 miles away.

Create an algorithm to help the student find suitable T-shirts.

```
OUTPUT "Please enter the colour of T-shirt."

colour ← USERINPUT
```

The user is asked to input the T-shirt colour and size and the distance to the shop.

The values entered are stored in variables.

```
OUTPUT "Enter size as S, M or L."

size ← USERINPUT

OUTPUT "Enter distance to shop in miles."

distance ← USERINPUT

IF (colour = "red" OR colour = "blue" OR colour = "white")
AND size = "M" AND distance ≤ 10 THEN
```

IF all of the variables meet the criteria, then this message is printed:

```
        OUTPUT "This T-shirt is suitable."
ELSE
```

IF all the variables do not meet the criteria, then this message is printed:

```
        OUTPUT "No. This T shirt is not suitable."
ENDIF
```

The 'ENDIF' statement must be placed after the 'IF, ELSE' code.

> **Tip**
>
> Study the *AQA Pseudo-code Guide* as you read through the following algorithm so that you understand the command words and how they have to be used.

> **Tip**
>
> The 'IF' statement is used to select the desirable characteristics.
>
> The items for colour selection are enclosed in brackets so that they are evaluated together.

Download Worksheet 1.4 from Cambridge Elevate

Complete Interactive Activity 1i on Cambridge Elevate

ACTIVITY 1.11

An 11–18 senior school would like you to design software to help with student administration. The software should allow the user to input the year and tutor group of each student. There are seven year groups designated from 7 to 13.

In each year, there are four tutor groups: red, green, blue and yellow.

Enter these details and check that the data entered is acceptable, that is, check that the year group or tutor group entered actually exists.

Nested 'IF' statements

A 'nested IF' refers to two 'IF' statements, one running inside the other.

A shop gives a discount of 5 per cent on purchases over £100, up to a maximum of £50. If the amount to be discounted would be greater than this, it has to be reduced back to £50.

`OUTPUT "Please enter the money spent in £."`	
`purchase ← USERINPUT`	The user is asked to enter the purchase price.
`IF purchase > 100 THEN`	IF the purchase price is greater than 100 the discount is calculated.
`discount ← purchase / 100 * 5`	The nested 'IF' is then used to check 'IF' the discount is more than 50.
`IF discount > 50 THEN`	Notice how the second 'IF' statement is indented.
`discount ← 50`	IF the discount is more than 50, it is reduced back to 50.
`ENDIF`	'ENDIF' for the inner 'IF'.
`ENDIF`	'ENDIF' for the outer 'IF'.

Download Worksheet 1.5 from Cambridge Elevate

'CASE' statements

As well as the 'IF' ... 'ELSE IF' ... 'ELSE' statements, this is another method which can be used for selection.

It is very useful where users have to select an item from a list.

Tip

Study the *AQA Pseudo-code Guide* to see the keywords for this method and how it is used.

In a multiple-choice question there are four possible answers, labelled **A**, **B**, **C** and **D**. To select the answer, the users have to enter one of these letters. They will then be informed if they are correct or incorrect. There should also be a method to inform if they enter a letter other than the four allowed. (In this example, the correct answer is option **C**.)

Using 'IF' ... 'ELSE IF' ... 'ELSE' statements, it could be coded as:

```
OUTPUT "Please select an option."

answer ← USERINPUT

IF answer = "A" THEN

        OUTPUT "Sorry. That is incorrect."
```

```
ELSE IF answer = "B" THEN

        OUTPUT "Sorry. That is incorrect."

ELSE IF answer = "C" THEN

        OUTPUT "Well done. That is the correct answer."

ELSE IF answer = "D" THEN

        OUTPUT "Sorry. That is incorrect."

ELSE

        OUTPUT "That option is not recognised."

ENDIF
```

This could also be written as:

```
IF answer = "A" OR answer = "B" OR answer = "D" THEN

        OUTPUT  "Sorry. That is incorrect."

ELSE IF answer = "C" THEN

        OUTPUT "Well done. That is the correct answer."

ELSE

        OUTPUT "That option is not recognised."

ENDIF
```

Using CASE it would be coded as:

```
OUTPUT "Please select an option."

answer ← USERINPUT

CASE answer OF

        "A": OUTPUT "Sorry. That is incorrect."

        "B": OUTPUT "Sorry. That is incorrect."

        "C": OUTPUT "Well done. That is the correct answer."

        "D": OUTPUT "Sorry. That is incorrect."

ELSE

        OUTPUT "That option is not recognised."

ENDCASE
```

ACTIVITY 1.12

A student is writing code to ask a user to enter the month number, for example: 1 = January and 12 = December. The user should then receive a message giving the name of the month.

Write an algorithm in pseudo-code, using 'CASE' statements, to solve this problem.

Remember

1. Pseudo-code is a generic, code-like language that can be easily translated into any programming language.
2. An operator is a symbol that tells the computer to perform a specific action on the data and manipulate it in a particular way.
3. An arithmetic operator is a mathematical function that can take one or two operands and performs a calculation on them.
4. Relational operators test the relationship between two values.
5. Boolean or logical operators test all the operands in a complex statement and return a value of true or false.
6. A 'nested IF' is a complete 'IF' statement running inside another 'IF' statement.
7. 'Switch/case' can be used to select from multiple options.

Practice question

1. Using pseudo-code examples, explain the following terms:

    a. variables
    b. relational operators
    c. Boolean operators
    d. nested IF statements.

Complete Interactive Activity 1j on Cambridge Elevate

Your final challenge

'We drive anywhere' is a taxi firm who have the following criteria when working out the customer charge.

The following rules apply:

- Between 8 am and 8 pm, passengers are charged £3 for the first mile and £2 for every further mile.

- If there are more than four passengers, there is a charge of £2 for each extra passenger.

- Between 8 pm and 8 am, the overall charge is doubled.

Design an algorithm that will allow the taxi drivers to input the required information that will then output the total charge.

Display your algorithm as a flowchart and as pseudo-code.

Download Self-assessment 1 worksheet from Cambridge Elevate (this content has not been approved by AQA)

2 Iteration

Learning outcomes

By the end of this chapter you should be able to:

- explain what is meant by iteration
- explain the difference between definite and indefinite iteration
- use 'FOR' loops
- use 'WHILE' loops
- use 'REPEAT...UNTIL' loops
- use nested loops
- analyse algorithms using trace tables
- use iteration when designing algorithms.

⭐ **Challenge: write an algorithm for a computer game**

- The computer games industry is huge, with over 50 per cent of the UK and United States population regularly playing.
- Top selling games earn more than Hollywood blockbusters and have 'red carpet' premieres.
- Your challenge is to write an algorithm for a new computer game.

Everything we learn, from walking to playing sports and driving a car, requires iteration until we have mastered the skills.

Why iteration?

Iteration is the act of repeating a process until there is a desired result.

- Iteration is used in education. To master a new topic we repeat activities and assessments until we reach the desired result.

- We learn poetry or the script of a play by repeating the lines over and over again until we can quote the text without making any mistakes because that is the desired result.

- When we practise sports skills we are using iteration. We execute actions over and over again until we can perform them perfectly every time. Like always scoring from the penalty spot!

What is iteration used for?

We mentioned iteration when we looked at simple algorithms using flowcharts. Iteration means that a procedure or a set of statements or commands is repeated for a set number of times or until there is a desired outcome.

We use iteration in our daily lives for actions such as learning to do something: it is called practice!

We do the action over and over again until we can do it properly or better than we did before. In a computer program, iteration is used so that a section of code is repeated to check on a condition, for example the temperature, until it reaches one that the programmer has selected, for example the temperature equals 20°C.

Program constructs that cause iteration are called loops and there are several different types of loop. Loops are explained in detail in the following sections.

There was even a popular film made about iteration.

'Groundhog Day' is about a person caught in a *loop*. Visit the IMDb website to watch a trailer of the film.

For a range of time the main character has to live the same day over and over again.

He has to live the same day over and over again *until* there is a desired outcome.

While he does the wrong thing he has to go back to the start over again.

All of the words in red used to describe the film are also used in algorithms, pseudo-code and actual programming languages.

> **Key term**
>
> loop: part of a program where the same activity is repeated over and over again for a fixed number of times or until a condition is met. Usually the condition is stated within the loop itself

Definite iteration

In these types of loops, the number of iterations is known before the execution of the loop is started, for example it may be set to three or five times and it will execute that number of times whatever the *conditions* – unless there is a command to break out of the loop.

Definite iteration can be achieved with a FOR, WHILE or REPEAT loop, but the FOR loop is specifically designed for this purpose.

> **Key term**
>
> execution: when a program or part of a program is run by the computer

'FOR' loop

The 'FOR' loop basically states 'For a set number of times, do something'.

Here is an example written in pseudo-code:

Code

`FOR index ← 0 TO 10`	There is a 'FOR' statement with a variable (in this case with the identifier 'index') and the range of values it must count through.
`   OUTPUT index`	The action that should be done at each iteration.
`ENDFOR`	An end statement to trigger the next turn of the loop.

In this case the printed output would be:

| 0 | 1 | 2 | 3 | 4 | 5 | 6 | 7 | 8 | 9 | 10 |

'WHILE' loop

Definite iteration can also be accomplished using a 'WHILE' loop set for a predetermined number of turns.

An example in pseudo-code:

Code

Code	Description
`index = 0`	The variable index is initialised as 0.
`WHILE index ≤ 10`	While 'index' is less than or equal to 10, it will be printed.
`  OUTPUT "The number is " + index` `  index ← index + 1`	At each turn of the loop, index is incremented by 1.
`ENDWHILE`	The 'ENDWHILE' statement is placed at the end of the loop and will transfer the processing back to the top of the loop.

The loop will run while the condition (≤ 10) is still true.

The 'WHILE' and 'FOR' loops can both be used for definite iteration and produce the same result. A 'REPEAT' loop could also achieve the same result.

> **Tip**
>
> The output statement could just have been 'index' but text has been added to make it more user-friendly. Notice how the added text is in speech marks and the statements are joined by '+' symbols.

WORKED EXAMPLE

Write an algorithm in pseudo-code to ask a user to input a number. The algorithm should then print out the times table for that number.

Code	Description
`OUTPUT "Please enter a number: "` `number ← USERINPUT`	The user is asked to enter a number for the times table. It is stored in a variable called 'number'.
`FOR index ← 1 TO 12`	The 'FOR' loop is started.
`  OUTPUT index + " x " + number + " = " +` `  number * index`	This is printed while the loop is running.
`ENDFOR`	The end of the loop.

The text to be printed looks quite complicated but we have met all of the constructs before. Let's go through them. We will assume that the user entered the number 9 and index has reached a value of 6.

```
OUTPUT index + " x " + number + " = " + number * index
```

What will be printed	Explanation
6	Index is now equal to 6
6 x	As we have already seen, a '+' in an output statement will join two items together. In this case it will add the letter 'x' to stand as a multiplication sign.
6 x 9	Now 'number' is added. That is the number 9.
6 x 9 =	Now the equals symbol is added.
6 x 9 = 54	Now 54 is added as that is equal to number * index or 9 * 6.

ACTIVITY 2.1

Write the above algorithm using a 'WHILE' loop.

Download Worksheet 2.1 from Cambridge Elevate

Complete Interactive Activity 2a on Cambridge Elevate

Indefinite iteration

In indefinite iteration, the number of iterations is not known before the loop is started. The iterations stop when a certain condition becomes true or false. There are two main variants of this type of loop, depending on where in the block of code the comparison is made.

'WHILE' loop

The loop continues *while* a certain condition remains true.

The condition is checked *before* the code is executed.

It is written as:

Code

```
WHILE a condition is true

    ...

    Block of code to be executed

    ...

ENDWHILE
```

WORKED EXAMPLE

A 'WHILE' loop can be used to check that a password is correct by comparing it with a password that is stored.

`storedPassword ← password that is stored`	The password stored in the system is assigned to the variable 'storedPassword'.
`password ← ""`	The variable 'password' is going to be used in the 'WHILE' loop and it must be declared before the loop is set up. It is given the value of an empty text string by using the speech marks with nothing between them as the 'WHILE' loop is going to run while the string is empty.

```
WHILE password = ""
```
The 'WHILE' loop is started and will run while the variable 'password' has the value of an empty string.

```
    OUTPUT "Please enter a password"
    password ← USERINPUT
```
The user is asked to enter the password.

```
    IF password ≠ storedPassword THEN
```
This checks the password variable against the stored password. It is checking to see if it is **not** equal to it (≠).

This selection ('IF' statement) is nested within the 'WHILE' statement.

We could also have written this as:

IF NOT(password = storedPassword)

```
            password = ""
```
If the passwords do not match, then the password variable is changed to empty text so that the loop will run again.

```
    ENDIF
```
This ends the 'IF' block.

```
ENDWHILE
```
This ends the 'WHILE' loop and directs processing back to the 'WHILE' statement.

This loop will run forever until the correct password is entered when the loop will be exited.

The flowchart in Chapter 1 illustrates an algorithm that allows a user only three failed attempts before stopping the program. The previous pseudo-code could be modified to allow this:

Code

```
storedPassword ← password that is stored
```
The password stored in the system is assigned to the variable 'storedPassword'.

```
attempts ← 0
```
The variable 'attempts' is assigned the value of 0.

```
password ← ""
```

```
WHILE password = "" AND attempts <3
```
This time there are two conditions for the loop to run. The variable 'attempts' has to have a value of three or less.

```
    OUTPUT "Please enter a password"

    password ← USERINPUT

    IF password ≠ storedPassword THEN

            password ← ""

            attempts ← attempts +1
```
As they are not the same, the variable 'attempts' is increased by 1.

```
    ENDIF

ENDWHILE
```

ACTIVITY 2.2

A student wants to find the sum of a series of numbers. Write an algorithm that would allow him to enter the numbers needed and would then print out their sum. (Hint: how could the algorithm be informed that all of the numbers had been entered?)

Complete Interactive Activity 2b on Cambridge Elevate

'REPEAT...UNTIL' loops

A 'REPEAT...UNTIL' loop is similar to the 'WHILE' loop but the comparison is not done until the end of the code block.

It is written as:

Code
```
REPEAT

    execute this code

UNTIL this condition is met
```

Because the condition is checked at the end of the code block, it is always run at least once.

The loop will run while the condition remains unmet.

WORKED EXAMPLE

The password entry example could be written using a 'REPEAT...UNTIL' loop.

`storedPassword ← password that is stored`	The password stored in the system is assigned to the variable 'storedPassword'.
`attempts ← 0`	
`REPEAT`	
`    OUTPUT "Please enter the password"`	
`    password ← USERINPUT`	
`    attempts ← attempts + 1`	The variable 'attempts' is incremented by 1. So it will equal 1, then 2 and finally 3
`UNTIL password = storedPassword OR attempts = 3`	The loop will run until the password is correct or 'attempts' is equal to 3 (because once 'attempts' equals 3 the user will have had 3 attempts).

Tip

In this Worked example, the 'REPEAT...UNTIL' loop is more efficient than the 'WHILE' loop.

For both, the variable 'password' has to be introduced before the comparison is made.

In the 'WHILE' loop, the variable has to be introduced before the loop code block because the comparison is made at the start. However, for the 'REPEAT...UNTIL' loop, where the comparison is not made until the end, the variable can be introduced by the 'USERINPUT' statement in the code block. Therefore fewer lines of code are needed!

Download Worksheet 2.2 from Cambridge Elevate

WORKED EXAMPLE

A client would like an algorithm for a computer game with the following specification:

- The computer generates a random number between 1 and 100.

- The user is asked to enter a number.

- If the guess is too high, then the user is told told 'Your guess is too high'.

- If the guess is too low, then the user is told told 'Your guess is too low'.

- If the guess is correct, then the user is told told that they are right.

`mysteryNumber ← RANDOM_INT(1,100)`	This will generate a random number between 1 and 100.
`guess ← 0`	The variable 'guess' is assigned the value of 0.
`WHILE guess = 0`	A 'WHILE' loop is set to run while 'guess' is equal to 0.
`    OUTPUT "Please enter a number between 1 and 100."`	The user is asked to input a number that is assigned to the 'guess' variable. Therefore 'guess' is no longer equal to 0.
`    guess ← USERINPUT`	
`    IF guess > mysteryNumber THEN`	If the guess is greater than the random number…
`        guess ← 0`	…guess is changed back to 0 so that the loop will run again and…
`        OUTPUT "Your guess is too high."`	…the user is informed.
`    ELSE IF    guess < mysteryNumber THEN`	If the guess is less than the random number…
`        guess ← 0`	…guess is changed back to 0 so that the loop will run again and…
`        OUTPUT "Your guess is too low."`	…the user is informed.
`    ENDIF`	This ends the 'IF' block.
`ENDWHILE`	This ends the 'WHILE' loop and processing is sent back to the start if the guess has been changed back to 0.
`OUTPUT "Well done. You guessed correctly!"`	If the guess is equal to the random number, then the variable 'guess' will not be equal to 0 and so the loop will be exited and this print statement will be executed.

ACTIVITY 2.3

The client would now like an improvement to the game. They would like the user to be given an option to play the game again: a 'Y' key press to play the game again and any other key to exit.

Adapt the code above to incorporate this and to also print a message for the user when they finally quit the game. Add comments to explain how your algorithm works.

Nested loops

One loop can be run inside another loop. This is referred to as 'nesting', so these loops are called 'nested loops'. You can also have nested 'IF' statements.

WORKED EXAMPLE

The following algorithm will print out all of the times tables from 2 to 12.

`FOR index ← 2 TO 12`	The first 'FOR' loop is set up to run from 2 to 12.
`    OUTPUT "This is the " + index " times table."`	This prints a message telling the user which times table is being printed.
`    FOR times ← 2 TO 12`	The second, inner loop is set up, also to run from 2 to 12.
`        OUTPUT times + " x " + index + " = " + index * times`	The second loop will run from 2 to 12 and each time will multiply the value for 'index' by the value for 'times'.
`    ENDFOR`	This ends the inner loop.
`ENDFOR`	This ends the outer loop.

Therefore:

- The first loop runs and index = 2.

- A message is printed saying that this is the index times table.

- The second loop starts with times = 2 and index is multiplied by times (2 x 2).

- The second loop now runs to completion, that is times = 3, then times = 4, etc.

- When the second loop has finished control is given back to the first loop which runs for a second time with index = 3.

- This continues until index = 12.

So the second loop has to work much harder. For every single turn of the first loop, it has to do 11!

It does 122 to the first loop's 11.

```
This is the 2 times table
2 × 2 = 4
3 × 2 = 6
4 × 2 = 8
5 × 2 = 10
6 × 2 = 12
7 × 2 = 14
8 × 2 = 16
9 × 2 = 18
10 × 2 = 20
11 × 2 = 22
12 × 2 = 24
This is the 3 times table
2 × 3 = 6
3 × 3 = 9
4 × 3 = 12
5 × 3 = 15
6 × 3 = 18
7 × 3 = 21
8 × 3 = 24
9 × 3 = 27
10 × 3 = 30
11 × 3 = 33
12 × 3 = 36
```

Download Worksheet 2.3 from Cambridge Elevate

ACTIVITY 2.4

Write an algorithm like the one shown in the previous worked example but allow the user to input the range of tables they want, for example from 5 to 9. Explain how your algorithm works.

Infinite loops

These are also called *endless loops* because they go on repeating and never stop.

Sometimes they are intentional, for example if you want the algorithm to check the temperature over and over again, indefinitely or until there is an override to exit the loop. However, infinite loops are often unintentional. A common cause is to place a condition in a 'WHILE' loop that will always be true.

Code

```
index ← 1
WHILE index <10
        OUTPUT index
ENDWHILE
```

In this example, the programmer has forgotten to increment the variable index before the end of the loop. It will always remain with the value of 1 and therefore it will always be less than 10.

Code

```
index ← 1
WHILE index <10
        OUTPUT index
        index ← index -1
ENDWHILE
```

In this example, the programmer has changed the variable index before the end of the loop but has written – 1 instead of + 1 so it will always be less than 10.

Remember

1. Iteration means that a procedure or a set of statements or commands is repeated a set number of times or until there is a desired outcome.
2. In definite iteration, the number of iterations is known before the execution of the loop is started and can be run with 'FOR' loops and, if needed, 'WHILE' loops or 'REPEAT' loops.
3. In indefinite iteration (conditional iteration), the number of iterations is not known before the loop is started. The number of iterations depends on a condition becoming true or false.
4. Conditional 'WHILE' loops run until a condition becomes false.
5. 'REPEAT…UNTIL' loops run until a condition becomes true.
6. 'WHILE' loops are tested at the start of a loop.
7. 'REPEAT…UNTIL' loops are tested at the end of a loop.
8. Nested loops run completely inside another loop.
9. Infinite loops run forever. They might be deliberate or accidental.

Complete Interactive Activity 2c on Cambridge Elevate

Trace tables

When programs are being coded, errors often occur. Some of these may be syntax errors. Each program must be written in a particular way and use certain keywords, depending on which programming language is being used.

Programming languages have rules of grammar, just like any other language.

Syntax errors do not impact algorithms. They can be written in pseudo-code for human use and are not meant to be understood by a computer. Therefore, pseudo-code is far more forgiving. You could have incorrect capital letters, missing punctuation marks and missing indents and it would still be understandable because it will be followed by a human, instead of a computer.

Algorithms and their expression in pseudo-code are intended to allow a programmer to create a logical solution to a problem that can then be translated into any actual programming language that a computer can understand.

Algorithms can suffer from the second type of error: logical error. There might be a blip in the programmer's thinking and the algorithm doesn't produce the output or solution expected.

For example, a 'WHILE' loop might have been set up incorrectly or an 'IF' block doesn't select what it was expected to select. One way to trap these errors is to do a dry run of the algorithm using sample data which can be tracked through the algorithm using a trace table.

Analysing the algorithm with a trace table will show whether it achieves what it was intended to, that is whether it is fit for purpose.

A trace table has columns for each of the variables and rows for each of the steps in the algorithm.

WORKED EXAMPLE

Here is a trace table for the previous nested loop algorithm. However, so that the trace table isn't too large it will just cover the times tables for 2.

```
FOR index ← 2 to 2

    OUTPUT index

    FOR times ← 2 TO 12

        OUTPUT index * times

    ENDFOR

ENDFOR
```

index	Output	times	Output
2	2		
2		2	4
2		3	6
2		4	8
2		5	10
2		6	12
2		7	14
2		8	16
2		9	18
2		10	20
2		11	22
2		12	24

There are two loops: one for 'index' and an inner loop for 'times'. When the outer loop starts, index is equal to 2.

The next command is to output the value of index.

Then times runs in a loop from 2 to 12. On each turn of this loop, the value of index*times has to be output.

While the inner loop is running, the value of index remains at 2.

WORKED EXAMPLE

The following algorithm allows a user to enter test scores and calculates the numbers that qualify for a pass or a fail.

```
OUTPUT "Enter the number of scores to be input"
number ← USERINPUT
pass ← 0
fail ← 0
FOR entry ← 1 TO number
        OUTPUT "Please enter the score"
        score ← INPUT
        IF score >= 5 THEN
                pass = pass +1
        ELSE
                fail = fail + 1
        ENDIF
ENDFOR
OUTUT pass, fail
```

This algorithm could be tested with sample data such as 6, 9, 5, 3, 10.

number	entry	score	pass	fail	output
5			0	0	
5	1	6	1	0	
5	2	9	2	0	
5	3	5	3	0	
5	4	3	3	1	
5	5	10	4	1	4, 1

At the start the values of 'pass' and 'fail' are 0 and 'number' is 5 as 5 entries are to be made.

The values of 'entry', 'pass' and 'fail' change as the loop is running according to the relational operator.

WORKED EXAMPLE

The following algorithm would allow the user to input numbers over and over again and the sum of the numbers is found. The loop will stop when the user enters a zero as the loop runs while the number is greater than 0. (It would also stop if the user entered a negative number.)

```
total ← 0

number ← USERINPUT

WHILE number > 0

        total ← total + number

        number ← USERINPUT

ENDWHILE

OUTPUT total
```

This algorithm could be tested with sample data such as 3, 13, 21, 28, 0.

The trace table would be:

total	number	Output
0	3	
3	13	
16	21	
37	28	
65	0	65

At the start total = 0 and the first test number, 3, is entered.

Therefore total = 3 when the second number, 13, is added.

The loop should stop when the user enters 0. At that time, the total should be 65 and that will be the output.

WORKED EXAMPLE

Here is another algorithm.

```
Y ← 2

FOR X ← 1 TO 6

        Y ← Y + X

ENDFOR

OUTPUT Y
```

GCSE Computer Science for AQA

X	Y	Output	Explanation
	2		At the start of the algorithm Y = 2.
1	3		When the loop starts, X becomes 1 and Y becomes equal to 3 (2 +1).
2	5		When X is incremented to 2, Y is equal to 5 (2 + 3) – as Y is equal to 3 from the previous loop.
3	8		When X is incremented to 3, Y is equal to 8 (5 + 3)
4	12		Explanations as above.
5	17		
6	23	23	The final value of Y is output.

Tip

At the start, turns = 0 and x = 3.

On each turn of the loop, x is changed to x*3 and turns is changed to turns + 3.

The loop will run while turns < 22.

Download Worksheet 2.4 from Cambridge Elevate

ACTIVITY 2.5

Use a trace table to track the variables and the output from the following algorithm.

```
turns ← 0
X ← 3
WHILE turns < 22
        turns ← turns + 3
        X ← X * 3
ENDWHILE
OUTPUT x
OUTPUT turns
```

Here is the start of the trace table.

turns	X	Output
0	3	
0	9	
3	27	

Remember

1. Trace tables use sample data to track the values of variables through an algorithm.
2. Trace tables have columns for variables and outputs, and rows for steps in the algorithm.

Complete Interactive Activity 2d on Cambridge Elevate

38

Determining the purpose of an algorithm

When you study an algorithm written by someone else it's not always obvious what it should do. Completing a trace table will help you understand its purpose.

WORKED EXAMPLE

Describe the purpose of the following algorithm.

```
OUTPUT "Enter weight of parcel."

weight ← USERINPUT

IF weight ≤ 2 THEN

        cost ← 8

ELSE

        extraWeight ← weight - 2

        IF extraWeight ≤ 10 THEN

                cost ← 8 + (extraWeight * 2.50)

        ELSE

                cost ← 8 + (10 * 2.50) + (extraWeight - 10 * 3.50)

        ENDIF

ENDIF

OUTPUT "The cost for" + weight + "Kg is £" + cost
```

The rules behind the calculation can be investigated by using a trace table and applying different inputs.

The inputs used will be 1, 2, 6, 12 and 13.

weight	extraWeight	cost	output
1		8	8
2		8	8
6	4	18	18
12	10	33	33
13	11	36.5	36.5

The algorithm calculates the cost of sending a parcel where the cost depends on the weight of the parcel.

The inputs used in the trace table show that:

- There is a standard charge of £8 up to a total of 2 kg.
- If the weight is over 2 kg, there is an additional charge of £2.50 for each extra kg, up to a total of 10 kg extra (so a total weight of 12 kg).
- When the weight exceeds this additional 10 kg, there is a charge of £3.50 for each extra kg.

ACTIVITY 2.6

Describe the purpose of the following algorithm.

Create a trace table using the following inputs:

13, 42, 3, 6, 9, 0

```
even ← 0
odd ← 0
sumEven ← 0
sumOdd ← 0
REPEAT
       number ← USERINPUT
       IF number MOD 2 = 0 THEN
              even ← even + 1
              sumEven ← sumEven + number
       ELSE
              odd ← odd + 1
              sumOdd ← sumOdd + number
       ENDIF
UNTIL number = 0
OUTPUT even, sumEven, odd, sumOdd
```

Efficiency of algorithms

Different programmers will create different algorithms to solve the same problem: for every problem, there can be many solutions.

Although they might successfully solve the problem, some algorithms might be more *efficient* than others: they might have fewer lines of code or produce the solution in less time. In other words, some algorithms have greater efficiency. In Chapter 4, we will be looking at algorithms for sorting and searching data and seeing that some algorithms can do this far more quickly than others.

Key term

efficiency: efficiency can be assessed by:
- How long it takes a program to generate a result.
- How much code has been written to generate the result.
- How much memory it uses.

Software development

Creating an algorithm is only one stage in developing software to meet the needs of a particular situation. In Chapter 6 we will be looking in detail at all of the stages that need to be carried out in order to achieve a successful outcome. Briefly, these stages are:

- identification and analysis of the problem
- design
- implementation
- testing
- documentation
- evaluation
- maintenance.

In this chapter we have only looked at stages within the design phase. It is crucial to get the design of the solution right before proceeding to coding which is done during the implementation stage.

> **Tip**
>
> In the AQA specification these stages are listed as:
>
> - Design
> - Implementation
> - Testing
> - Evaluation/refining

Implementation

This is the stage where the algorithm, either in a flowchart or pseudo-code, is translated into an actual programming language. Pseudo-code allows the programmer to concentrate on the logic of the solution without having to think about the way the actual programming language has to be written with its rules and syntax.

It's similar to making notes of your ideas and then writing them out in 'proper' English with all the correct spellings, punctuation marks and rules of grammar.

WORKED EXAMPLE

Here is the algorithm of the guessing game that we looked at earlier.

```
mysteryNumber ← RANDOM_INT(1,100)
```
This will generate a random number between 1 and 100.

```
guess ← 0
```
The variable 'guess' is assigned the value of 0.

```
WHILE guess = 0
```
A 'WHILE' loop is set to run while 'guess' is equal to 0.

```
    OUTPUT "Please enter a number between
    1 and 100."
```
The user is asked to input a number which is assigned to the 'guess' variable. Therefore 'guess' is no longer equal to 0.

```
    guess ← USERINPUT
```

```
    IF guess > mysteryNumber THEN
```
If the guess is greater than the random number…

```
        guess ← 0
```
…guess is changed back to 0 so that the loop will run again and…

```
        OUTPUT "Your guess is too high."
```
…the user is informed.

```
    ELSE IF guess < mysteryNumber THEN
```
If the guess is less than the random number…

```
      guess ← 0
```
…guess is changed back to 0 so that the loop will run again and…

```
    OUTPUT "Your guess is too low."
```
…the user is informed.

```
  ENDIF
```
This ends the 'IF' block.

```
ENDWHILE
```
This ends the 'WHILE' loop and processing is sent back to the start if the guess has been changed back to 0.

```
OUTPUT "Well done. You guessed correctly!"
```
If the guess is actually equal to the random number, then the variable 'guess' will not be equal to 0 and so the loop will be exited and this print statement will be executed.

Now we will look at how the guessing game algorithm could be implemented in two different programming languages.

Python

Python is a programming language that was first released in 1991 and has become the most widely used language for teaching computer science in schools and universities. Python users have developed modules and libraries of functions so that it can be used for web and internet development, database access and networking.

WORKED EXAMPLE

Pseudo-code	Python 3

Pseudo-code:
```
mysteryNumber ← RANDOM_INT(1, 100)

guess ← 0
WHILE guess = 0
  OUTPUT "Please enter a number
  between 1 and 100."
  guess ← USERINPUT
  IF guess > mysteryNumber THEN
    guess ← 0
    OUTPUT "Your guess is too high."
  ELSE IF guess < mysteryNumber THEN
    guess ← 0
    OUTPUT "Your guess is too low."
  ENDIF
ENDWHILE
OUTPUT "Well done. You guessed correctly!"
```

Python 3:
```
import random
mysteryNumber = random.randint(1, 100)

guess = 0
while (guess == 0):
  guess = int(input("Please enter a number
  between 1 and 100: "))

  if guess > mysteryNumber:
    guess = 0
    print("Your guess is too high.")
  elif guess < mysteryNumber:
    guess = 0
    print("Your guess is too low.")
print("Well done. You guessed correctly!")
```

Notice the following differences:

1. This language has its own terminology for generating a random number.

2. For the 'WHILE' loop there is no 'ENDWHILE'. Python uses indentation to show when a block starts and ends.

3. Python also uses indentation for 'IF' blocks.

4. Notice how the following commands require a colon after their statements. This is an example of the language's syntax:

```
while(guess==0):

if guess > mysteryNumber:
```

5. Notice how the program has to be told that the value that is input is an integer number:

```
guess = int(input("Please enter a number between
1 and 100: "))
```

> **Key term**
>
> syntax: the rules of spelling, punctuation and grammar of a language so that the meaning of what is being communicated is clear (humans can make allowances if the rules are broken, but computers can't!)

JavaScript

JavaScript is a computer programming language commonly used to create interactive effects within web browsers. It is used with HTML to produce interactive web pages. HTML provides the user interface and JavaScript provides the brains.

> **Key term**
>
> HTML: hypertext markup language (HTML) is used to write web pages for the internet as well as for ebooks. The algorithm would be interpreted differently in JavaScript to create a version of the game that could be played in a web browser

Guessing game

Play   Try it

Enter a number between 1 and
100 and click the button.   **39**

Your guess is too low.

When the correct number is entered.

Guessing game

Play   Try it

Enter a number between 1 and
100 and click the button.   **45**

**Well done.
You guessed correctly!**

An actual loop does not have to be programmed as the user is doing it all themselves.

All that is needed is code attached to the action buttons.

> **Tip**
>
> This code is attached to the 'Play' button to generate the random number.
>
> Notice the semi-colon required at the end of each statement.

Code

```
var mysteryNumber = Math.floor((Math.random() * 100) + 1);
```

WORKED EXAMPLE

This code is executed when the 'Try it' button is pressed.

JavaScript code	Explanation
`var m = document.getElementById('message');`	This line creates a variable for the text box on the page where the messages will be displayed. Notice how a variable needs the 'var' keyword. This isn't needed in Python.
`var guess = document.getElementById('myguess').value;`	This stores the number (value) that the user has just entered in an entry box named 'myguess'.
`if(guess > mysteryNumber) {`	An 'if' statement. Notice how the block of the 'if' statement is enclosed in *braces* (curly brackets).
`m.innerHTML = ('Your guess is too high.');`	This is the message displayed if the guess is too high.
`document.getElementById('myguess').value = '';`	
`}`	Brace at end of 'if' block.

`else if (guess < mysteryNumber) {`
`m.innerHTML = ('Your guess is too low.');`
`document.getElementById('myguess').value = '';`
`}`
	This block checks if the number entered is too small.

`else {`
`m.innerHTML = ('Well done. You guessed correctly!');`
`}`
	If the number is not too large or too small, it must be just right!

The algorithm is interpreted differently for these two programming languages which produce different visual displays, but the basic logic was the same.

That basic logic was developed from the algorithm.

Remember

1. There can be many different algorithms to solve a particular problem.
2. Some algorithms are more efficient than others in terms of execution speed, amount of code and how much computer memory is needed.
3. Algorithms displayed as flow diagrams or pseudo-code have to be coded into programming languages.

Practice question

1. Complete the trace table for the following algorithm.

   ```
   number_1 ← 3
   number_2 ← 2
   FOR X ← 1 TO 5
        number_1 ← number_1 * X
        number_2 ← number_2 * (X + 1)
        total ← number_1 + number_2
   ENDFOR
   OUTPUT total
   ```

X	number_1	number_2	total	Output
	3	2	0	
1	3	4	7	

Complete Interactive Activity 2e on Cambridge Elevate

Your final challenge

You have been asked to create an algorithm for a game with the following specification:

- The player starts the game with £5.
- Each round of the game costs 20p. If the player has not got 20p, then they are informed and have to quit the game.
- For each game, the player has to roll three dice with six faces with numbers 1 to 6.
- If two dice have the same number, then the player wins £1.
- If all three dice have the same number, then the player wins £2.
- The player is informed if they have won any money and how much.
- They are also told how much money in total they have.
- The player is asked after each game whether they want to play again or quit.
- If they quit, they are told how much money they have.

Your task is to create an algorithm for this game. You can illustrate it using either a flowchart or pseudo-code.

Even if you are going to present your solution in pseudo-code, a flowchart might be useful for determining the information flow. The start of a possible flowchart is provided.

- Read through the specification until you understand exactly what you have to do.
- Make notes about the key points.

Here are some initial ideas:

- £5.00 to start the game.
- Ask if they want to play.
- Check if they have at least 20p.
- Deduct 0.20 if they play.
- Roll three dice.
- Check numbers on dice.
- Check if they have won any money.

Remember to:

- List the variables that you will use.
- List the inputs and outputs that will be required.
- Consider where selection and iteration will be required.

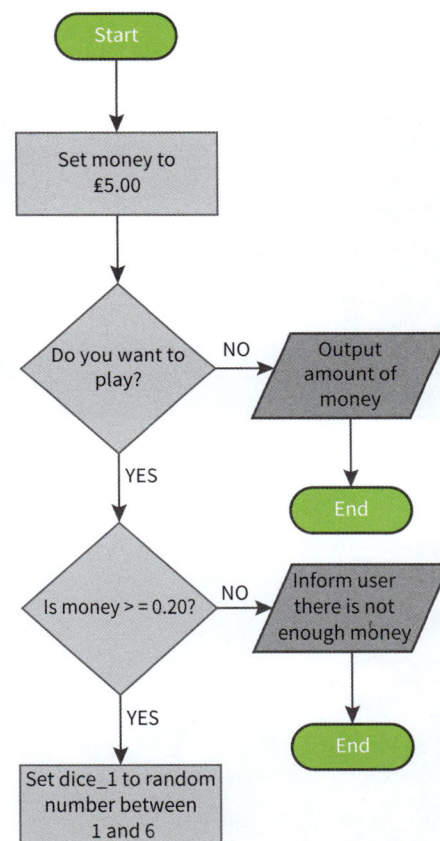

Download Self-assessment 2 worksheet from Cambridge Elevate (this content has not been approved by AQA)

3 Data types and structures

⭐ **Challenge: encode and decode messages with an encryption key**

- Throughout history people have sent secret messages by using invisible ink, ciphers and codes.
- Computers have enabled people to quickly encode and transmit messages using public and private encryption keys.
- Your challenge is to create an algorithm to encode and decode messages using an encryption key!

Why data types and structures?

- We saw in Chapter 1 that data is stored in variables. There are different types of data and therefore the computer must be told what type each variable is storing. This process is called 'declaring' the variable.
- Data can take many different forms, depending on the type of information that is being stored, for example the data might be different kinds of numbers, text data or logical data.
- How groups of related data items are organised and stored is the data structure. Data structure allows data to be grouped together so that links can be made between them and they can be processed in some way. For example, a school uses data structure to group data about their students and lessons. Data can be quickly processed to print a list of all the students in a particular lesson at a particular time.
- Data are held electronically all around us. This makes it easier for us to access. If we are ill whilst on holiday, a doctor can access our medical notes almost instantly.
- It is important to organise data. Dictionaries are organised alphabetically so that we can find the word we need. Digital data are the same: we need to put the data into categories in databases. Websites combine data from different databases all the time. An online bookshop will have data about books and customers, and each time you buy a book, a link will be made.

When you go to the doctor, information about what is wrong with you and the treatment you need is stored as data on computers.

Different data types

Examples of different data types can be seen in this screenshot from a video game. The image shows the information page of a computer game displaying the user's progress.

A variable will have to be declared as a 'string' to store name data.

Name: Alice Smith

Level	Complete	Score
1	Yes	900
2	Yes	650
3	Yes	775
4	Yes	850
5	No	0
6	No	0

A variable to hold whole numbers will be declared as an "integer".

Average Score: 793.7

A variable to hold one of two values– 'yes' or 'no' is a Boolean variable.

A variable to hold a number with decimal places is declared as a floating point variable or just 'float' for short.

In a computer program, a variable is used to hold data that can be used or manipulated in certain ways.

Computers need to be told what type of data it is, so they know how it can be manipulated and represented.

For example:

- A student created a variable called 'firstName' to hold the letters of a person's first name and declared it as a **string variable**, so that the computer would interpret the 1s and 0s as letters. It then won't try to use this variable in a mathematical equation because you can't multiply text.

- Similarly, a variable called 'length' is declared as a **numeric variable**, and can be multiplied by another number variable, for example 'width' to give the area.

Data type	Description of data type	Example
Integer	An integer is a numeric variable without a decimal. Integers are whole numbers and can be positive or negative. Sometimes a distinction is made between short and long integers, referring to how much data storage is used for the number. In most programming languages, the word 'int' is used to designate an integer type, but in some programming languages the word integer must be used.	3

Data type	Description of data type	Example
Real	Real numbers include all of the integer numbers that exist to infinity plus all of their fractions and decimals. Therefore $3, 6\,000\,001$ and 3.124569 are all real numbers. They do this using a data type called 'floating point', float or real.	3.25
Character	A character data type is used to store a single, alphanumeric character: a character representing a letter, number or symbol.	C 3 *
String	A string is more useful than the character data type as it can hold a list of characters of any length: it therefore represents alphanumeric data and symbols. When data are entered in a string variable they are enclosed with single or double quote marks, for example: firstName ← "David"	"David" "2015" "April 1"

Boolean	The Boolean data type can only represent two values: true or false.	This data type is very useful in loops, for example:
		
		`correct ← False`
		`mysteryNumber ← RANDOM_INT(1, 10)`
		`WHILE correct = False`
		`   OUTPUT "Please enter a number."`
		`   guess ← USERINPUT`
		`   IF guess = mysteryNumber THEN`
		`      correct ← True`
		`   ENDIF`
		`ENDWHILE`
		`OUTPUT "You guessed the number."`

Download Worksheet 3.1 from Cambridge Elevate

Complete Interactive Activity 3a on Cambridge Elevate

Key terms

integer: a whole number without decimals (can be positive or negative)

real: a numeric variable which can have a fractional value; it will have digits on either side of a decimal point. Commonly used to store currency values, for example 1.5 for £1.50

character: often abbreviated to 'char', it is a variable that holds one letter, number or symbol

In some languages, you have to explicitly state the data type of a variable, for example `int age` to declare the variable 'age' as an integer.

Other programming languages assume what the data type should be from the data that is input or stored, for example:

Code
```
variable ← 5 + 5
```

Some languages would assume that this was an integer, even though it is not specified, because the variable is made up of integers.

Code
```
OUTPUT variable
```

would return 10. And:

Code
```
variable ← '5 + 5'

OUTPUT variable
```

would return '5 + 5'.

The language would assume that this was a string, because of the quote marks.

ACTIVITY 3.1

This is part of the pseudo-code for a program designed to enrol new members to a club.

```
OUTPUT "Please enter your first name."

firstName ← USERINPUT

OUTPUT "Please enter your last name."

lastName ← USERINPUT

OUTPUT "Please enter the initial of your middle name."

initial ← USERINPUT

OUTPUT "Please enter your age in years."

age ← USERINPUT

IF age < 18 THEN

    OUTPUT "Sorry" + firstName + " " + initial + " " +
    lastName + "but you are not old enough to join the club."

ELSE

    OUTPUT "Welcome to the club."

ENDIF
```

List the variables used in this code and suggest suitable data types for them.

Working with strings

If a variable is a string data type, the computer knows to interpret the 1s and 0s that make up the data as characters. The computer also knows the ways in which the data can be manipulated.

There are many useful operations that can be performed on strings. Here are a few.

The length of a string

An important property of a string is its length. In fact, this is one of the most important properties. All programming languages have a method of finding the length of a string and in pseudo-code it is written as:

Code

```
LEN(stringName)
```

Here is an example of its use:

Code

```
name ← "Freda Smith"

OUTPUT LEN(name)
```

This would output the number 11 (don't forget to count the space!).

Here is the string with the index positions of the characters.

0	1	2	3	4	5	6	7	8	9	10
F	R	E	D	A		S	M	I	T	H

Although there are 11 characters, in many languages they are numbered 0 to 10.

WORKED EXAMPLE

In the following example, we will work out the number of times that a particular character occurs in a string.

The algorithm needs to use a loop to go through the string one letter at a time looking for the character. This is called string traversal. The algorithm will therefore need to know the length of the string.

In this example, the string is stored in a variable named 'myString' and it is searching for the letter 'c'.

Key term

string traversal: moving through a string, one item of data at a time; sometimes this might just mean counting

Code

`times ← 0`	A variable assigned the value 0. This variable will be used to count the number of occurrences.
`FOR index ← 0 TO LEN(myString) - 1`	A 'FOR' loop is started. This will go through the string starting at index 0. It will run until it reaches the last index which is equal to the length of the string minus one. For example, if the length of the string is 13, then it will have to run from index 0 to index 12. Note that 12 is the length minus 1.
`IF myString[index] = "c" THEN` `times ← times + 1`	If the letter at position index is a 'c', 'times' is incremented by 1.
`ENDIF`	This ends the 'IF' block.
`ENDFOR`	This is the end of the loop. Processing will be directed to the start until the condition is met.
`OUTPUT times`	This will display the value of the variable 'times'.

Download Worksheet 3.2 from Cambridge Elevate

ACTIVITY 3.2

Create an algorithm that will count the number of times that a particular character, entered by a user, occurs in a string also entered by the user.

Splitting up strings

A string may need to be split up into substrings. In the example we are using, the variable contains the full name:

0	1	2	3	4	5	6	7	8	9	10
F	R	E	D	A		S	M	I	T	H

If this variable is being used to display information to the user, printing 'Hello Freda' would be far more friendly than printing 'Hello Freda Smith'.

WORKED EXAMPLE

Create an algorithm that will create two strings, one containing the first name and one containing the surname, from a string that contains the full name.

What we need to do is to find the space. Everything before this is the first name and everything after this will be the surname. A loop is needed. In this example, the variable 'fullName' contains the whole name.

```
OUTPUT "Please enter the full
       name with a space
       between the first name
       and surname."
```

```
fullName ← USERINPUT
firstName ← ""
lastName ← ""
```
Two variables are declared and given the values of empty strings so that they can be added to later.

```
FOR index ← 0 TO LEN(fullName)
- 1
      IF fullName[index] = " "
      THEN
         position ← index

      ENDIF
ENDFOR
```
This 'FOR' loop will traverse the string…

…to find the index position of the space.

This index position is stored in the variable 'position'.

This ends the 'IF' block.

This is the end of the loop. Processing will be directed to the start until the condition is met.

```
FOR index ← 0 TO position-1
      firstName ← firstName +
      fullname[index]
ENDFOR
```
This loop traverses the 'fullName' string up to the character before the space and adds them to the 'firstName' string.

```
FOR index ← position + 1 TO
LEN(fullName) - 1
      lastName ← lastName +
      fullName[index]
ENDFOR
```
This loop traverses the 'fullName' string from the character after the space up to the last character and adds them to the 'lastName' string.

There will now be two new strings:

firstName	Freda
lastName	Smith

Finding substrings

An instance of one or more characters in a string in known as a substring: a string within a string.

In these examples, we have traversed a string looking for a single character. But what if we needed to find a substring that consisted of more than one character? This can again be found by using a loop. But it is more complicated!

This is our previous string example:

0	1	2	3	4	5	6	7	8	9	10
F	R	E	D	A		S	M	I	T	H

We could find if the substring 'RED' occurred and be notified of the index of its first letter. We would have to start at index 0 and check if characters 0, 1 and 2 were equal to 'RED'. We would then start at index 1 and see if 1, 2 and 3 were equal to 'RED'. Then start at index 2 and so on.

But we cannot continue beyond index 8 because if we started at index 9, we would have to check indexes 10 and 11. But there is no index 11 so we would get an error message!

```
myString ← "FREDA SMITH"
```
The name is assigned to the variable 'myString'.

```
found ← "No"
```
This variable will be changed to "Yes" if the substring is found.

```
FOR index ← 0 TO LEN(myString) - 3
```
A 'FOR' loop is set up to start from index 0 to 2 before the end of the string. We need to use – 3 as the last index in the string is the length – 1.

```
    testString ← ""
```
This variable is set to the value of an empty string so that it can be added to later at the start of each loop.

```
    FOR test ← 0 TO 2
```
A loop is set up to add the character at the index position plus the next two characters to the variable 'testString'.

```
        testString ← testString + myString(index + test)
    ENDFOR

    IF testString = "RED" THEN
```
If testString is equal to 'RED', then the variable 'found' is assigned the value 'Yes' and the variable 'position' is assigned the value of the start index.

```
        found ← "Yes"

        position ← index

    ENDIF

ENDFOR

IF found = "Yes" THEN
```
Messages are printed for the user informing them whether the substring has been found.

```
    OUTPUT "It was found at index" + position

ELSE

    OUTPUT "Sorry. Not found"

ENDIF
```

A student has made some notes in a text document on her computer and would like to check if she has used the word 'variable'.

Create an algorithm that would notify her if the word appears and also the number of times it is used.

Concatenation: joining strings together

In addition to cutting strings up into substrings, strings can also be joined together. This is called concatenation.

To concatenate two strings you would simply enter:

Code

```
stringOne + stringTwo
```

For example:

Code

```
firstName ← "Freda"

lastName ← "Smith"

fullName ← firstName + lastName

OUTPUT fullName
```

The output would be:

Code

```
FredaSmith
```

They would be concatenated without a space: the computer doesn't know how we write names! However, string variables can also be concatenated with literal text, as long as it is enclosed within speech marks. We could add a space as follows:

Code

```
firstName ← "Freda"

lastName ← "Smith"

fullName ← firstName + " " + lastName

OUTPUT fullName
```

Key term

concatenation: the placing together of two separate objects so that they can be treated as one, for example a string variable can be joined end-to-end to produce a larger string

We could add any other literal text:

Code
```
fullName ➡ firstName + " " + lastName + " is brilliant!"
```

Create an algorithm that would allow a user to enter their first name and their surname and would then print a message saying, 'Hello [first name surname]. How are you?'

Multiplying variables

Although we can't multiply string variables together, in the Python programming language we can use the * symbol to generate multiple copies of the same string. For example:

Code
```
myString ← "5"

OUTPUT myString * 5
```

This would return:

```
55555
```

Converting strings to numbers and numbers to strings

Casting refers to when strings are converted to numbers and numbers to strings.

Numeric data within a string may be needed for a mathematical calculation and must therefore be converted from string data type to a mathematical one, such as an integer or a real number.

This can be easily done.

Code
```
myNumber ← STRING_TO_INT(myString)
```
would convert numeric data into an integer.

```
myNumber ← STRING_TO_REAL(myString)
```
would convert it into a real number.

Obviously using the statement `myNumber ← STRING_TO_INT(myString)` in an actual programming language would produce an error message if myString contained the data 5.3. It could only be a whole number.

If you wanted an integer, you could do the following:

Code
```
myNumber ← int(STRING_TO_REAL(myString))
```

Key term

casting: converting one data type to another data type

Watch out

Sometimes the computer can become confused as to whether a variable is a number or a string and produce an error message when a string is used in a mathematical calculation.

These problems can be solved by explicitly casting the variables.

Converting a number (integers and floating point numbers) to a string is done in the following way using the AQA pseudo-code:

Code

```
myString = REAL_TO_STRING(myNumber)
```

OR

```
myString = INT_TO_STRING(myNumber)
```

Storing multiple items of data

So far we have stored data in variables, for example:

Code

```
firstName ← "David"

length ← 13

answer ← True
```

Each variable holds one, single item of information.

If you were writing an algorithm to store the names of all your friends, you could do something like this:

Code

```
name_1 ← "Catherine"

name_2 ← "Jack"

name_3 ← "Rosie"
```

Or you could use the USERINPUT command:

Code

```
OUTPUT "Please enter a name."

name_1 ← USERINPUT

OUTPUT "Please enter a name."
```

```
name_2 ← USERINPUT
OUTPUT "Please enter a name."
name_3 ← USERINPUT
```

But when you start, you may not know how many friends' names you have to enter. And what happens if you fall out with one of them? Or what if you use the program again on another day and forget how many friends' names you have already stored and so don't know what number the next name will be.

Wouldn't it be great:

- if you could store all of the names in one list that you could add to?

- if when you had to enter another name it could just be appended to the end, without having to remember what number it was?

It would be even better if each item was given an index number, like the characters in a string, so that they could be manipulated more easily.

Well, there is a solution! There are data structures called arrays that let you do some or all of these things.

Arrays

An array is a data structure that contains a group of linked elements that are usually of the same data type. An array allows the storing of multiple pieces of data in one variable.

Arrays can be either static or dynamic. A static array has a fixed size and when it is declared the number of items it can hold must be stated, for example:

Code

```
array friends [5]
```

In our pseudo-code, this will create an array with the identifier 'friends' that will hold 5 items.

Notice how square brackets are used with arrays.

The data at a specific index can be printed, for example:

Code

```
OUTPUT friends[3]
```

Watch the arrays animation on Cambridge Elevate

Key terms

array: a structure that contains many items of data of the same type. The data are indexed so that a particular item of data can be easily found

static array: an array that is of a set size

dynamic array: an array that has not had its size defined and can change as data are appended

Watch out

In most programming languages, indexes for arrays start at 0, as they do for strings. However, some languages start array indexing at 1 and pseudo-code can use indexing beginning at either 0 or 1. In this book array indexing in pseudo-code starts at 0.

Tip

Investigate the programming language you are using to see how to declare a dynamic array.

WORKED EXAMPLE

A teacher has set an online test with ten questions. Create an algorithm that would store a student's answers to each question in an array.

```
FOR index ← 0 TO 9
    OUTPUT ("Please enter your answer to
    question" + index )
    answers[index] ← USERINPUT
ENDFOR
OUTPUT "Test finished"
```

A loop is set up to store the 10 answers.

The student is asked to enter the answers. The loop runs from 0 to 9.

The student's answer is stored in the array.

The student is informed that the test is over.

ACTIVITY 3.5

Create an algorithm that will ask a user to enter the names of five cars into an array.

Whenever data are added to a static array the index must be stipulated, for example

```
cars[3] ← "Hyundai"
```

If this was in a programming language and not pseudo-code, and a user tried to add data to index cars [6] in this example, an error message would be generated. This is because it has been declared as having only five items at indexes 0 to 4.

If an array is declared as a dynamic array in a programming language, then an item cannot be inserted at a particular index position as there aren't any index positions until items have already been inserted! There has to be a method to add one to the end. This can be the 'append' keyword.

Code

```
array cars []

cars.append("Hyundai")
```

Therefore 'Hyundai' will be at the index position 0.

The append command (or a similar one) will be available in the programming language that you are studying, but it is not included in the AQA pseudo-code.

Array length

Like a string, arrays have a length property indicating the number of items they contain.

Using the previous example of the static array:

Code

```
LEN(cars)
```

would return the value 5.

Once the length is known, a loop can be used to traverse the array.

The loop could be used to see if a value was present in the array and also return its index.

Code

```
FOR index ← 0 TO LEN(array) - 1

    IF cars[index] = "Renault" THEN

        OUTPUT "Renault is in the list at
        index." + index

    ENDIF

ENDFOR
```

A 'FOR' loop is set up to run from the first index (0) to the last (the length) - 1.

The user is looking for all items with the value 'Renault'.

If 'Renault' is at the index, a message is printed along with the index number.

ACTIVITY 3.6

Create an algorithm that would print all of the items stored in an array named 'cars'.

(Remember that the numbering starts at 0 and that you can use the 'LEN' method.)

> **Tip**
>
> The length method can be used for arrays as well as strings.

ACTIVITY 3.7

An array contains all of the lower case letters of the alphabet in alphabetical order. Create an algorithm that would return the array indexes of all the letters in the following string: 'computer'.

> **Tip**
>
> You will have to go through the string one character at a time and then search for the character in the array.

Max, min and mean

If you have an array of number values, you can traverse it to find the maximum or minimum value.

Here is an algorithm that will find the maximum value. The values are stored in an array called 'results'.

Code

```
max ← 0

FOR index ← 0 TO LEN(results) - 1

    IF results[index] > max THEN

        max ← results[index]

    ENDIF

ENDFOR

OUTPUT max
```

A variable named 'max' is assigned a value of 0.

This loop will go through each item in the array.

If the data item has a value greater than is currently stored in 'max', then 'max' is assigned this value. So if any item is greater than currently stored, this item replaces the previous 'max'.

Maths skills

To find the mean, the values are added together and then divided by the number of values added. Although the marks may be integers, the mean may be a float or a real number.

ACTIVITY 3.8

A student has all of her computer science marks stored in an array. Create an algorithm that would allow her to find:

a. the minimum value.

b. the mean of the marks.

Slicing an array

An array can be cut up, or sliced, into smaller arrays in the same way as a string.

WORKED EXAMPLE

Here is an array that contains seven data items:

```
colours ← ["red", "orange", "yellow", "green", "blue", "indigo", "violet"]
```

If we wanted to create a smaller array with just the first three items, we could use the following algorithm:

```
colours ← ["red", "orange", "yellow", "green",
"blue", "indigo", "violet"]
FOR index ← 0 TO 2

    someColours[index] ← colours[index]
ENDFOR
```

Here is the original array named 'colours'.

A loop is set up which will run from 0 to 2, that is the first three items.

The items are copied from the colour array to the 'someColours' array.

The new array will contain the colours red, orange and yellow.

Tip

When declaring the new array, in some languages including Python you can use a variable instead of an actual number.

ACTIVITY 3.9

A student has an array that stores all of his computer science marks:

```
[6, 9, 2, 5, 8, 3, 9, 9, 10, 9, 5, 7, 10]
```

Create an algorithm, using pseudo-code, which would create a new array called 'pass' and copy all the marks of 5 and over into this new array.

Complete Interactive Activity 3c on Cambridge Elevate

Changing data items in an array

Changing a data item in an array is quite straightforward. The method is to create a loop to find the data item and then assign a new value at that index.

A student has been carrying out a survey of cars passing the school between certain times. The make of each car has been stored in an array called 'cars', but the student realises that he has misspelt 'Vauxhall', and has entered 'Vauxall' instead. The spelling mistakes can be corrected by using a loop:

```
FOR index ← 0 to LEN(cars) - 1

    IF cars[index] = "Vauxall" THEN

        cars[index] ← "Vauxhall"

    ENDIF

ENDFOR
```

A loop is set up to search through the indexes of the array. The 'length' method has been used to find the length of the array. If 'Vauxall' is found, it is changed to 'Vauxhall'.

A teacher has created an array called 'exam1' to store the student marks for an exam. He discovered he had made a mistake in the mark scheme and results under 50 should be increased by five marks and results over 50 should be increased by ten marks. Create an algorithm that would amend all of the results.

Complete Interactive Activity 3d on Cambridge Elevate

Multi dimensional arrays

In this array, `cars ← ["Ford", "Renault", "Vauxhall"]`, there is only one item of information at each index position, the name of the manufacturer.

Wouldn't it be great if we could store several pieces of information about the data item at each index position and access them using the index? We can do this by using a multi dimensional array if we want to arrange data into a table format.

A multi dimensional array is an 'array of arrays': each item at an index is another array.

If we wanted to declare an array to store the scores for five users of a game we would use this statement:

Code ───────────────────────────────────
```
array scores [5].
```
───

If the game has three levels and we want to store these scores for each user we could create a two-dimensional array. We would declare it as:

Code

```
array scores [5] [3]
```

This would create an array at each index to store three items of information.

The scores for the three levels for each user can be stored.

Rows and columns

We can visualise a two-dimensional array as a matrix of rows and columns. The scores array would look like this with the rows representing the users and the columns the scores for each level:

	0	1	2
0	76	58	35
1	78	70	56
2	69	85	93
3	86	76	89
4	67	45	45

Each item of information has two indexes. The value of scores [2][1] is 85.

ACTIVITY 3.11

State the values at the following indexes.

a. scores [2][0]

b. scores [3][1]

Entering data into a two-dimensional array

Here is how a user could be asked to enter data into a two-dimensional array to store the first names and surnames of their friends.

Code

```
FOR index ← 0 TO 4

    OUTPUT "Please enter first name"

    friends[index] [0] ← USERINPUT

    OUTPUT "Please enter surname"

    friends[index] [1] ← USERINPUT

ENDFOR

OUTPUT "Thank you. You have entered
all five friends."
```

A loop is set up running from 0 to 4 so that five entries can be made.

The entries are made at index 'index' which will run from 0 to 4. The first one will be at [0][0] and the second at [0][1]

Saving the arrays

Time is taken entering data into an array and then the computer is turned off and all that data are lost. All that time was wasted!

Wouldn't it be great if the arrays could be saved to a disk file and then read in again?

Well, they can. They can be saved as text files.

This is covered in Chapter 5.

Other data structures

Programming languages use many other data structures; some are common but some are specific to each language. Examples include lists, tuples, namedtuples, records and dictionaries.

ACTIVITY 3.12

Investigate the programming language that you are studying to find out if any of these data structures are supported.

Records

A record is a collection of data elements about a particular entity.

For example, records could be created about cars. Each record could have data elements for make, model, maximum speed, etc. The elements can be of different data types.

Each record that is created has the same structure and is a collection of the same elements.

The elements can be indexed by using numbers (as in arrays) or by names called field names.

Databases

When large amounts of linked data need to be stored, a database is usually created using database management software. This structures and manages the storage of the data by allowing users to edit and sort data and, more importantly, to search or query data.

Key terms

entity: something recognised as being capable of an independent existence, which can be uniquely identified, and about which data can be stored. It can be a physical object, for example a car, person, student or book. It can also be a concept, for example a customer transaction

field: one item of information. For example, the make, model and maximum speed of a car are all fields

Key term

table: a collection of rows and columns forming cells which is used to store data and user information in a structured and organised manner

The records are stored in **tables** as shown in the figure.

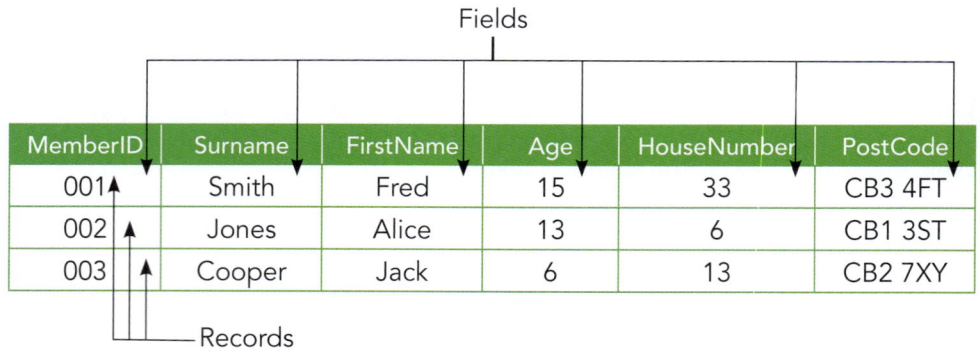

Fields

MemberID	Surname	FirstName	Age	HouseNumber	PostCode
001	Smith	Fred	15	33	CB3 4FT
002	Jones	Alice	13	6	CB1 3ST
003	Cooper	Jack	6	13	CB2 7XY

Records

Each record is a collection of data elements: Member ID, Surname, FirstName, etc. Each element is identified by a field name.

Some programming languages allow users to create a similar data structure and the records are sometimes referred to as 'structs'. When these are set up, the data type for each element is usually stipulated as the elements can be of different data types.

In the C programming language a struct could be set up to store records containing the following elements in the following way:

```
struct club {
    int  MemberID;
    char  Surname[25];
    char  FirstName[25];
    int   age;
    char   PostCode[8]
};
```

In Python, one way of creating records is to use 'namedtuples'. Here is an example of a namedtuple record structure.

`from collections import namedtuple`	
`Pets = namedtuple('Pets', 'animal name age')`	A data structure named 'Pets' is defined and created. The field names of the data items are 'animal', 'name' and 'age'.
`Dottie = Pets(animal = 'cat', name = 'Dottie', age = 10)`	A record with the unique identifier of 'Dottie' is created.
`Jack = Pets(animal = 'cat', name = 'Jack', age = 9)`	And two more are created.
`Lassie = Pets(animal = 'dog', name = 'Lassie', age = 13)`	

These records can be printed and even searched. For example, a loop could be used to examine each record and count the number of cats.

Watch out

In the AQA pseudo-code, there are no commands for creating records.

Similarly Python does not have 'records' but complex data structures, using field names, can be created using 'namedtuples'.

Complete Interactive Activity 3e on Cambridge Elevate

Practice question

1. For a science experiment, Ann recorded the air temperature three times per day (morning, noon and evening) for a week (beginning with Sunday). She stored the data in a two-dimensional array.

	0	1	2
0	6	13	5
1	5	12	6
2	9	17	8
3	9	20	9
4	7	15	6
5	6	13	6
6	7	13	6

   a. State the data type Ann should use for this data.
   b. If Ann wants to output the temperature at noon on Monday, she would write the following code:

   `OUTPUT temperature[1][1]`

   i. State the temperature that would be output.
   ii. Write the code that she would use to output the temperature in the evening on Wednesday.
   c. Ann needs to calculate the average temperature for each day and the average for the week. Using a flowchart or pseudo-code create an algorithm that would do this.

Remember

1. An array is a data structure that contains a group of linked elements which are of the same data type.
2. Arrays allow the storing of multiple pieces of data in one variable.
3. Arrays can be either static or dynamic.
4. Each data item stored in an array has an index.
5. The length of an array states the number of indexes used.
6. Arrays can be traversed and sliced.
7. Data items can be edited and deleted.
8. In a multi dimensional array more than one index is used to reference each data item.

Your final challenge

Computers have enabled people to quickly encode and transmit messages using public and private keys. One method is to shift the letters of the alphabet to the right or left by a set number of places. The number of 'shifts' that are made is called the key. For example, with a left shift and a key of 2, the alphabet would be changed to that shown on the bottom row:

A	B	C	D	E	F	G	H	I	J	K	L	M	N	O	P	Q	R	S	T	U	V	W	X	Y	Z
Y	Z	A	B	C	D	E	F	G	H	I	J	K	L	M	N	O	P	Q	R	S	T	U	V	W	X

Notice how the letters at the end move to the start of the alphabet.

So if the message was:

PLEASE SEND MORE TROOPS

The encrypted version would be:

NJCYQC QCLB KMPC RPMMNQ

If the recipient knew the key used, they could decrypt the message.

What you have to do:

- Design an algorithm using a flowchart or pseudo-code to encode and decode messages in this way.
- You should then code and test the program using the programming language that you are studying.

Good luck!

Tip

This is quite a difficult challenge and so here are some hints and tips.

- The message to be encrypted or decrypted will be in a string.

- All of the letters of the alphabet can be stored in a string. If you are using upper and lower case, you could use two strings.

- When encrypting, each letter has to be moved to the left: the number to be moved depends on the key used and vice versa for decrypting.

- The most difficult part is at the end of the alphabet, for example using an encryption key of 4 an 'A' would be encrypted as a 'W' and a 'W' would be decrypted as an 'A'.

Download
Self assessment 3 worksheet from Cambridge Elevate (this content has not been approved by AQA)

4 Searching and sorting algorithms

Learning outcomes
By the end of this chapter, you should be able to:
- explain why sorted lists are of more value than unsorted lists
- understand the bubble sort and merge sort algorithms and compare and contrast them
- use these algorithms to sort lists into ascending and descending order
- understand the linear and binary search algorithms and compare and contrast them
- use these algorithms to search sorted and unsorted lists
- write code for the implementation of these algorithms.

⭐ **Challenge: write an algorithm to find the top ten!**

Every week the UK Top 40 is worked out by taking into account sales of CDs and vinyl, digital downloads and the number of times the music has been streamed.

The total sales are collated and the final amounts sorted into order.

At the end of this chapter, you will write a program to analyse the data to find the top ten!

If a train timetable wasn't sorted into order according to the times the trains left, you would have to read each one until you found the correct train and time.

Why search and sort?

Searching and sorting algorithms are used in lots of programs to make data easier to access and understand.

- Computer game leader boards are sorted from the *highest* score to the *lowest* score to make it easy to find the winner and your position in the list.
- Search engines like Google use special algorithms to help find us the most useful search results.
- Online shopping websites order their products by type, so that you can click straight to the department you're looking for, rather than searching through the whole site.

🔑 **Key terms**

searching: looking through a file to see if particular data are there
sorting: putting items of data into a precise order, for example alphabetical or numerical

Sorting

Sorting makes it easier to **search** for the data you need. Look at this football league table. The table hasn't been sorted according to points won. Time yourself to see how long it takes you to find the team in 13ᵗʰ position.

CompSci League 1				
	Played	Won	Drawn	Lost	Points
Naciri Orient	38	24	7	7	79
Walton Wanderers	38	10	8	20	38
Salisbury Hotspur	38	7	9	22	30
Whiscombefield	38	25	7	6	82
Axe Vans Albion	38	13	6	19	45
McGarvey Club Rovers	38	21	9	8	72
Campbell Palace	38	9	5	24	32
Valpy Harriers	38	10	7	21	37
St Smart Rangers	38	26	6	6	84
Fradford United	38	27	5	6	86
Watkins Athletic	38	19	7	12	64
Fayebury Town	38	15	4	19	49
Porterfield Green	38	8	9	21	33
Cunningham Town	38	15	11	12	56
Farr County	38	13	11	14	50
Stevens Town Park	38	10	8	20	38
Linghorn Lions	38	11	9	18	42
Mantovani United	38	21	6	11	69
Howardsmith Stanley	38	7	15	16	36
Walford Thistle	38	11	7	20	40

If data is *sorted* into a relevant order you can generally *search* it far more quickly.

> **Tip**
>
> Data can be sorted into either
> **ascending order**: sorted from smallest to largest, e.g. 123456789 or ABCDEF
> or
> **descending order**: sorted from largest to smallest, e.g. 987654321 or FEDCBA

Sorting algorithms

When sorting data items it is essential to compare them with each other so that they can be put into the correct order.

There may be millions of items of data to compare, so sorting algorithms must carry out the task as efficiently as possible so as not to cause a bottleneck – another part of the program may not be able to run until the sorting has been carried out.

> **Key term**
>
> compare: assess how items of data are similar or different to each other, to help decide which order they should go in

Watch the **bubble sort** algorithm animation on Cambridge Elevate

Key term

adjacent items: items of data that are next to each other

Bubble sort

This algorithm is used to sort an unordered list by comparing adjacent items. It works like this:

1. Start at the beginning of the list of values.

2. Compare the first and second values. Are they in order? If so, leave them; if not, swap them.

3. Compare the second and third values. Are they in order? If so, leave them; if not, swap them.

4. Now move on to the third and fourth values, then the fourth and fifth values. Continue in this way to the end of the list, comparing each pair of values. Working through the list once is called the first pass.

5. Go through the list of values for a second time (which will be the second pass), a third time (the third pass), and so on, repeating steps 1–4 until there are no more swaps or passes to be made.

WORKED EXAMPLE

Sort this list into *ascending* order using the bubble sort algorithm.

6 3 1 2 7 4 5

In the following explanation, the swaps in each pass are shown.

First pass:

6	3	1	2	7	4	5	First and second values – wrong order – swap
3	6	1	2	7	4	5	Second and third values – wrong order – swap
3	1	6	2	7	4	5	Third and fourth values – wrong order – swap
3	1	2	6	7	4	5	Fourth and fifth values – correct order – leave
3	1	2	6	7	4	5	Fifth and sixth values – wrong order – swap
3	1	2	6	4	7	5	Sixth and seventh values – wrong order – swap
3	1	2	6	4	5	7	**End of first pass**

After the first pass the final number will be in the correct position, as it has been pushed along by comparing it with the other numbers. After the second pass, the second to last number will be in the correct position, and so on. So for each pass the number of comparisons needed is reduced by 1.

The **bubble sort** gets its name because the numbers tend to move up into the correct order like **bubbles** rising to the surface.

3	1	2	6	4	5	7	First and second values – wrong order – swap
1	3	2	6	4	5	7	Second and third values – wrong order – swap
1	2	3	6	4	5	7	Third and fourth values – correct order – leave
1	2	3	6	4	5	7	Fourth and fifth values – wrong order – swap
1	2	3	4	6	5	7	Fifth and sixth values – wrong order – swap
1	2	3	4	5	6	7	Sixth and seventh values – correct order – leave
1	2	3	4	5	6	7	**End of second pass**

Although the values are in the correct order after two passes, the algorithm would still have to do a third pass, as it repeats the comparisons until there are no swaps in the pass it has just completed.

ACTIVITY 4.2

Produce a table showing the results of the passes when sorting the following numbers into ascending order.

20 15 3 13 9 2 6

Coding the bubble sort algorithm

Now you know what bubble sort is and how to use it, but you need to write the code to be able to implement it.

In addition to flow diagrams and as a different method-writing a program, algorithms can also be expressed using pseudo-code. Pseudo-code is a kind of structured English for describing algorithms. It is a generic, code-like language that is independent of, and can be easily translated into, any programming language.

Below is pseudo-code for the bubble sort algorithm. The pseudo-code is in the left column, with the explanations in the right column.

Complete Interactive Activity 4a on Cambridge Elevate

Watch out

If you are using Python, there is no term *array*. You should use the term *list*.

Tip

We met Boolean variables in Chapter 3. They can hold the value of either 'true or 'false'.

`S ← List of items`	The items in the list are assigned to the variable S, which is the array.
`N ← length of list`	The variable N is needed to set the number of comparisons to be made.
`swapped ← true`	A Boolean variable (swapped) is defined and is set to true.
`WHILE swapped = true`	This WHILE loop will run while swaps have occurred in the last pass.
`swapped ← false`	Set the variable back to false ready for this pass.
`FOR X ← 1 to N - 1`	Set up a loop to go through the list. N − 1 is used as the actual list numbering will start at 0 and not at 1 i.e. the first item on the list will be at position 0.
`IF S[X - 1] > S[X] THEN`	This compares two numbers next to each other. In the first run of the loop it will compare the number at position 0 with that at position 1 (the one at 1 with the one at 2). If it is larger, then the following stages will occur.

```
            temp    ←   S[X - 1]        A variable named temp is assigned the value of the first number.

            S[X - 1]    ←    S[X]       The second number is swapped to the position of the first number.

            S[X]   ←   temp             The second number is now assigned the original number of the first.

            swapped    ←    true        If a swap has occurred then the Boolean variable is set to 'true' so that
                                        the 'WHILE' loop will run again when the FOR loop is complete.

        ENDIF                           End of IF selection.

      ENDFOR                            The 'FOR' loop will be repeated but the value of the variable X will
                                        be incremented by 1 each time it is run until it is equal to N.

  ENDWHILE                              The WHILE loop will run again as long as swapped is true.
```

ACTIVITY 4.3

This pseudo-code above will check through the entire list during each iteration of the WHILE loop.

Write the code for a bubble sort (you could use pseudo-code or a programming language) and amend it so that it does not check the numbers at the end of the list, which are already in their correct positions each time it carries out a pass.

If you use a programming language, run your program to check that it is working as you intended it to.

Download Worksheet 4.1 from Cambridge Elevate

Tip

A 'divide and conquer' algorithm works by dividing a problem into smaller and smaller sub-problems until they are easy to solve. The solutions to these are then combined to give a solution to the complete problem.

A 'brute force' algorithm does not include any techniques to improve performance, but instead relies on sheer computing power to try all possibilities until the solution to a problem is found.

Watch the merge sort algorithm animation on Cambridge Elevate

Remember

The bubble sort algorithm:

1. If there is only one item in the list, then stop.
2. Compare the first two values. If they are not in the correct order, swap them.
3. Repeat for the second and third values.
4. Compare each pair until the end of the list and swap if necessary.
5. Repeat steps 2 to 4 until no swaps have been made.

Merge sort

The merge sort algorithm is used to sort an unordered list by repeatedly (recursively) dividing a list into two smaller lists until the size of each list becomes one. This is why it is called a 'divide and conquer' algorithm. The individual lists are then merged. It works like this:

1. If there is only one item in the list, then stop.

2. Divide the list into two parts.

3. Recursively divide these lists until the size of each becomes one.

4. Merge the lists with the items in the correct numerical order.

The key thing to remember is that when the lists are merged, two at a time, they are merged with the items in the correct order.

WORKED EXAMPLE

Sort the following list into ascending order.

6 2 5 4 3 7 1

| 6 | 2 | 5 | 4 | 3 | 7 | 1 |

This is the original list.

| 6 | 2 | 5 | 4 | | 3 | 7 | 1 |

It is divided into two.

| 6 | 2 | | 5 | 4 | | 3 | 7 | | 1 |

It is divided again.

| 6 | | 2 | | 5 | | 4 | | 3 | | 7 | | 1 |

It is divided again until the size of each list becomes one.

| 2 | 6 | | 4 | 5 | | 3 | 7 | | 1 |

The individual lists are now merged, with the items in the correct numerical order.

| 2 | 4 | 5 | 6 | | 1 | 3 | 7 |

| 1 | 2 | 3 | 4 | 5 | 6 | 7 |

ACTIVITY 4.4

Produce a diagram showing the swaps required to sort the following numbers into ascending order using the merge sort method.

20 15 3 13 9 2 6

Complete Interactive Activity 4b on Cambridge Elevate

Remember

The merge sort algorithm:

1. If there is only one item in the list, then stop.
2. Divide the list into two parts.
3. Recursively divide these lists until the size of each becomes one.
4. Merge the lists with the items in the correct numerical order.

Tip

You might wonder why the merge sort would be necessary because it seems to be a complicated way of sorting. The answer can be seen in the next example where the algorithms are compared.

Download Worksheet 4.2 from Cambridge Elevate

Which algorithm should I use?

Choosing which sorting algorithm depends on what you want to do.

	Advantages	Disadvantages
Bubble sort	Simplest and easiest to code	Slowest
Merge sort	Fastest	More difficult to code

So if you have a very large list (for example, of more than 1000 items) and speed of execution is important, it is worth spending the extra time coding the merge sort algorithm. However, if you have a list of less than 1000 items, then the time saved in execution is so small that it is negligible and so you could use a bubble sort which is easier to code.

The following graph shows the times taken for the algorithms to sort lists of different lengths. As you can see, with small lists the differences are less than one second.

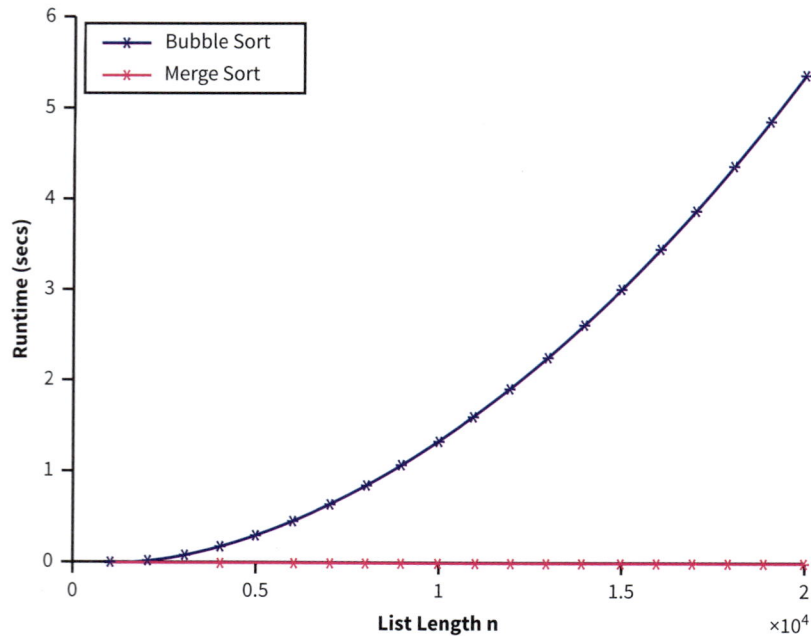

Searching algorithms

To find specific data, a list must be searched. The searching process will usually be far more efficient if the list has already been sorted into ascending or descending order.

Linear search

A **linear search** is a simple, sequential search. It starts at the beginning of the list and moves through the items, one by one, until it finds a matching value or reaches the end without finding one.

Linear searches are easy to code and have one great advantage: they do not require the list to be sorted. They are frequently used by programmers because they are easy to code and the code doesn't have to be written to sort the list first.

Key term

sequential: starts at the beginning and moves through the list one-by-one

Tip

Although a linear search doesn't need the list to be sorted, it takes far longer to find the required item. This could be a very serious problem when the amount of data being searched is very large. Users often search for data on internet sites and they would not be prepared to wait for the slower linear sort.

The linear search algorithm works like this:

1. Start at the first item in the list.

2. Compare the list item with the data you are looking for (the search criterion).

3. If they are the same, then stop. If they are not the same, then move to the next item.

4. Repeat steps 2 through 4 until the end of the list is reached.

ACTIVITY 4.5

An unsorted array contains the names of the 100 most popular names for children born last year.

Write the code, in the programming language you are studying, that would inform a user whether the name they had entered was, or was not, on the list.

Run your program to check that it is working as you intended it to work.

> ### Key term
>
> ordered: the data in the list are already in order

> ### Remember
>
> The linear search algorithm:
>
> 1. Start at the first item in the list.
> 2. Compare the list item with the search criterion.
> 3. If they are the same, then stop.
> 4. If they are not the same, then move to the next item.
> 5. Repeat steps 2, 3 and 4 until you reach the end of the list.

Binary search

The **binary search** algorithm searches an ordered list to find an item by looking at the middle item (the median) and comparing it with the search value. It works like this:

You must first decide on the target value you are searching for (your search criterion) and ensure your list is ordered.

1. Select the middle item (the median).

2. Compare this value with your search criterion. If they are equal, then stop.

3. If your search criterion is lower, then repeat with the left-hand side of the list; if it is higher, repeat with the right-hand side of the list.

4. Repeat these steps until the search criterion is found or there are no more items in the list to search.

> ### Maths skills
>
> The median is the middle number, for example if there are nine numbers, then the fifth number is the median.
>
> If there is an even number of items, then for the search algorithm, choose the item to the left of (or above, depending on whether you're working across or down a list) the middle, for example if there are eight numbers, then choose the fourth as the median. It can be found using integer division.
>
> Median = (length of list + 1) / 2 e.g. for a list of 10 items the median would be 11/2 = 5. The median is the fifth number.

> **Watch the binary search algorithm animation on Cambridge Elevate**

> ### Tip
>
> The binary search can only be used on sorted lists.

WORKED EXAMPLE

Find the value 9 from the following list:

3 6 8 9 12 15 18 24 27

| 3 | 6 | 8 | 9 | (12) | 15 | 18 | 24 | 27 | Find the median of the sorted list. |

| 3 | (6) | 8 | 9 | | | | | | The target (9) is less than the median so select the sub-list to the left and find its median. |

| | | (8) | 9 | | | | | | The sub-list does not include the number you have just tried. It was the median of the list in the previous step in the algorithm so you know that it is not the number that you are searching for.
Note, if there are an even number of values select the one to the left of the middle. |

| | | (9) | | | | | | | |

ACTIVITY 4.6

Use the binary search algorithm to find the letter 'g' in the following list using a table as in the Worked example.

a d g h k m p r s u w x z

Tip

A binary search will also work with a sorted list of strings as 'Green' is less than 'Smith' ('G' comes before 'S' in the alphabet) and 'Smyth' is greater than 'Smith' ('y' comes after 'i').

ACTIVITY 4.7

A student wrote down the following list of numbers and asked a friend to think of one of the numbers without telling them which one.

3, 5, 6, 8, 9, 12, 15, 21, 23, 45, 56, 63, 69

The student then used the binary search algorithm to find the number.

Here are the results:

- The first guess was too low.
- The second guess was too high.
- The third guess was too low.
- The fourth guess was correct.

What was the number?

ACTIVITY 4.8

Before writing the code to perform a binary search of a list, a student wrote down a list of statements so that they understood exactly what they had to do.

Here are their statements but they are not in the correct order.

Write out the statements so that they are in the correct order.

- Enter a number.
- If middle is less than number entered, then start equals middle + 1.
- Inform the user that the number is not present.
- End of search items equals length of array – 1.
- End of while loop.
- Middle equals (start + end) / 2 using integer division.
- Find the length of the array.
- If middle is greater than number entered, then end equals middle – 1.
- While start is less than or equal to end.
- If middle is equal to number entered tell the user and stop the loop.
- Start (of search items) equals 0.

ℹ Remember

The binary search algorithm (for a list in ascending order):

1. Select the median item of the list.
2. If the item is equal to the search criterion, then stop.
3. If the item is larger than the search criterion, then repeat steps 1 and 2 with the sub-list to the left.
4. If the item is smaller than the search criterion, then repeat steps 1 and 2 with the sub-list to the right.
5. Repeat steps 3 and 4 until the search criterion is found or there are no more items in the list to search.

Linear search vs binary search

How efficient are the algorithms?

Suppose we have a sorted list of 100 items (from 1 to 100 in ascending order).

For a linear search, the best case would be for the search item to be the first item of the list and so require only one comparison. The worst case would be for the item to be at the end of the list and so it would have to examine all of them and 100 comparisons would be needed.

For a binary search, the best case would be for the search item to be the middle item of the list.

The worst case would be for the item to be the last possible division, that is the median items selected could be: 50, 75, 88, 94, 97, 99, 100.

Therefore in the worst case, the binary search would find the search item after only seven comparisons.

1. Check the median number:

1	50	100

2. Too small, so check the new median:

51	75	100

3. Still too small, so again use the sub-list to the left:

76	88	100

4. Still too small, so repeat the process:

89	94	100

5. Need to repeat again:

95	97	100

6. Still too small. So another comparison is needed.

98	99	100

7. If this one is too small, there is only one number left.

100	

Worst case for a search of 100 items	
Linear search	100
Binary search	7

Download Worksheet 4.3 from Cambridge Elevate

Remember

Linear search versus binary search:

1. For a binary search, the list must be sorted.
2. For a sorted list, the binary search will be more efficient with smaller, average search times.

We use a binary search algorithm when finding a word in a dictionary.

Practice question

1. A student has stored the names of their friends in a file as shown:

Jane	Stephen	Matthew	Mary	David	Catherine	Maureen	Francesca	Alice	Carol

a. Show the stages of a bubble sort when applied to the data above.
   When the data were sorted, they were in the following order:

Alice	Carol	Catherine	David	Francesca	Jane	Mary	Matthew	Maureen	Stephen

b. Show the stages of a binary search to find the name 'Matthew' when applied to the data above.

Complete Interactive Activity 4c on Cambridge Elevate

Download Worksheet 4.4 from Cambridge Elevate

Your final challenge

In an official charts list, the performers' names and their total sales have been saved in an appropriate data structure.

- Write and test a program, using the language you are studying, that would sort the list into ascending order according to total sales.

- The user would like to enter a performer's name and be given their chart position. Write and test a program that would do this.

- Write and test a program that would allow the user to find out how many performers had total sales equal to or higher than a number entered, and display the result as a percentage of the total number of performers.

Download Self-assessment 4 worksheet from Cambridge Elevate (this content has not been approved by AQA)

5 Input and output

⭐ **Challenge: write a program to create and manage logins**

- To use computer systems and social networking sites users need to register for accounts, submit their details and create login names and passwords.
- They must then input their details to access the systems.
- Their names and passwords need to be authenticated each time they log in.
- Your challenge is to write a program in pseudo-code or a programming language that will allow users to:
  - create an account and password
  - allow them to change their password.

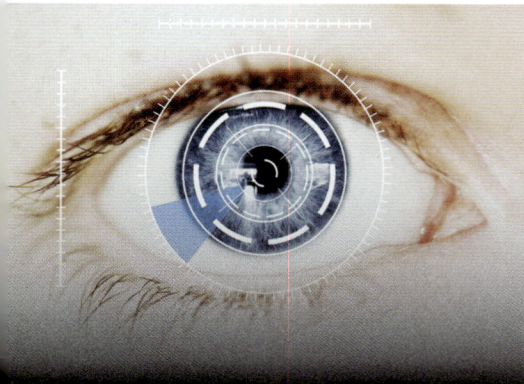

Why input and output?

Input and output devices are incredibly important as they allow us to interface with computer systems providing ease of use and security.

- The two most common methods are data input by keyboard and mouse which enable us to create complex files quickly and easily.

- Data can be entered or browsed using a touchscreen.

- Users can enter data to prove their identities using their bodies, for example fingerprint characteristics, eye colour and size and speech.

- Data about products can be entered automatically without users needing to type or point, using barcode scanners.

- Quick Response (QR) codes are barcodes that are machine readable, for example by smartphones. They contain information about the objects to which they are attached and can automatically connect the smartphone to websites, texts and emails.

- Contactless payment allows the input of card details using radio: Radio Frequency Identification (RFID).

- RFID microchips can be attached to any object and even implanted into pets so they can be tracked and identified.

Eye gaze devices can be used by people with limited mobility to allow them to navigate and control their computer with only their eyes.

Watch the inventive use of input devices on mobile phones animation on Cambridge Elevate

Input process output loop

In general, programs are created to process data. That's what they are for. The figure below shows how data is input, stored and processed into information which is output to the user.

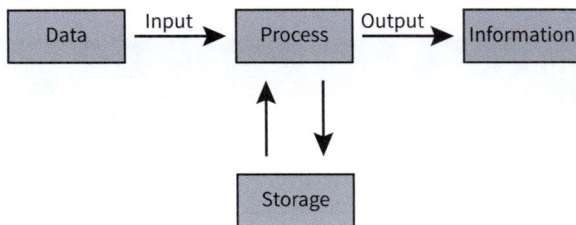

Data are input and processed by the software running on the computer. The data that are input must be meaningful and correct. This is illustrated by the acronym GIGO which stands for **G**arbage **I**n **G**arbage **O**ut. If the input data are incorrect, then so will any information that the program outputs to the user.

The computer executes the software and it must function as expected: it must be free from logical and syntax errors.

Complete Interactive Activity 5a on Cambridge Elevate

Validating data input

Validation routines are essential whenever data are input if the output is to be meaningful. For example, if a user has to enter a number into a variable called 'length' in a program to calculate the area of a rectangle, then entering 'don't know' is going to produce a strange result unless the data entry is validated. When data are validated, they are checked to ensure that the input is sensible.

> **Tip**
>
> See Chapter 1 for information on designing algorithms that function correctly and efficiently, and on turning the algorithms into error-free executable code.

> **Key terms**
>
> logical error: a problem in the design of the algorithm
>
> validation: the process through which the program checks that data is sensible and reasonable and appropriate to be processed by the program

> **Tip**
>
> Validation does not check that data are *correct*, that is that the user did not enter the wrong data. That would be impossible. Only a person could do that by checking the entered data against the original version. Even when data pass a validation test they might still be *incorrect*.
>
> For example, if a user enters '6' into a variable for the length of a rectangle, it could pass a validation check as it is a number but the length might, in fact, be 5 and not 6. The validation check would not find this error.

Presence check

This is the most basic and obvious check. It ensures that the person who is using the program has made a choice so that some data have been entered. It should ensure that the program will not continue until the data have been entered. You can include it in your algorithms and programs.

An example of where it could be included would be in a multiple-choice question asking the user to enter a letter between A and D. If the user does not make a choice, the program will not show the next question.

> ⚑ **Watch out**
>
> Take care with this kind of data entry. The choice from the user might be a letter rather than a number so it would need to be entered as a 'string' variable.

Code

`letter ← ""`	The variable letter is assigned the value of an empty string.
`WHILE letter = ""`	A 'WHILE' loop is set up which will run while the variable 'letter' contains an empty string.
`    OUTPUT "Please enter your selection:"`	The user is asked to input their selection. If they enter any text, then the string will no longer be empty and the loop will stop.
`    letter ← USERINPUT`	
`    IF letter = "" THEN`	The variable 'letter' is checked to see if anything has been entered. If nothing has been entered, it will still contain an empty string.
`        OUTPUT "You have not entered anything."`	This message will be output for the user.
`    ENDIF`	This closes the 'WHILE' loop and sends processing back to the start if no entry has been made.
`ENDWHILE`	

This output would be generated by the above code:

Code

`Please enter your selection:`
`You have not entered anything.`
`Please enter your selection:`
	Here is the error message displayed for the user. Notice how processing has moved back up to the start of the loop and the user is asked again to enter a selection.

> 💼 **Complete Interactive Activity 5b on Cambridge Elevate**

Range check

Often when data are entered, it would be expected to fall within a certain range.

Continuing the above example, the letter must be in the range A to D. Again this validation check can be included in your programs.

Code

Code	
`letter ← ""`	The variable name is assigned the value of an empty string.
`while letter <= "A" OR letter >= "D"`	A 'WHILE' loop is set up and it will run while the variable 'letter' contains a; letter other than A, B, C or D.
	Text values can be compared in this way as they are represented by sequential numeric codes.
`    OUTPUT "Please enter your selection:"`	The user is asked to input their selection. If they enter an A and B and C and D, the loop will stop.
`    letter ← USERINPUT`	
`    IF letter <= "A" OR letter >= "D" THEN`	The variable 'letter' is checked to see if an acceptable letter has been entered.
`        OUTPUT "The letter is not recognised."`	This message will be output for the user.
`    ENDIF`	
`ENDWHILE`	This closes the 'WHILE' loop and sends processing back to the start if a letter outside the range has been entered.

Range checks are more commonly performed on numeric data, as illustrated in Activity 5.1.

This screen would be generated from the above code:

```
Please enter your selection: E
The letter is not recognised.
Please enter your selection:
```

ACTIVITY 5.1

A student is applying for a driving licence for which the minimum age is 17. Write a validation routine that would check that the age entered fell within the correct range. Use a programming language of your choice. Run your program to check that it is working as intended.

Length check

When we are asked to choose a password, we are often informed that it must have a certain number of characters. Obviously there must be a routine in the software to check the length of the text that is entered. Text is entered into a string variable (recall that in Chapter 2 we looked at the keyword that is used to find the length of a string).

ACTIVITY 5.2

A user is asked to enter a password of at least 9 characters and no more than 12. Write a routine that would validate their chosen password.

Download Worksheet 5.1 from Cambridge Elevate

> **Tip**
>
> As the letter 'E' has been entered, the user is asked to make another entry.

> **Tip**
>
> Computers haven't got a 'not equals' sign as used by mathematicians. 'Not equals' is written as != or <> in computer programs. In AQA pseudo-code it is written as ≠.

> **Remember**
>
> 1. If data that are input are incorrect, then the output will also be incorrect.
> 2. GIGO: **G**arbage **I**n **G**arbage **O**ut.
> 3. Validation checks that the data are sensible.
> 4. Validation checks include presence checks, range checks and length checks.
> 5. Data can pass validation checks but can still be incorrect.

Authentication

The most common method for users to authenticate themselves (to prove they are who they say they are) is by entering a username and password that are stored on the system.

Authentication is the process that a system uses to verify that a username with its associated password exist in the database. Usernames and passwords are used to authenticate user identities for social networking sites, online banking and online ordering sites. They do not verify that the person entering the data are the person to whom they were issued.

Stealing usernames and passwords is an example of 'identity theft'.

An authentication routine can be built into a program. It would require:

- a list of all the registered usernames and passwords
- data input for the username
- a routine to check that the username is registered
- data input for the user's password
- a routine to check that the password is correct.

A list of usernames with their passwords could be stored in an array (for more information on arrays, see Chapter 3).

The following algorithm assumes that usernames and passwords are stored in a two-dimensional array with username in one column and password in the other.

Code

```
users ← [[user1, password1], [user2, password2], [user3, password3]]
```

```
userEntry ← ""
```
The variable 'userEntry' is assigned the value of an empty string.

```
foundName ← False
```
This variable is used as a flag. It will be set to True if the username is found.

```
WHILE userEntry = ""
```
A 'WHILE' loop is set up and it will run while the variable 'userEntry' contains an empty string.

```
OUTPUT "Please enter your username:"

userEntry ← USERINPUT
```

Please enter your username:

The user is asked to input their name. If they enter any text, then the string will no longer be empty and the loop will stop.

```
usersLen ← LEN(users)
```

The length of the array is stored in the variable 'usersLen'.

```
FOR index ← 0 TO usersLen - 1
```

A 'FOR' loop is set up to go through all of the indexes in the array.

```
    IF userEntry = users[index][0] THEN
```

The first item at each index of the two-dimensional array is checked to see whether it matches the one the user entered. If it does, then the password is checked.

```
        foundName ← True
```

The flag is set to True if the username is found in the array.

```
        OUTPUT "Please enter your password:"

        passwordEntry ← USERINPUT
```

Please enter your username: David Please enter your password:

The user is asked to enter a password.

```
        IF passwordEntry = users[index][1]
        THEN
```

It is checked with the second item at the index of the username (i) and if it is the same...

```
            OUTPUT "Username and password
            are correct."
```

Please enter your username: David Please enter your password: **correctpassword** Username and password are correct.

The user is informed that all is correct.

```
        ELSE
```

But if it is not the same...

```
            OUTPUT "Sorry the password is
            incorrect."
```

Please enter your username: David Please enter your password: **Incorrect** **password** Sorry the password is incorrect. Please enter your password:

The user is informed that the password is incorrect and processing goes back to the start of the 'WHILE' loop.

```
            userEntry ← ""
```

The variable 'userEntry' is set back to an empty string so that the while loop will run again.

85

`ENDIF`	The inner 'IF' block (for checking the password) is closed.
`ENDIF`	The outer 'IF' block for checking the username is closed.
`ENDFOR`	This re-runs the loop with the variable 'index' incremented by 1.
`IF foundName = False THEN`	If the flag has not been set, the user must be informed that the username has not been recognised.
`OUTPUT "Username not recognised."`	

```
Please enter your username: Incorrect
username
Username not recognised.
Please enter your username:
```

If the loop finishes and the username entered does not match any of those in the array, then the user is informed and processing goes back to the start of the 'WHILE' loop.

`userEntry ← ""`	The variable 'userEntry' is set back to an empty string so that the while loop will run again.
`ENDIF`	
`ENDWHILE`	This closes the 'WHILE' loop and will send the processing back to the start if the username or the password are incorrect.

Tip

You could easily add code like this into your own programs to authenticate users.

Tip

You could use nested loops (for more on nested loops, see Chapter 2).

This is a simple solution and could be expanded to allow the user to input their password more than once.

ACTIVITY 5.3

Adapt the algorithm so that the user can enter their password up to three times before they receive the error message. Use a programming language of your choice. Run your program to check that it is working as you intended.

Remember

Authentication is used to confirm the identity of a user.

Output to screen

The program processes the data that have been entered and displays the results as information to the user. These data should be presented in as clear a way as possible. If a list of users and passwords was printed on screen, then it should be formatted.

If it was printed without any breaks, it would be confusing:

user1 password1 user2 password2 user3 password3 user4 password4
user5 password5

A line break could be inserted between each user:

user1 password1

user2 password2

user3 password3

user4 password4

user5 password5

It would be even better presented if tab stops were used to line up the different data:

user1   password1

user2   password2

user3   password3

user4   password4

user5   password5

Programming languages have commands that allow on-screen formatting. Have a look at the commands in the programming language you are using for on-screen formatting.

Output to files

Data can be output to disk and stored in text files. The files of data can then be used to input data to programs when they need it.

Being able to do this is very useful because it means that data such as scores or usernames are not lost when a program is closed and can be loaded in again the next time the program is run.

There are no commands for using text files in the AQA pseudo-code and the following explanations will use the commands from the Python programming language.

You should research the programming language that you are studying to find out how text files are manipulated.

In most programming languages, to access a text file the file must first be given a file handle, for example 'myFile'.

Key term

file handle: a label that is assigned to a resource needed by the program. It can only access the file through the computer's operating system

Key terms

write mode: the program can 'write' to the file or in other words it can change the data in the file

overwritten: if a file exists on the computer and a new file is created with the same name, the new file is kept and the old file is written over and lost

Writing to a text file

When files are opened by programs, they can be opened in different ways. One of these ways is write mode. To write data to that file, the file must be opened in write mode, for example:

Code

```
myFile = open("samplefile.txt", "w")
(The 'w' stands for 'write')
```

Writing data

Data can be written to the file using the following command:

Code

```
myFile.write(Data to be written)
```

Watch out

If the file does not exist, then a file will be created. However, if the file does exist, then it will be overwritten. To prevent this, programming languages have an 'openAppend' command to add data to the file but this is not available in the pseudo-code.

Key term

closed: when the computer has finished using the file, closing it saves it safely on to the disk for permanent retention

Closing the file

In most languages, when you have finished writing to the file it must be closed:

Code

```
myFile.close()
```

WORKED EXAMPLE

Anil is a student who has created a program that allows him to input his computer science test scores into an array which he declared as scores[10].

He has now filled the array and wants to add code that will store the data in a text file called 'ComputerScienceScores'.

Python code	Explanation
`myFile = open("ComputerScienceScores.txt", "w")`	The file, with a handle of 'myFile' is opened in 'write' mode.
`for index in range (0, 10):`	A loop is set up to move through the array from index 0 to index 9. Python does not use 'for…to'. The 'in range' command means 'up to but not including' this number.
`myFile.write(str(scores[index]) + "\n")`	The data item at the index position must be converted to a string to be written to the text file. A line break "\n" is added so that each data item is on a new line.
`myFile.close()`	The file must be closed for the data to be written to it.

Reading data from a file
Data can be read in from a text file.

In most languages, to read data from a file, the file must be opened in read mode, that is:

Code
```
myFile = open("SampleFile.txt", "r")
```

Reading the data
Each item of data can be read using the following command:

Code
```
myFile.read()
```

Closing the file
In most languages, when you have finished reading from the file it must be closed:

Code
```
myFile.close()
```

Complete Interactive Activity 5c on Cambridge Elevate

Key term

read mode: the file is opened in such a way as to allow the data to be used by the program but not to allow the program to write any data to the file. Using read mode protects the data file from being accidentally changed by the program

Tip

Your programming language will probably have many more commands for file handling, so carry out research to find out other file handling commands and how they are written.

WORKED EXAMPLE

Anil now wants to add code to read the scores from the file 'ComputerScienceScores' back into the array declared as scores[10].

Python code	Explanation
`myFile = open("ComputerScienceScores.txt", "r")`	The file, with a handle of 'myFile' is opened in 'read' mode.
`scores = myFile.read().splitlines()`	Each line is read and appended to the array 'scores'. The 'splitlines()' method is used to get rid of the new line commands.
`myFile.close()`	

ACTIVITY 5.4

A student has coded a computer game which stores the five highest scores that have been attained while the program is running in an array. She now wants to save those scores to a file and load them back in when the game is run again.

Write a program that will save the array of scores to a suitable text file and then load them back in again. Run your program to check that it is working as intended.

Remember

1. Data can be output to and stored in text files on storage media.
2. Data can be written to the file and then read back in by a program running on the computer.
3. After writing to or reading from a file it must be closed.

Practice questions

1. Explain what is meant by validation.
2. A school with years 7 to 13 uses a computer program to enter student details. One of the items of data to be entered is the school year that the student is in. Using pseudo-code or a flowchart, illustrate an algorithm that would carry out:
   - a presence check
   - a range check

   when this data are entered.

Download Self-assessment 5 worksheet from Cambridge Elevate (this content has not been approved by AQA)

⭐ Your final challenge

Your final challenge is to create programs to:

- Create a new username which is unique and has not been used before. The username is to be based on the user's surname, gender, year of birth and postcode.
- Allow a user to enter a password of nine letters. This must be entered twice and be the same each time.
- Allow users to change their passwords.

You do not need to create one program with all these features. Instead you can write separate programs for each task. (We will be looking at linking these separate programs into one program in the next chapter.) The rules for creating a username are shown in the following flowchart:

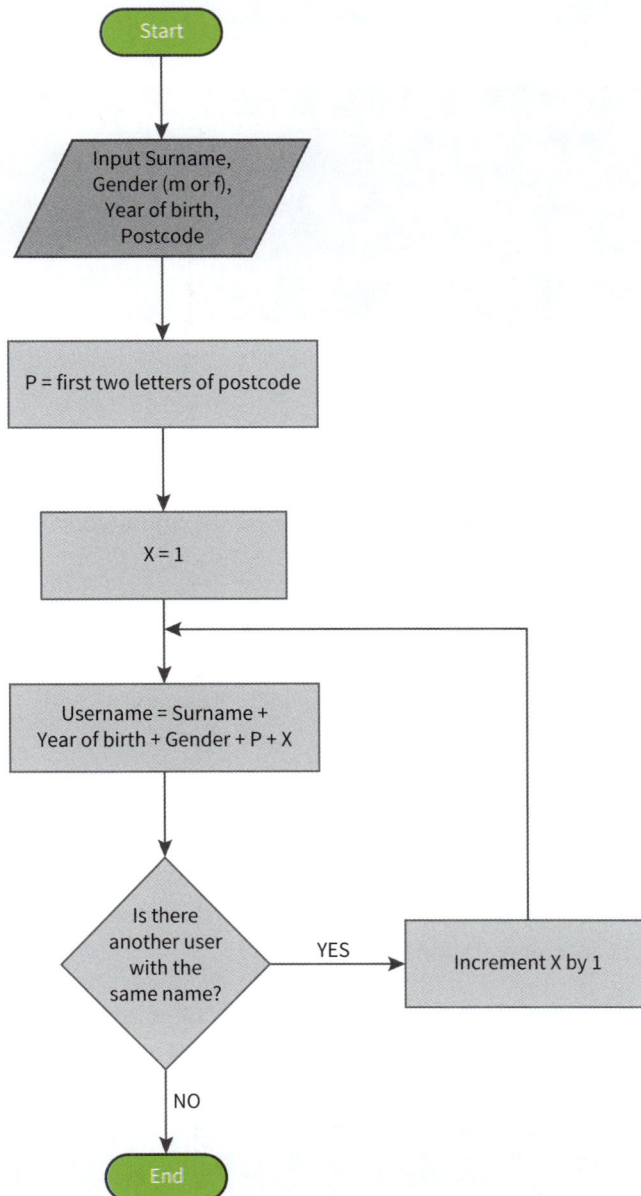

```
                    ┌──────────┐
                    │  Start   │
                    └──────────┘
                         │
                         ▼
              ╱─────────────────────╲
             ╱   Input Surname,      ╲
            ╱    Gender (m or f),      ╲
            ╲    Year of birth,        ╱
             ╲   Postcode             ╱
              ╲─────────────────────╱
                         │
                         ▼
         ┌──────────────────────────────────┐
         │ P = first two letters of postcode │
         └──────────────────────────────────┘
                         │
                         ▼
              ┌────────────────────┐
              │       X = 1        │
              └────────────────────┘
                         │
                         ▼◄──────────────────────────┐
         ┌──────────────────────────────┐            │
         │ Username = Surname +          │            │
         │ Year of birth + Gender + P + X │           │
         └──────────────────────────────┘            │
                         │                            │
                         ▼                            │
                    ╱─────────╲                ┌──────────────────┐
                   ╱ Is there   ╲     YES       │                  │
                  ╱ another user  ╲────────────►│ Increment X by 1 │
                  ╲  with the     ╱             │                  │
                   ╲ same name?  ╱              └──────────────────┘
                    ╲─────────╱
                         │
                         │ NO
                         ▼
                    ┌──────────┐
                    │   End    │
                    └──────────┘
```

6 Problem solving

Learning outcomes

By the end of this Chapter you should be able to:

* explain what is meant by computational thinking
* explain what is meant by decomposition and abstraction and use these to solve problems
* create algorithms to solve problems that you have analysed
* explain what is meant by top-down and bottom-up problem solving
* create structured programs using procedures
* follow the systems development cycle to analyse problems, design and implement solutions and test the outcomes.

⭐ **Challenge: write a program for ordering a pizza online**

* Practically everything we need we can order online: clothes, food, music, cars and books.
* We can select the items we want in the comfort of our own homes and have them delivered.
* Your challenge is to write a program for ordering a pizza online.

Why problem solving?

* All our lives we have to solve problems. How to make a cup of coffee? How to tidy up our bedrooms? How to do our maths homework? Our lives are one long problem to solve!

* When you were creating algorithms in Chapter 1, you had to think about problems in a particular way. You had to think about:

    * inputs and outputs
    * data and processes
    * sequence, selection and iteration.

* In Chapter 4, you had to compare the efficiency of different algorithms and which one would be better in a particular circumstance. Thinking in this way is referred to as computational thinking.

* Problem solving is essential for our survival and the techniques used in computational thinking are being applied to solve world-wide problems.

🎥 **Watch the thinking logically animation on Cambridge Elevate**

Problems such as global warming, pollution and the burning of fossil fuels are being tackled using computational thinking skills.

Problems and programming

A computer scientist's job can be divided into three areas:

1. defining and analysing problems

2. creating a structured solution or algorithm

3. coding the solution.

The first two parts contribute to what we think of as 'problem solving'. The third area, 'coding the solution' is what a computer scientist does after they have solved the problem.

Coding is not problem solving. It is merely translating the structured solution into a form that can be implemented by a computer. If the computer scientist has failed to solve the problem correctly, then no amount of advanced coding technique will produce a successful solution.

Computational thinking

The set of skills needed to solve problems is often referred to as computational thinking, a term coined by Jeannette Wing, a computer scientist at Carnegie Mellon University in the United States.

When you create an algorithm, you think in a computational way. For example, in Chapter 1, when you created an algorithm for making a cup of tea, you had to think about:

- the start state (empty kettle, cold water in tap, no tea bag in cup)

- the end state (what you had to end up with: hot water and tea bag in cup, milk in cup)

- the inputs needed (water, tea bag, milk, possibly sugar)

- the processes required and their correct sequence (fill kettle, turn on kettle, place tea bag into cup)

- selection (Is the kettle full? Is the water boiling?)

- iteration (checking and rechecking the water until it is boiling. Pouring water into cup until it is full).

Four important skills included in computational thinking are:

1. decomposition

2. abstraction

3. pattern recognition

4. algorithm design (see Chapter 1).

Let's look at these skills now.

> **Tip**
>
> The terms 'programming' and 'coding' are often used to mean the same functions but a programmer analyses the problem, creates an algorithm and then codes the solution whilst a coder just codes the solution; the algorithm could be created by someone else.

Decomposition

Decomposition is the ability to break down a problem into smaller and smaller sub-problems or components. It is far easier trying to solve a small problem than a large one and decomposing a problem shows how these various components fit together.

We decomposed a problem when we looked at getting up on a morning and going to school. The sub-problems included:

Getting out of bed.

Showering.

Getting dressed.

Making breakfast.

These can now be broken down even further. For example, to make breakfast:

Make tea.

Make toast.

And for each of these there are even more sub-tasks, such as boiling the water for the tea. Breaking down the problem into small parts allows greater focus on each one.

Download Worksheet 6.1 from Cambridge Elevate

ACTIVITY 6.1

You have been asked to create a program that would allow a user to calculate the approximate cost of a car journey. List the sub-tasks involved in solving this problem.

Abstraction

Abstraction means ignoring or filtering out the unnecessary details that are not so important for the current purpose to get to the essential features of something.

We use abstraction all of the time so that we are not constantly thinking about too many facts. If someone says to us that they have seen a 'car', we know what they mean as we have abstracted the essential features and have made a mental image of an object we call a car. We know that they mean something with four wheels, an engine and a steering wheel that uses fuel to transport people along a road. Imagine trying to have a conversation without abstraction. We would have to describe the car in minute detail, giving dimensions, number of wheels, etc. Then, we would have to explain what a wheel was and so on.

Would the minute details for the following tasks really matter when describing a general solution that could be used by anybody?

- the way you remove the duvet and covers

- the side of the bed you get out of

- putting on slippers

- how to get to the shower

- the colour of mug

- the type of tea bag to be used.

These facts may be important to you, but what if a person following the algorithm does not have a duvet? Or does not wear slippers? Or has a different route to the shower? Or does not have the type of tea bag that you use? The minute details would be confusing. Only the essential features matter.

⬇ **Download Worksheet 6.2 from Cambridge Elevate**

Pattern recognition

When you look at this picture what do you see? A young woman or an old one? How do you interpret the patterns?

We look at data and we can see patterns, often without thinking about it. For example, look at this sequence of numbers:

2, 4, 8, 16, 32, 64

Can you see a pattern? What are the next two numbers in the sequence?

We are always looking for patterns in human behaviour: if a person smiles at us, we assume they are going to be friendly.

When we see the patterns in the problem, we can use similar solutions. For example, we could recognise that iteration will be required and so we immediately know that loops will be required.

3D pattern recognition is an essential skill needed by anyone hoping to solve the Rubik's cube.

Complete Interactive Activity 6a on Cambridge Elevate

Maths skills

The cost of the journey can be calculated using the following formula:

(Length of journey in miles / miles per gallon of the car) x cost of one gallon of petrol

Algorithm design

This is the development of a step-by-step strategy for solving a problem and has been covered in Chapter 1.

WORKED EXAMPLE

Look at this relatively simple problem about calculating the approximate cost of a car journey.

In order to solve the problem, we need to decompose the problem into sub-problems and then we need to identify the tasks to solve them.

Create an algorithm that could be used to calculate the approximate cost of a car journey.

1. Decomposition

The following factors affect the cost and should be included in the algorithm:

- the length of the journey
- the efficiency of the car (how many miles the car travels on one gallon of petrol), that is the miles per gallon or mpg of the car (this value is given by the manufacturer so the user will know an average value from experience)
- the cost of one gallon of petrol
- the number of passengers
- the speed of the car
- the condition of the roads
- the amount of luggage carried
- the tyre pressure
- the use of the heater and air conditioning system
- the air temperature and air pressure.

2. Abstraction

We have identified many factors. The user will know some of the factors but not others. For example, before the journey the user will not know:

- the speeds they will be travelling at
- the condition of the road
- whether they will be using the heater or air conditioning
- the air temperature and air pressure.

For example, they will know:

- the number of passengers
- the tyre pressure.

But they probably will not know how these affect the efficiency of their particular car.

Because we are trying to find the *approximate* cost, we are going to have to do some abstraction.

The factors that will *most affect* the cost and which will most likely be *known* by the user are:

- the length of the journey

- the average miles per gallon for the car

- the cost of one gallon of petrol.

As we are trying to calculate the approximate cost of the journey, we will use these three factors.

We have abstracted the essential features and now we must represent them in an algorithm. We are in fact making a model of a car journey in an algorithm. We are converting a real-life event into a computer simulation of it.

3. Algorithm design

We can illustrate the algorithm using a flow diagram.

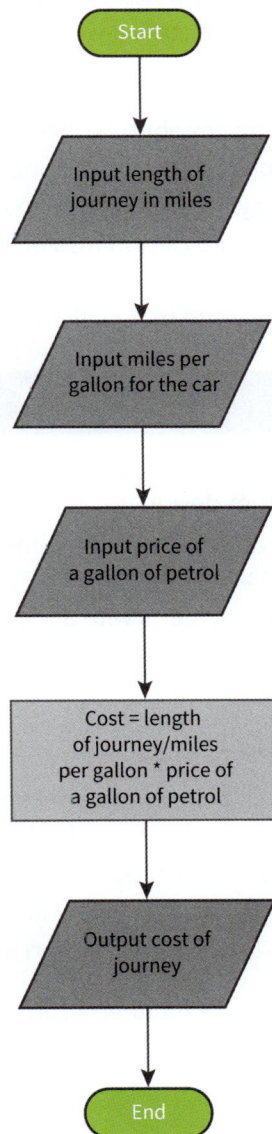

This algorithm will output the cost of the journey assuming that:

- distance is input in miles
- price is given per gallon.

ACTIVITY 6.2

Adapt the flow diagram so that if the price of petrol was entered as 'price per litre', the cost of the journey could still be calculated correctly.

Top-down problem solving

The solutions for the problems we have been looking at illustrate a *top-down* approach. This means that the problem has been broken down to gain an insight into the sub-problems that make it up.

Each sub-problem can then be broken down into further problems that may have to be solved.

Bottom-up problem solving is the opposite of the top-down approach and begins with specific details. These details are analysed and put into groups that are grouped into larger groups.

For example, a computer scientist might be asked to design a complete billing system for a company. They could start at the 'bottom', and look at all of the different bills that customers pay, for example full payment, part payment, discounts available, etc. They would design a solution for each one and then try to find similarities so that any code used to solve one could be used for the others. However, there is no certainty that all the solutions will fit together.

Remember

1. Computational thinking involves decomposition, abstraction, pattern recognition and algorithm design.
2. Top-down problem solving starts with the main problem and breaks it down gradually into smaller sub-problems.
3. Bottom-up problem solving starts with a collection of small problems and tries to combine them together to form a larger system.

Structured programming

The top-down approach shows that any problem consists of sub-problems and so it follows that any solution can be built up of sub-solutions or modules. It is often helpful for modules to be coded separately as subroutines. They can be then be called and used in the program as many times as needed without having to rewrite the code each time. They can be re-used in different programs.

This type of programming is called *structured programming* (or modular programming) and it makes a program more logical, easier to edit and far easier for another person to understand.

Login and password control

In Chapter 5, we looked at algorithms to allow users to create usernames and passwords and to change their passwords. Using a top-down approach, we can look at the tasks and sub-tasks involved:

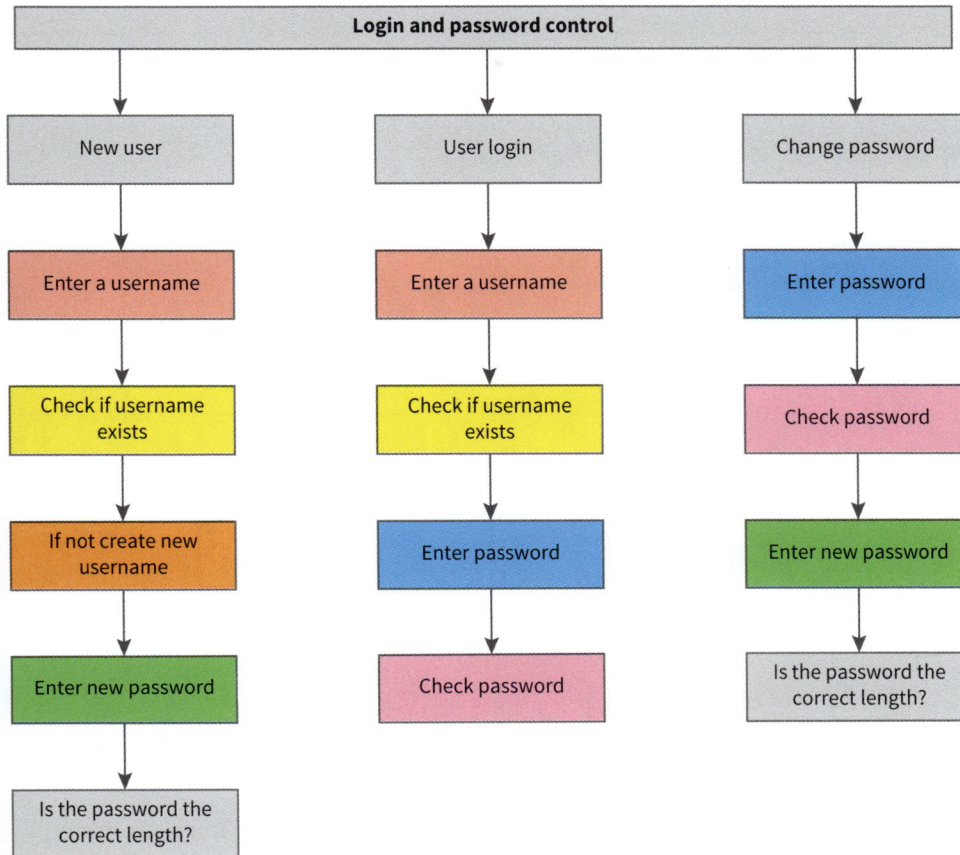

In the diagram whole problem has been divided into 3 sub-tasks. The first of these has been divided into 5 sub-tasks and the second and third are each divided into four sub-tasks.

In total there are 16 sub-tasks that need to be coded, but many are used more than once. If we used a structured programming approach, we could create a subroutine for each of these sub-tasks and use and re-use them. Each of these subroutines can be called and used when they are needed.

If a user wants to create a new login, the process is:

- call 'Enter a username' subroutine

- call 'Check if username exists' subroutine

- call 'If not create new username' subroutine

- call the 'Enter new password' subroutine

- call the 'Is the password the correct length?' subroutine.

Four existing subroutines can be reused and only 'If not create new username' is unique to this section.

> **Tip**
>
> To change their password, the user would have to use the subroutines for 'User login' and then the ones for 'Change password'.

Procedures and functions

There are two types of subroutine: *procedures* and *functions*.

Functions are called from an expression in the main program and return a value to it, for example:

Code

```
area ← findArea()
```

Where 'findArea' is the name of the function.

Procedures are called from a statement in the main program, but do not return any value to it. They just do something and then the main program continues, for example this statement:

Code

```
count()
```

would call the following procedure:

Code

```
SUBROUTINE count()

    FOR x ← 1 TO 1000

    ENDFOR

ENDSUBROUTINE
```

The procedure would just count to 1000 and then return to the main program. Most programming languages have ready-made functions built-in.

Here is a list of functions in the Python programming language:

Built-in Functions			
abs()	divmod()	input()	staticmethod()
all()	enumerate()	int()	str()
any()	eval()	isinstance()	sum()
basestring()	execfile()	issubclass()	super()
bin()	file()	iter()	tuple()
bool()	filter()	len()	type()
bytearray()	float()	list()	unichr()
callable()	format()	locals()	unicode()
chr()	frozenset()	long()	vars()
classmethod()	getattr()	map()	xrange()
cmp()	globals()	max()	zip()
compile()	hasattr()	memoryview()	_import_()
complex()	hash()	min	
delattr()	help()	next()	
dict()	hex()	object()	
dir ()	id()	oct()	

Notice how each function is followed by open and close brackets for you to enter the data that you want the function to work on.

We have already used some of these functions in the pseudo-code that we have been using, for example LEN(). When the LEN function is called, the string to be used is enclosed within the brackets.

Using these functions is another example of abstraction. They can be called to carry out an action without a programmer actually knowing how they do it. When the LEN function is used, the programmer does not need to know all of the commands used by the function to count the number of characters in the string.

We use this type of abstraction in our daily lives. For example, a car driver does not need to know how the engine and the gears work or how the car starts when the key is turned. They can still drive the car without knowing or understanding these things.

Creating functions
In addition to using these built-in functions, programming languages allow us to write our own.

> ### Tip
> When functions are created, they should be given meaningful names relating to the action they perform. It is easier to remember what they are for if they are given meaningful names.

WORKED EXAMPLE

Kim is creating a game in which users have to throw two dice and add the results together to find the total score. This has to happen many times in the game and, without using functions, the code to do this would have to be re-written many times. But by using a function, it would only have to be written once and then it could be called when it was needed.

```
SUBROUTINE dice()
```
This defines a function named 'dice'.

```
    number1 ← RANDOM_INT(1, 6)
```
The variable 'number1' is assigned a single value of between 1 and 6 produced by the built-in RANDOM_INT() function. The two numbers given to the function (1, 6) indicate the lower and upper limits of the number to be generated.

```
    number2 ← RANDOM_INT(1, 6)
```

```
    number ← number1 + number2
```
The variable 'number' is assigned the value of the sum of number1 and number2.

```
    RETURN number
```
The value of the variable 'number' is what the function has to return to the main program. In AQA pseudo-code, the use of the RETURN command indicates that the subroutine is a function not a procedure.

```
ENDSUBROUTINE
```
This statement ends the function definition.

Kim has used her powers of abstraction to work out the essential features of a dice: that it will return a random number between 1 and 6. Any other features such as colour or the material it is made of are unimportant. She has then represented them in pseudo-code. She has made a computer model of a real-life event.

The function is an abstraction.

This function will return a value. So if number1 = 3 and number2 = 6 then number will be 9.

Therefore whenever the dice need to be thrown in the program, all that is needed is the following line of code:

```
score ← dice()
```

The variable 'score' will be assigned the value returned by the function.

Watch out

The total of the two dice is stored in two different variables. In the main program which calls the function it is stored in the variable 'score' but in the actual function it is stored in a variable named 'number'.

Key terms

argument: the name for the data that is passed to a subroutine by the main program

parameter: the names of the variables that are used in the subroutine to store the data passed from the main program as arguments

ACTIVITY 6.3

In your chosen programming language, create and test a game, using a function, in which a user is asked to throw three dice to find the total. The game should keep the highest score and notify the user if they have beaten it. The user should be able to keep throwing the dice until they select an option to stop playing the game.

Arguments and parameters

In the dice example, a value was returned to the main program by the function when it was called.

In a similar way values, stored in the main program, can be passed to the function. These are called arguments.

Watch the arguments and parameters animation on Cambridge Elevate

WORKED EXAMPLE

In this example, a user is asked to enter their first and second names. The procedure is used to print a message.

```
SUBROUTINE message(one, two)
```
This defines the procedure. It uses two variables named 'one' and 'two'. These are called the parameters of the procedure. They signal that values will be passed from the main program.

```
    OUTPUT "Hello " + one + " " + two
```
The procedure then prints a welcome message using these two variables.

Until the procedure is run, the variables are empty; they have no value. The values for these variables have to be passed to it from the main program when it is called.

```
ENDSUBROUTINE
```

```
OUTPUT "Please enter your first name"
```
The user is asked to enter their first name.

```
firstName ← USERINPUT
```

```
OUTPUT  "Please enter your surname"
```
The user is asked to enter their surname.

```
secondName ← USERINPUT
```

```
message(firstName, secondName)
```
The procedure is called and the values stored in these two variables (the arguments) are passed to the procedure's parameters. The procedure uses them in the order they are given, that is 'one' assumes it has to have the value of firstName and 'two' the value of 'secondName' as they are passed in that order.

Rewrite the message function and the calling program so that it prints the welcome message with the surname before the first name.

Several arguments passed and several values returned

In the previous example, two arguments were passed to the subroutine but nothing was returned. Just as more than one argument can be sent to the function, more than one value can be returned.

In the following example, a function used to calculate the area and perimeter of a rectangle, there are two arguments and two values returned.

> **Tip**
>
> The term 'interface' is used to refer to the values passed between a subroutine and the code that is calling it.

Code

```
SUBROUTINE rectangle (length, width)
```
This function has two parameters, 'length' and 'width'.

```
    area ← length * width
```
The area of the rectangle is assigned to the variable 'area'.

```
    perimeter ← (length * 2) + (width * 2)
```
The perimeter of the rectangle is assigned to the variable 'perimeter'.

```
    RETURN area, perimeter
```
The values of these variables are returned to the main program.

```
ENDSUBROUTINE
```

```
OUTPUT "Please enter the length."
```
The user enters the length of the rectangle.

```
rectLength ←USERINPUT
```

```
OUTPUT "Please enter the width"
```
And now the width.

```
rectWidth ←USERINPUT
```

```
rectArea, rectPerimeter ← rectangle(rectLength, rectWidth)
```
The function 'rectangle' is now called in this statement and the values of the two variables ('rectLength' and 'rectWidth') are passed to it as arguments.

Main program	Function rectangle
rectLength	⟶ length
rectWidth	⟶ width
rectArea	⟵ area
rectPerimeter	⟵ perimeter

The two variables 'rectArea' and 'rectPerimeter' are created and will be given the values of the two variables (area and perimeter) which are returned from the function.

Key terms

local variable: a variable that is used only within a subroutine. When the subroutine has completed its work, the local variable is discarded

global variable: a variable that is used in the main program. It can be used by any of the commands or subroutines in the program

Local and global variables

In the previous example, different variables have been used to hold the same data.

Data	Variable in the main program	Variable in the function
Area of rectangle	rectArea	area
Perimeter of rectangle	rectPerimeter	perimeter

The variable in the subroutine exists only within the subroutine and is called a local variable. Data stored in the local variable are only available for manipulation in the subroutine. That is why they are called 'local'.

In the main program the same data are stored in another variable and they can be used by other commands in the main program. They are available to all and are therefore said to be global.

If you added another statement to the main program, such as the one below, then an error message would be shown because 'area' and 'perimeter' have not been declared in the main program. They exist only in the subroutine.

Code

```
OUTPUT "The area is: " + area + " and the perimeter is " +
perimeter
```

You could actually use the same variable names in the subroutine as in the main program, but we could easily get into a muddle with our logic and mix them up.

It is good practice to use local variables for that and the following reasons:

- You cannot change the value of the local variable by mistake somewhere else in the program.

- You could use the same variable name in different subroutines, and each is treated as a separate variable.

- You free up memory as when a subroutine containing a local variable finishes executing, the memory used by the variable is freed up.

- Subroutines are easier to move between programs as they do not rely on global variables.

ACTIVITY 6.5

Shown below is a function:

```
SUBROUTINE calculate(input1,input2)
        solution ← int((input1 * input2) / (input1 + input2))
        WHILE solution < 3
                solution ← int((input1 * input2) / (input1 + input2))
                input1 ← input1 + 1
                input2 ← input2 + 1
        ENDWHILE
        RETURN input1, input2
ENDSUBROUTINE
```

Complete a trace table for this function when it is called with the following arguments:

```
calculate(3, 6)
```

Subroutines and menus

Subroutines are useful when using **menus** in a program. When a user selects a menu option, they can be sent to a particular function or procedure.

> **Key term**
>
> **menu**: a set of options to help a user find information or use a program function

WORKED EXAMPLE

For a system login and password control, the main program could have a menu system like this:

1. Register as a new user

2. Login

3. Change your password

4. Exit

Now that we are using structured programming using subroutines, it is relatively easy to direct a user to the part of the program they need.

The user enters a number between 1 and 4 and is directed to the correct section:

```
OUTPUT "1. Register as a new user."
OUTPUT "2. Login."                          The on-screen menu is set up.
OUTPUT "3. Change your password."
OUTPUT "4. Exit."
choice ← USERINPUT                          The user enters a menu number.
IF choice = "1" THEN
    newUser()
ELSE IF choice = "2" THEN
    login()                                 The user is directed to a different function depending on their
ELSE IF choice = "3" THEN                    choice.
    changePassword()
ELSE IF choice = "4" THEN
    exit()
ELSE
    OUTPUT "Incorrect option. Try again."   This message will be displayed if the entry is not one of the above.
ENDIF
```

Owners often want to know the 'human equivalent' of their pet's age. Here are two rules for calculating this for dogs and cats:

- Assume that a one-year-old dog is equal to a 12-year-old human and a two-year-old dog is equal to a 24-year old human. Then add four years for every year after that.

- Assume that a one-year-old cat is equal to a 15-year-old human and a two-year-old cat is equal to a 24-year-old human. Then add four years for every year after that.

Your task is to design an algorithm for a program to allow a user to find the 'human equivalent age' of their dog or cat and then code it in the language you are studying.

It should have a menu system to allow them select the type of animal and use functions for the calculations.

Extension
Allow the user to use the menu as many times as they want until they select an option to quit.

The benefits of using subroutines
Subroutines are a natural way of implementing top-down design because some of the tasks identified can be allocated to a subroutine. They, therefore, assist with decomposition and abstraction.

Repeated sections of code need only be written once and called when necessary. This shortens the development time of a program and means that the finished program will occupy less memory space when it is run.

Subroutines also improve the structure of the code, making it easier to read through and follow what is happening. It is easier to check your code if you use subroutines because each subroutine can be coded and tested independently. The program is easier to debug as each subroutine can be inspected independently. If changes have to be made at a later date it is easier to change a small module than having to work through the whole program.

In large development teams, different members can be working independently on different subroutines. They can use and develop standard libraries of subroutines that can be reused in other programs.

Remember
1. In structured programming a program consists of distinct blocks of code that are linked together.
2. A function is a subroutine that can return a result to the command that called it.
3. Procedures do not return a result.
4. Subroutines can accept parameters or values that they can use.

Download Worksheet 6.4 from Cambridge Elevate

Software development

Software is developed for a purpose. For example, if there is a problem or someone thinks that something could be done more efficiently, then software or whole systems of software are developed to meet that need.

The problem is that lots of this development results in failure and billions of pounds are wasted in Britain each year.

In order to maximise success, various schemes or methods have been developed detailing the way software development should be done.

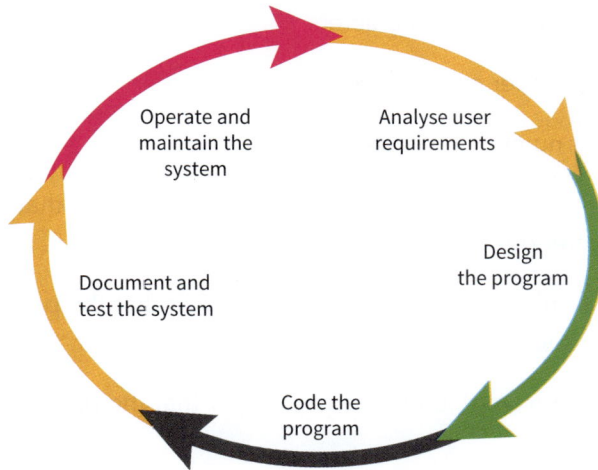

All of these schemes are variations of the systems development cycle, a step-by-step process for planning, creating and testing, and deploying and maintaining a system.

We will look through these stages using the following problem:

Password creation

You have been asked to create a system to assess and accept or reject passwords entered by users.

Passwords should be at least six, and no more than 12, characters long. If a password does not meet these criteria, the user should be told why and be allowed to re-enter a password. If the password is acceptable, the user must be informed.

After the password has been accepted, the user should also be informed of the strength of the password based on the following rules:

weak: if the password is all lower case or all upper case or all numeric characters

medium: if two of the above types are used

strong: if all three types are used.

Problem identification and analysis

The first thing any software developer needs to do is to fully understand the problem. They should read and re-read the problem until they have identified all of the details about what is required.

Key term

systems development cycle: a defined process of planning, designing, creating, testing and deploying an information system

107

The developer can then decompose the problem into tasks and sub-tasks. Notetaking and identifying links (pattern recognition) are very important.

The following are some of the tasks and sub-tasks involved:

- Data entry for user's password.

- Check if it is 6 to 12 characters in length:

  o If it is not, then inform user and allow them to re-enter.

  o If it is, then check password characters:

    – Count lower case characters.

    – Count upper case characters.

    – Count numeric characters.

      • If all are greater than 0, then inform the user that the password strength is strong.

      • If only one is 0, then inform the user that the password strength is medium.

      • If two are 0, then inform the user that the password strength is weak.

As the developer is decomposing the problem into tasks and sub-tasks, they will be thinking ahead about how some of these can be solved. For example:

- How can I count the number of characters?
- How can I allow the user to go back to re-enter if there are not sufficient characters?
- How can I count the number of lower case characters?

These are just three of many questions raised by the identification and analysis stage and in the next stage the developer plans how to solve them by doing what you are already brilliant at: creating algorithms.

Design

This is the creative section, where the developer can design solutions to the problems. Although developers will use the same tools (algorithms, flowcharts, pseudo-code) they will probably end up with different designs. There are always many different solutions for a problem!

The analysis identified the tasks and sub-tasks and showed how different modules or subroutines can be used to contribute to the complete solution.

In the design, the data types and structures are identified and the programmers have to decide the best way of implementing them in the high level language they are using.

The following shows a flowchart that could be used to illustrate an algorithm for password entry.

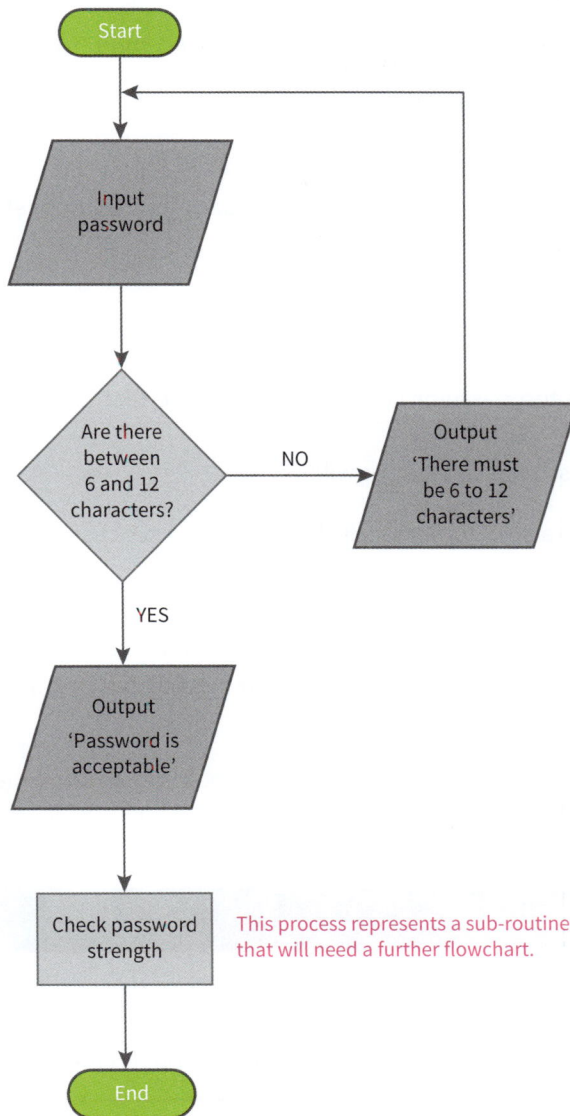

The flowcharts show the logical structure and navigation of the algorithm, where selection, iteration, input and output will be used.

This can be refined using pseudo-code.

Using pseudo-code will enable the developer to identify the variables and functions that will be required and decide on suitable names and data types.

The following shows sample pseudo-code for the flowchart shown above:

Code ───

`password ← ""`	The variable 'password' is assigned the value of an empty string.
`WHILE password = ""`	A loop is set up which will run while 'password' contains an empty string.
`    OUTPUT "Please enter a password of between 6 and 12 characters"`	The user is asked to enter a password which is stored in the variable 'password'.
`    password ← USERINPUT`	

`IF LEN(password) < 6 OR LEN(password) > 12 THEN`	If the length of the password entered is less than six characters or more than 12 then…
`    OUTPUT "The password must be between 6 and 12 characters. Please enter a different password."`	…the user is given a message asking them to choose another password.
`    password ← ""`	The variable 'password' is set back to an empty string so that the loop will run again.
`    ENDIF`	
`ENDWHILE`	
`OUTPUT "The password is acceptable."`	As the password entered 'passed the test' the user is informed.

In the design phase, the developer will:

- Design the data structures needed to store and process the data.

- Design the modules which will be used.

- Design the interface. Will a graphical user interface be used with input boxes for password entry or will it be purely text based? If it is graphical, then the complete input form will be designed.

- Design the output. The text for the user should be as unambiguous and clear as possible. Will different fonts be used? Will the text be in different colours?

Key term

unambiguous: this means that the instruction cannot be misunderstood and the correct action will always be performed. All instructions given to a computer must be unambiguous or it won't do anything!

Watch out

Everyone is human and we can make errors in our design. It is important to check for logical errors (see Chapter 1) at this stage because they are easier to identify and correct than when the code has been written.

Tip

Using pseudo-code allows the programmer to concentrate on the logic of the solution without having to think about the way the actual programming language has to be written with its rules and syntax.

Implementation

This is the stage where the algorithm, either in a flowchart or pseudo-code, is translated into an actual programming language.

Now the developer has to produce a solution that works in a particular programming language on a computer with a specific operating system.

It is important that there are no syntax errors.

Since computer programs must follow strict syntax to compile correctly, any aspects of the code that do not conform to the syntax of the programming language will produce a syntax error.

Integrated development environments

If we make mistakes with our spelling, punctuation or grammar, then the person reading our work will probably still be able to understand it. They can make allowances.

If you make one mistake in an essay, your English teacher does not immediately refuse to read it and give you zero marks. But computers are not so forgiving. One mistake in a program and they will not be able to continue to run the program.

We have already looked at logic errors, but other errors causing programs to malfunction are syntax errors such as misspellings, missing brackets, statements not indented, missing colons or semi-colons. The list is endless.

Programmers therefore need all the help they can get. They get no help if they write their code in a word processor or text editor but thankfully integrated development environments (IDE) have been developed. An IDE is a software application that provides facilities to computer programmers for software development. It typically consists of a source code editor, debugger, complier or interpreter and might well have a graphical user interface (GUI). Using an IDE will help to prevent syntax errors.

> **Watch the debugging animation on Cambridge Elevate**

Source code editor

A source code editor is a text editor designed specifically for the writing and editing of source code for computer programs. They should provide facilities such as syntax highlighting, which displays source code in different colours and fonts according to the category of terms (e.g. commands, variables and strings enclosed in quotation marks). It improves the readability of the text and makes it easier to spot if a delimiter such as a bracket or quote mark has been omitted.

Code

```
Import random
mysteryNumber = random.randint (1, 100)
guess = 0
while (guess == 0):
        guess = int( input ( "Please enter a number between
        1 and 100:"))
        if guess > mysteryNumber:
                guess = 0
                print("Your guess is too high.")
        elif guess < mysteryNumber:
                guess = 0
                print("Your guess is too low.")
print("Well done. You guessed correctly.")
```

> **Tip**
>
> Different categories have different coloured fonts.

Autocomplete or word completion

This involves the source code editor predicting a word or phrase that the user wants to type in without the user actually typing it in completely, for example if the user types a 'p', the editor might suggest the word 'print'.

Bracket matching

Bracket matching is a syntax highlighting feature that highlights matching sets of delimiters such as brackets or quote marks. The purpose is to help the programmer navigate through the code and also spot any delimiters that do not match.

Auto indentation

This feature will automatically indent the next line if it is required when the Return key is pressed. In some languages, indentation is a requirement.

Debugger

This is used to test the code and highlight and remove programming errors. When an error is found, it will show its location in the code.

Step by step or single-stepping

This allows the code to be run and inspected one line at a time. It allows the effects of that single statement or instruction to be evaluated in isolation.

Breakpoints or pauses

Breakpoints, or pauses, are the intentional stopping of the program at a specified place so that the programmer can inspect the code and see if the program is functioning as expected up to that point. They are useful if there is an overall problem so that the code can be tested bit by bit.

Variable tracing

This feature allows the programmer to see the values of variables at any stage in the running of the program. The programmer can see if the values are as expected.

Auto documentation

This feature allows the automatic documentation of all the variables and modules in a text file. This is especially useful when teams of programmers are working on the same project to ensure that they all understand the coding.

As the solution is coded, extensive use should be made of comments or explanations of the code.

Remember that comments are used by the programmer to explain the code to other users, even to themselves at a later date. When the program is executed, these comments are ignored because they are enclosed within specific identifiers.

All programming languages allow comments, but they use different symbols to denote them. Often forward slashes are used (//) or the hash symbol (#).

In the following programming language, multiple line comments are enclosed with three quote marks (''') and a single line comment with a hash symbol.

Here is an example of a Python program with comments:

Code ───

```
'''
This is part of a program developed
to demonstrate part of a
menu system
'''

def menu(): #This is the start of a function named menu.

    print ("1. Register as a new user.")
    print ("2. Login.")
    print ("3. Change your password.")
    print ("4. Exit.")
    response = input("Please select an option: ")
    if (response == "1"):
        newUser()
        run = True
        return run
    elif (response == "4"):
        run = False
        return run

def newUser(): #This is the function for a new user to enter
a user name.
    new = input ("Please enter a user name: ")
    return new
```

Testing

The software is tested to ensure that:

- It is technically correct, it does not contain any bugs, and it produces the expected results.

- It meets the needs of the user. It might function perfectly, but does it actually do what the user needed? Is it easy to use? Can data be input and output in a convenient way?

Alpha testing

The first phase of testing, called alpha testing, is carried out by the actual programmers. It is intended to find any errors or bugs in the program. Test data is used to ensure that the program produces expected results.

The testing plan should include the data to be used, the expected results, the actual results and the corrective action taken.

Key terms

normal test: ensures that the correct result will be produced with the expected data (sometimes called an 'in-range test')

boundary test: where the highest or lowest acceptable numbers and those just inside or outside the acceptable range are entered; these check any logical errors that might have been introduced using the <= and >= operators

erroneous test: data that should be rejected are deliberately input to check that validation routines are functioning as expected (sometimes called an 'out-of-range test')

beta testing: testing done by a selected group of individuals to receive their feedback about how well the program works

For example, part of a program might ask a user to enter a number between 1 and 10 and the square of that number is then output. Here is part of a test plan for this function:

Test number	Test data	Expected result	Actual result	Type of test
1	3	9	9	Normal or in range test
2	1	1	1	Boundary test
3	10	100	100	Boundary test
4	12	Message stating that the number should be between 1 and 10	The message was displayed as expected	Erroneous or out of range test.

Beta testing

Beta testing is the second phase of testing, where a selected group of potential users are given a pre-release version to operate in a working situation and report bugs and improvements. They use their normal operating data. Their comments are used to correct and refine the software.

Evaluation

During the evaluation stage of software development, the developer writes an evaluation report comparing their finished software with the requirements identified in the problem analysis phase. It should include details of improvements made in the light of testing and user feedback.

Remember

1. Software should be developed using the systems development cycle.
2. Software development has the following components:
   a. problem identification and analysis
   b. design
   c. implementation
   d. testing
   e. evaluation

   The components do not have to be done in a rigidly linear fashion as some subroutines and parts of the solution might be coded before others have been fully specified and designed.

Practice question

A student has been asked to design an algorithm to analyse any sentence that a user inputs.
The algorithm should analyse the sentence to find how many times each of the vowels (a, e, i, o, u) has been used.
Design the algorithm so that the analysis is carried out by a function and the main program then outputs the vowels and the number of times they have been used.

⭐ **Your final challenge**

The pizza shop offers the following ingredients for buyers to design their own pizza.

Bases

Small   £1.00

Medium   £1.50

Large   £2.00

All bases are supplied with tomato sauce.

Toppings

Pepperoni	Spicy minced beef
Chicken	Anchovies
Cajun chicken	Tuna
Mushrooms	Peppers
Red onions	Jalapeños
Sweetcorn	Cheese
Ham	Green chillies

All toppings cost 50p and a customer can order as many as they want.

Your task is to design and create a program that will allow a customer to:

• Order a base.

• Select and order all the toppings that they want.

When they have finished ordering, the customer should be informed of the following:

• The type of base and all of the toppings they have ordered.

• The total cost of their pizza.

The customer should then be asked if they are going to collect the pizza or want it delivered. If they are collecting the pizza there is a 10 per cent discount and they should be informed of the new cost.

⬇ **Download Self-assessment 6 worksheet from Cambridge Elevate (this content has not been approved by AQA)**

7 Representing numbers

Challenge: write a program that will convert between different number formats

- Computers can manipulate and use numbers only if they are in binary format. Trying to remember strings of 1s and 0s is very difficult for humans. We are used to our decimal numbering system.
- We can shorten the strings by using hexadecimal but it is still difficult for us.
- Your challenge is to write a program that will allow users to enter numbers in decimal, binary or hexadecimal and convert them into the other number formats.

All computer programs and the data that computers store have to be converted into billions of 1s and 0s as that is all that computers can work with.

Why binary?

- The microprocessor contains the central processing unit which carries out all of the program instructions by carrying out millions of calculations each second.

- These calculations are performed by billions of transistors acting as switches. They are either on or off. They have only two states: they either transmit an electric current or they do not.

- Any system involving two states is called a binary system.

- As there are only two states (off or on), they can be represented by the two digits of the binary system: 0 and 1.

- All computer programs are lists of instructions switching transistors off or on and therefore they can be represented by the digits 0 and 1.

Binary data

The digits, 0 and 1 are known as binary digits or *bits* for short. These are used because computers are digital so the inputs and outputs to devices can only be electrically 'on' or 'off'. If the input or output is 'on', then we represent that by a 1 and we represent 'off' by a 0.

Series of combinations of 'on' and 'off', that is 0s and 1s, are used to represent numbers in the binary number system.

If there are only two digits, then how can we communicate complex data and commands to a computer?

We are able to communicate complex concepts and ideas using only the 26 letters of our alphabet.

We do this by combining the letters into words and the words into phrases and sentences.

In a similar way, the two bits, 0 and 1, can be combined to represent different meanings.

If each 'word' consisted of two bits, there could be four different 'words': 00, 11, 01 and 10.

With three bits there are eight possible 'words': 000, 001, 010, 011, 100, 110, 101, 111.

> **Key term**
>
> **binary digits**: computers can only communicate directly in 0s and 1s; series of 0s and 1s represent the codes for instructions and data

ACTIVITY 7.1

Write down all of the possible combinations if the bits were arranged in groups of four, for example 0000, 0001, 0010, etc.

Can you use your pattern recognition skills to see the relationship?

Number of bits used	Number of combinations
2	4
3	8
4	16
5	32
6	64
7	128
8	256

> **Maths skills**
>
> $2^2 = 2 \times 2$
>
> $2^3 = 2 \times 2 \times 2$

Yes. It is 2 (the number of different bits) to the power of the number used in combination.

Number of bits used	Number of combinations
2	2^2
3	2^3
4	2^4
5	2^5
6	2^6
7	2^7
8	2^8

Tip

All commands and data processed by a computer, including text, images and sound are represented by strings of 0s and 1s; often billions of them.

Therefore in order to communicate with a computer we must 'talk' to it in words made up of strings of 0s and 1s.

On a computer the string 'hello' would be represented by the following digits:

0110100001100101011011000110110001101111

Quite a mouthful!

An image as it would appear to us.

```
0 1 0 1 0 1 0 0 0 1 1 0 1 0 0 0 0 1 1 0 1 0 0 1 0 1 1 1 0 0 1 1
0 0 1 0 0 0 0 0 1 1 0 1 0 0 1 0 1 1 1 0 0 1 1 0 0 1 0 0 1 0 0 0 0 0
0 1 1 1 0 1 0 0 0 1 1 0 1 0 0 0 0 1 1 0 0 1 0 1 0 0 1 0 0 0 0 0
0 1 1 1 0 1 0 0 0 1 1 1 0 1 0 1 0 1 1 1 0 1 0 0 0 1 1 0 1 1 1 1
0 1 1 1 0 0 1 0 0 1 1 0 1 0 0 1 0 1 1 0 0 0 0 1 0 1 1 0 1 1 0 0
0 0 1 0 0 0 0 0 0 1 1 1 0 1 0 0 0 1 1 0 1 1 1 1 0 0 1 0 0 0 0 0
0 1 1 0 1 1 0 0 0 1 1 0 0 1 0 1 0 1 1 0 0 0 0 1 0 1 1 1 0 0 1 0
0 1 1 0 1 1 1 0 0 0 1 0 0 0 0 0 0 1 1 0 0 0 1 0 0 1 1 0 1 0 0 1
0 1 1 0 1 1 1 0 0 1 0 0 0 0 0 1 0 1 1 1 0 0 1 0 0 1 1 1 1 0 0 1
0 0 1 0 1 1 1 0 0 0 1 0 0 0 0 0 0 1 0 0 1 0 0 1 0 0 1 0 0 1 0 0
0 1 1 0 1 0 0 0 0 1 1 0 1 1 1 1 0 1 1 1 0 0 0 0 0 1 1 0 0 1 0 1
0 0 1 0 0 0 0 0 0 1 1 1 1 0 0 1 0 1 1 0 1 1 1 1 0 1 1 1 0 1 0 1
0 0 1 0 0 0 0 0 0 1 1 0 0 1 0 1 0 1 1 0 1 1 1 0 0 1 1 0 1 0 1 0
0 1 1 0 1 1 1 1 0 1 1 1 1 0 0 1 0 0 1 0 0 0 0 0 0 1 1 0 1 0 0 1
0 1 1 1 0 1 0 0 0 0 1 0 0 0 0 1
```

Part of the image as it would appear to a computer.

Humans are not very good at communicating using the binary system. We use a different number system.

Humans use the decimal or decimal system which comprises 10 digits: 0, 1, 2, 3, 4, 5, 6, 7, 8 and 9. This originated because we learnt to count on our 10 fingers.

Number systems

Watch the number systems animation on Cambridge Elevate

Key term

base 10: each place value is ten times bigger than the place to its right

In most numbering systems, the position of a digit determines the value associated with it.

Decimal system

Our decimal system is said to be base 10 because the position assigns a value that is *ten times the value of the position to the right*.

For example here is a number:

369

Reading from the right, the '9' is in the first position and has a value of 9 x 1.

The '6' directly to its left has a value of 6 x 10.

The '3' therefore has a value of 3 x 100.

The total number is therefore 300 + 60 + 9 which is equal to 369.

The values of the digits are called their place values.

The following table shows some of these place values:

Place values of the decimal system					
100000	10000	1000	100	10	1

The place value is ten times the value of the place value to the right.

These place values are equal to powers of 10.

Place values of the decimal system					
10^5	10^4	10^3	10^2	10^1	10^0
100000	10000	1000	100	10	1

Therefore 369 is equal to:

10^2	10^1	10^0
100	10	1
3	6	9

$(3 \times 10^2) + (6 \times 10^1) + (9 \times 10^0) = 300 + 60 + 9$

Binary system

The binary system also has place values and the value at any position will be *two times the value at the position to the right*: it is base 2. As in the decimal system, the place values increase but as powers of 2.

Place	2^4	2^3	2^2	2^1	2^0
Decimal equivalent	16	8	4	2	1

Remember that bits are combined into groups to represent data. The basic group is one of eight bits and is called a byte.

The following table shows the place values and the decimal equivalents for each bit in a byte.

Place	2^7	2^6	2^5	2^4	2^3	2^2	2^1	2^0
Decimal equivalent	128	64	32	16	8	4	2	1

To aid our understanding, we can translate binary into decimal.

Key term

place value: the value that a digit's position in a number gives it, for example (for decimal) in the number 356, the digit 5 has a value of 50 whereas in the number 3560, the digit 5 has a value of 500

Maths skills

Any number to the power of 0, for example 10^0 or 2^0, is equal to 1.

Key terms

base 2: each place value is two times bigger than the place to its right

byte: a group of eight bits

WORKED EXAMPLE

The following is a byte of bits:

10011010

This has meaning for the microprocessor but we need it to be translated into our decimal system.

We can use the above table to do this:

Place	2^7	2^6	2^5	2^4	2^3	2^2	2^1	2^0
Decimal equivalent	128	64	32	16	8	4	2	1
Byte	1	0	0	1	1	0	1	0

Just as we did for the decimal system above, we can work out the overall value of this byte by using the place values of each bit.

1×2^7	128
0×2^6	0
0×2^5	0
1×2^4	16
1×2^3	8
0×2^2	0
1×2^1	2
0×2^0	0
	154

Therefore **10011010** in binary is equivalent to **154** in decimal.

ACTIVITY 7.2

Convert the following 8-bit binary numbers into decimal ones.

a. 11001101   b. 01000100   c. 10101010   d. 11110000   e. 10111100

Converting decimal numbers to binary

Decimal numbers up to 255 can be converted into 8-bit binary ones.

WORKED EXAMPLE

Convert the decimal number 113 to binary.

Method 1

Use a table to make your conversion clear.

- Start at the left (here with 2^7 or 128) and ask if the number is equal to or greater than this place value.

- If the number is less than the place value, place a 0 at that position.

- If the number is greater than or equal to the place value, place a 1 and subtract that value from the place value to find the remainder.

Place	2^7	2^6	2^5	2^4	2^3	2^2	2^1	2^0
Decimal equivalent	128	64	32	16	8	4	2	1
Byte	0							
Byte	0	1						
Remainders		49						
Byte	0	1	1					
Remainders		49	17					
Byte	0	1	1	1				
Remainders		49	17	1				
Byte	0	1	1	1	0	0	0	
Remainders		49	17	1	1	1	1	
Byte	0	1	1	1	0	0	0	1
Remainders		49	17	1	1	1	1	0

113 < 128, so place a 0 in the place value.
113 > 64, so place a 1
Remainder is 113 − 64 = 49
49 > 32, so place a 1
49 − 32 = 17
17 > 16, so place a 1
17 − 16 = 1
The remainder is now 1 and that is less than 8, 4 and 2.
1 = 1, so place a 1

Therefore 113 in decimal is equivalent to 01110001 in binary.

Method 2

Using this method the number is continually divided by 2 and the remainders are found.

Number	Result of division by 2	Remainder
113	56	1
56	28	0
28	14	0
14	7	0
7	3	1
3	1	1
1	0	1

Now add these remainders to the table but in **reverse order** starting at 2^0

Place	2^7	2^6	2^5	2^4	2^3	2^2	2^1	2^0
Decimal equivalent	128	64	32	16	8	4	2	1
Byte	0	1	1	1	0	0	0	1

As only 7 bits have been calculated from the remainders, a 0 is added for the 8th bit.

Brilliant! Both methods have returned the same binary equivalent!

ACTIVITY 7.3

Convert the following decimal numbers into 8-bit binary ones.

a. 13   b. 69   c. 131   d. 199   e. 245

Counting in binary

The following shows the sequence in binary of counting up to 15 in decimal.

Decimal	0	1	2	3	4	5	6	7	8	9	10	11	12	13	14	15
Binary	0	1	10	11	100	101	110	111	1000	1001	1010	1011	1100	1101	1110	1111

ACTIVITY 7.4

Try counting up to 31 in binary using the fingers of one hand. The raised fingers represent a 1 and the lowered fingers a 0. Here is how to start: look how the pattern of fingers is the same as the binary underneath:

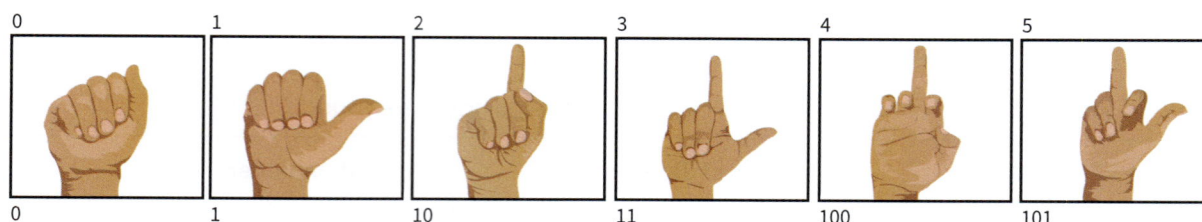

Groups of bits

A byte is a group of 8 bits. The word byte is represented by upper case B and bit by lower case b. People are often confused by claims made by internet service providers as they quote bandwidth in kbit or mbit (kilobits and megabits) which are a lot less than kB or MB!

Obviously lots of bytes are needed to represent programs and data and so largerunits are needed.

The next in size is the kilobyte or kB. Historically this was 1024 bytes, but as the prefix 'kilo' represents 1000, by modern standards a kB is 1000 bytes.

Then in order of magnitude:

1 Megabyte (MB)   1000 Kilobytes

1 Gigabyte (GB)   1000 Megabytes

1 Terabyte (TB)   1000 Gigabytes

ACTIVITY 7.5

a. Calculate how many bits there are in a gigabyte.

b. Express 2000MB in gigabytes.

c. Express 1 terabyte in kilobytes.

Bit

×8

Byte

×1000

Kilobyte

×1000

Megabyte

×1000

Gigabyte

×1000

Terabyte

Remember

1. If there are 8 bits in a byte, one megabyte is equal to 8 megabits.
2. Bits are **BI**nary digi**Ts** – they have single binary values of either 0 or 1.
3. The bits can be combined into groups in the same way that letters are combined into words.
4. All commands and data processed by a computer consist of groups of bits.
5. In any number system the value of a digit is partially determined by its place value.
6. Binary is a base 2 number system.
7. Binary numbers can be converted to decimal and vice versa.

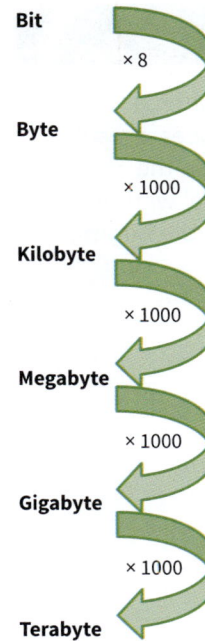

Binary sums

Addition

Here is a simple decimal addition. Beginning with the column on the right, if the total of one column is greater than 9 (e.g. 13, as below), then the 10 is carried over to the next column and the remainder (3) is written as the total in this column.

Calculations can be made the same way with binary numbers. The only difference is that where a '10' is carried over in decimal, a '2' is carried in binary.

Carry over	1		1	
		9	6	5
		3	2	8
Total	1	2	9	3

WORKED EXAMPLE

Carry out the following binary addition:

01011 + 00111 + 00100

Carry over	1	1	1	1	
	0	1	0	1	1
	0	0	1	1	1
	0	0	1	0	0
Total	1	0	1	1	0

In the same way that a '10' is carried in decimal, a '2' is carried in binary.

In binary, 1 + 1 = 10 (2 in decimal). The '1' is carried and the '0' is placed in this column.

In binary 1 + 1 + 1 = 11 (3 in decimal). The '1' on the left is carried and the other '1' is placed in this column.

When adding three binary numbers there is also the case of 1 + 1 + 1 + 1. In this case a 1 is carried two places to the left.

When computers are processing binary, they may only be able to cope with a fixed number of bits.

Look at this addition being performed by an 8 bit processor.

Carry over	1	1	1	1	1	1		1	
		1	0	0	1	1	1	0	1
		1	1	1	1	0	1	0	1
Total		1	0	0	1	0	0	1	0

Key term

overflow error: when a calculation produces a result that is greater than the computer can deal with or store in the available number of bits

But there is a problem. All eight bits have been used and the 1 that was carried over in the last column has nowhere to go – it has been *carried out*. Therefore the result of the calculation would be wrong!

This is called an **overflow error**. When this occurs, the microprocessor is informed that an error has occurred.

Complete Interactive Activity 7b on Cambridge Elevate

ACTIVITY 7.6

Complete the following binary additions.

a.
0	0	1	1	1	0	1	1
0	1	0	1	0	0	0	1
1	0	0	1	0	1	1	0

b.
0	1	0	0	1	1	1	1
0	1	0	1	0	1	1	1
1	0	0	1	0	1	0	0

c.
1	1	0	1	0	0	1	1
1	1	1	0	1	1	1	1
0	0	0	1	0	1	0	0

Download Worksheet 7.3 from Cambridge Elevate

The most famous disaster caused by an overflow error was the crash of the Ariane 5 space rocket launched by the European Space Agency in 1996.

Binary shifts

Multiplication

In decimal, when we want to multiply by 10 we add a 0, for example:

15 x 10 = 150

We have done a *left shift*: we have shifted the digits to the place values to their left.

10^2	10^1	10^0
100	10	1
	1	5

Will become:

10^2	10^1	10^0
100	10	1
1	5	0

If we multiplied by 100, then we would shift the digits two places to the left, and multiplying by 1000 would result in a shift three places to the left. A left shift is used when multiplying by powers of ten. Similarly, we can also use a left shift in binary when we are multiplying by powers of 2. If we multiply the 8-bit binary number 00001011 (decimal 11) by the binary number 10 (decimal 2), we could do one left shift.

2^7	2^6	2^5	2^4	2^3	2^2	2^1	2^0
128	64	32	16	8	4	2	1
0	0	0	0	1	0	1	1
0	0	0	1	0	1	1	0

Therefore 00001011 x 10 = 00010110.

We can check this in decimal: 11 x 2 = 22.

Division

A division of a binary number by powers of 2 is very easy. You just shift the bits to the right. So if the binary number 10011011 is divided by 2, the bits are shifted to the right one place and the one at the right end drops off and is removed. The result would be 01001101. We can test this:

2^7	2^6	2^5	2^4	2^3	2^2	2^1	2^0
128	64	32	16	8	4	2	1
1	0	0	1	1	0	1	1
0	1	0	0	1	1	0	1

If you convert the numbers to decimal, you can see that 10011011 (155) divided by 2 gives the result 77 using the right shift method. The result is not precise as it should be 77.5. Using right shift leads to a loss of accuracy.

ACTIVITY 7.7

State the results of the following binary left shifts:

a. 00101101 left shift by 3

b. 10001101 left shift by 4

c. 10110111 left shift by 2.

Watch out

As bits are lost there is a loss of accuracy and precision.

This method can also be used for any number that is a power of 2. For example if the number is divided by 16 (which is 2^4), there should be a shift of four places to the right.

2^7	2^6	2^5	2^4	2^3	2^2	2^1	2^0
128	64	32	16	8	4	2	1
1	0	0	1	1	0	1	1
0	0	0	0	1	0	0	1

The result in decimal is 9, and 16 multiplied by 9 is equal to 144 and not 155.

Therefore, the result given is the nearest, lower integer.

Complete Interactive Activity 7c on Cambridge Elevate

ACTIVITY 7.8

State the results of the following binary right shifts.

a. 00101101 right shift by 3

b. 10001101 right shift by 4

c. 10110111 right shift by 2.

Hexadecimal

Hexadecimal is a base 16 number system: there are 16 digits, 0 to 15.

As we only have 10 single digits in decimal (0 to 9), we use uppercase letters A to F for the remaining six digits.

Therefore hexadecimal digits and their decimal equivalents are:

Decimal	0	1	2	3	4	5	6	7	8	9	10	11	12	13	14	15
Hexadecimal	0	1	2	3	4	5	6	7	8	9	A	B	C	D	E	F

Why do we need hexadecimal numbers?

We need hexadecimal numbers because of our human limitations! Computers do not understand or use hexadecimal, they only understand and use binary. Hexadecimal is used because people get confused with large binary numbers, so we simplify binary numbers by representing them in hexadecimal notation, meaning that fewer digits are used. A byte is represented by just two digits in hexadecimal.

Here is a byte of 8 bits:

1	1	0	1	0	0	1	1

Saying that is quite a mouthful, but it is easier if it is represented as hexadecimal.

Converting binary to hexadecimal

To convert the binary to hexadecimal the byte is split into two halves of 4 bits each. These are called nibbles.

1	1	0	1

Nibbles

0	0	1	1

Key term

nibble: half a byte

Each nibble is now converted into its decimal number. Here are the nibbles with their place values.

8	4	2	1
1	1	0	1

8	4	2	1
0	0	1	1

Therefore the decimal numbers are: 13 and 3.

Therefore the hexadecimal representation is: D3.

It is far easier to say and remember D3 than 11010011.

As we will see later, hexadecimal numbers are used to simplify colour codes, which consist of 24 bits. It is far easier to colour code as six hexadecimal digits rather than 24 binary ones.

Here are some colours with their hexadecimal codes.

#FF66FF		#CC66FF		#9966FF	
#FF66CC		#CC66CC		#9966CC	
#FF6699		#CC6699		#996699	
#FF6666		#CC6666		#996666	
#FF6633		#CC6633		#996633	
#FF6600		#CC6600		#996600	
#FF33FF		#CC33FF		#9933FF	
#FF33CC		#CC33CC		#9933CC	
#FF3399		#CC3399		#993399	
#FF3366		#CC3366		#993366	

ACTIVITY 7.9

Investigate the hexadecimal codes for the different colours that can be used.

Hexadecimal is also used in assembly language programming and in error messages. When anything is represented by a hexadecimal number, a # sign is used, for example #FF0000 is the hexadecimal for red.

Using hexadecimal raises another problem. We have to be able to convert from binary and decimal into hexadecimal and vice versa. Converting from binary to hexadecimal has been shown previously, but we will now look at the other conversions.

Converting decimal to hexadecimal

Here is a decimal number: 213.

To convert to hexadecimal we must progressively divide by 16 until the result is 0 and remember the remainders.

Number	Result of dividing by 16	Remainder
213	13	5
13	0	13

D 5

Therefore 213 in decimal in hexadecimal is: D5

We can check this if we create a table showing place values for base 16.

16^3	16^2	16^1	16^0
4096	256	16	1
		D	5

Therefore D5 is equal to (13 x 16) + 5 which is 213.

Converting hexadecimal to decimal

Here is a hexadecimal number: CD. We can convert it to decimal using the table.

16^3	16^2	16^1	16^0
4096	256	16	1
		C	D

Therefore the decimal is equal to: (12 x 16) + (13 x 1) which is equal to 192 + 13.

Therefore 'CD' in hexadecimal equals '205' in decimal.

Converting hexadecimal to binary

We will use the same hexadecimal number: CD.

First convert each digit to decimal.

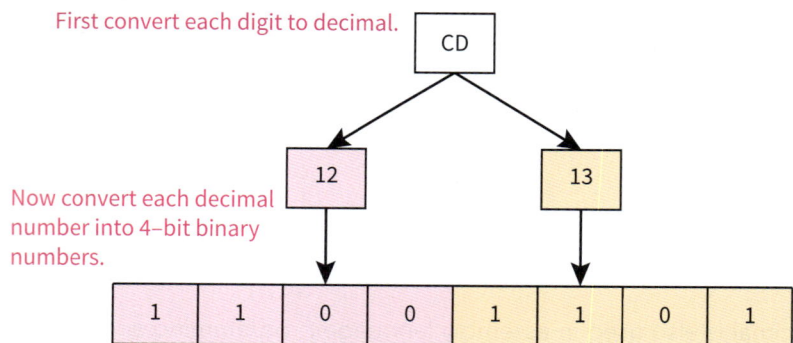

Therefore CD in hexadecimal is 11001101 in binary.

Complete Interactive Activity 7d on Cambridge Elevate

Download Worksheet 7.4 from Cambridge Elevate

ACTIVITY 7.10

Convert the following hexadecimal numbers to decimal and binary.

a. C4   b. 46   c. FA

Convert the following decimal numbers to hexadecimal.

d. 96   e. 201   f. 141

Remember

1. Additions, subtractions, multiplications and divisions can be carried out on binary numbers in the same way as on decimal numbers.
2. When multiplying or dividing binary numbers by powers of 2, a left or right shift can be used.
3. Hexadecimal numbers are used to represent binary numbers because they are easier for humans to remember and use.

Practice questions

1. Convert the binary number 01101101 to decimal.

2. Carry out the following binary addition:

0	0	1	0	1	0	1	1
0	1	1	1	0	1	0	1

3. Convert the decimal number 213 to

   a. binary
   b. hexadecimal.

Your final challenge

You have been asked to create a program to help people who are struggling with binary and hexadecimal representations of numbers.

- The user should be able to enter a number in hexadecimal, binary or decimal.
- The number should be between 0 and 255.
- You will need some validation to ensure the numbers fall within the required range.
- The program should then display that number in the other two number systems.
- You could use a menu system to allow the user to select the number system for entering the number.
- The user should be able to keep using the converter until they select an option to quit.

Download Self-assessment 7 worksheet from Cambridge Elevate (this content has not been approved by AQA)

8 Representing text, graphics and sound

Learning outcomes

By the end of this chapter you should be able to:

- explain how characters are represented in binary
- calculate the ASCII code for any character
- calculate the size of a text file
- explain how images are represented in binary
- calculate the size of an image file
- explain how sound is represented in binary
- calculate the size of an audio file
- explain the disadvantages of large image and audio files
- explain how file compression reduces the size of files
- explain the differences between lossless and lossy file compression.

Challenge: create a program to compress and decompress image files for a social media site

- Millions of image, video and sound files are uploaded and downloaded each day.
- On Facebook alone more than 200 million images are uploaded each day! It is in everyone's interest to compress these files as much as possible.
- Your challenge is to create a program to compress and decompress image files.

Why binary representation?

- Computers operate and communicate using binary.
- All instructions and data have to be represented by strings of 1s and 0s.
- All text, images and sound have to be reduced to combinations of 1 and 0: they have to be represented by binary.
- To the computers on which this book was written, edited and produced the book is nothing more than billions of bits: 1s and 0s.
- The bits have to be arranged so that they can be interpreted as text, images or sound.

Representations of text

Recall from an earlier chapter that all characters are processed by a computer as binary codes. When we enter a letter from the keyboard, a stream of bits is transmitted to the processor. It cannot recognise the letter 'A' or an exclamation mark, only a set of 1s and 0s. The list of these binary codes that can be recognised by the computer hardware and software is known as its character set.

Digital sound recording has allowed anyone to record and distribute their music from their homes without needing to use expensive studios.

ASCII code

At first, different manufacturers used their own codes for their computers. However, they soon realised that if computers wanted to share information, they needed to also share a common encoding system for text. The first character-encoding scheme to be used as a common standard for all computers was called ASCII (which stands for 'American Standard Code for Information Interchange').

ASCII was originally a 7-bit code and the 128 possible code sequences represent English characters and control actions such backspace, shift on, shift off and carriage return. The following table shows the printable characters of the ASCII code with their decimal and 7-bit binary values.

> **Key term**
>
> **character set**: the list of binary codes that can be recognised by computers as being usable characters

Decimal	7-bit binary	ASCII	Decimal	7-bit binary	ASCII	Decimal	7-bit binary	ASCII
space	0100000	32	@	1000000	64	`	1100000	96
!	0100001	33	A	1000001	65	a	1100001	97
"	0100010	34	B	1000010	66	b	1100010	98
#	0100011	35	C	1000011	67	c	1100011	99
$	0100100	36	D	1000100	68	d	1100100	100
%	0100101	37	E	1000101	69	e	1100101	101
&	0100110	38	F	1000110	70	f	1100110	102
'	0100111	39	G	1000111	71	g	1100111	103
(	0101000	40	H	1001000	72	h	1101000	104
)	0101001	41	I	1001001	73	i	1101001	105
*	0101010	42	J	1001010	74	j	1101010	106
+	0101011	43	K	1001011	75	k	1101011	107
,	0101100	44	L	1001100	76	l	1101100	108
-	0101101	45	M	1001101	77	m	1101101	109
.	0101110	46	N	1001110	78	n	1101110	110
/	0101111	47	O	1001111	79	o	1101111	111
0	0110000	48	P	1010000	80	p	1110000	112
1	0110001	49	Q	1010001	81	q	1110001	113
2	0110010	50	R	1010010	82	r	1110010	114
3	0110011	51	S	1010011	83	s	1110011	115
4	0110100	52	T	1010100	84	t	1110100	116
5	0110101	53	U	1010101	85	u	1110101	117
6	0110110	54	V	1010110	86	v	1110110	118
7	0110111	55	W	1010111	87	w	1110111	119
8	0111000	56	X	1011000	88	x	1111000	120
9	0111001	57	Y	1011001	89	y	1111001	121
:	0111010	58	Z	1011010	90	z	1111010	122
;	0111011	59	[	1011011	91	{	1111011	123
<	0111100	60	\	1011100	92	|	1111100	124
=	0111101	61	]	1011101	93	}	1111101	125
>	0111110	62	^	1011110	94	~	1111110	126
?	0111111	63	_	1011111	95	DEL	1111111	127

The codes are grouped according to function:

0–31	Control codes (non-printing)
32–47	Printable symbols such as ! / \ &
48–57	**The digits 0 to 9**
58–64	Printable symbols such as < > =
65–90	**Upper case characters A to Z**
91–96	Printable characters including [ ]
97–122	**Lower case characters a to z**
123–127	Printable characters including { }

ACTIVITY 8.1

Translate this ASCII code message into English. The decimal codes of the characters have been used. So 65 would be upper case 'A' and 97 would be lower case 'a'.

84 104 101 32 65 83 67 73 73 32 99 111 100 101 32 114 101 112 114 101 115 101 110 116 115 32 99 104 97 114 97 99 116 101 114 115 46

Converting string characters to ASCII code and vice versa

To a computer, a character in a string is just a number; a number representing one of the characters in the ASCII code. An algorithm might need to find the ASCII code for a character. All programming languages have commands for doing this.

The following examples will use the AQA pseudo-code.

Code ———————————————

```
CODE_TO_CHAR() to return a character from a number.

CHAR_TO_CODE() to return a number from a character.
```

Therefore:

Code ———————————————

```
myString ← CODE_TO_CHAR(67)

OUTPUT myString
```

Would return the letter upper case C as 67 is the ASCII code for that letter.

Entering:

Code ———————————————

```
myNumber ← CHAR_TO_CODE('D')

OUTPUT myNumber
```

would return the number 68 as that is its number in the ASCII code.

Size of ASCII files

Because one byte is used for each character, the size of a plain text file in bytes should be equal to the number of characters. Although ASCII is a 7-bit code, characters are usually stored in 8-bits, i.e. one per byte.

Here is a picture of a text file:

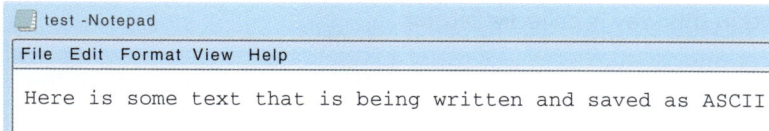

```
test -Notepad
File  Edit  Format  View  Help
Here is some text that is being written and saved as ASCII.
```

This file consists of 59 characters, including spaces, and so the size should be 59 bytes.

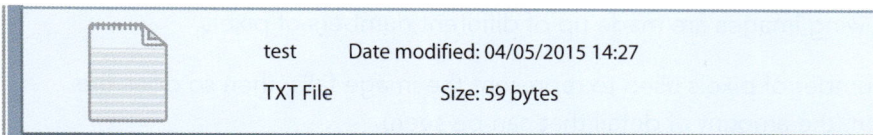

```
test        Date modified: 04/05/2015 14:27
TXT File         Size: 59 bytes
```

The file size is shown as 59 bytes.

The extended ASCII code

In the ASCII code, there are 96 printable characters but there was always a need for more characters in order to accommodate foreign languages, mathematical symbols and special symbols for drawing pictures.

As computers process data in 8-bit bytes, it was sensible to extend ASCII to an 8-bit code, which allows 256 codes. Unfortunately there was no standardisation and different manufacturers such as IBM and Apple created their own versions with different characters represented by the same codes. With the huge popularity of home computing in the 1980s and the proliferation of manufacturers such as Atari and Commodore, each creating their own operating system, there were many different versions of extended ASCII.

Unicode

To overcome the problem of multiple versions of ASCII, the Unicode Consortium was founded to develop and promote a Unicode standard which can represent and handle text in most of the world's writing systems. Unicode has become the universal standard recognised and used by the major hardware and software manufacturers such as IBM, Apple, Microsoft, Oracle and Sun.

Unicode encodings include UTF-8 with an 8-bit fixed width encoding and UTF-16 and UTF-32 with 16 and 32 bits. A 32-bit character set can have 4,294,967,296 possible characters, enough for all known languages.

Unicode can represent the characters in all known languages. For compatibility and because ASCII was the recognised standard, Unicode characters 0 to 127 are the same as ASCII. In English-language documents, Unicode is represented using the same codes as in 8-bit ASCII.

Complete Interactive Activity 8a on Cambridge Elevate

ACTIVITY 8.2

Create an algorithm asking a user to input a sentence and then print the codes (in decimal) for each of the characters or symbols with each one printed on a new line. Code and test the algorithm in your programming language.

Remember

1. A character set is a defined list of characters recognised by the computer hardware and software.
2. The ASCII code is a 7-bit code and the 128 possible code sequences represent English characters and control actions.
3. Extended ASCII uses 8 bits and was developed to cater for foreign language and graphics characters.
4. Unicode can represent characters in all known languages and writing systems.

ACTIVITY 8.3

Create an algorithm that will allow a user to enter a sentence or phrase and will then inform them of the size of the text file (in bytes) created.

Download Worksheet 8.1 from Cambridge Elevate

Representations of images

Computers also represent and store images as binary code.

A digital image is composed of many small points of colour or picture elements, pixels, for short. Each pixel is represented by a number of bits. Programs can indicate where each pixel is placed on the screen and what colour it is to be. An image represented in this way is called a bitmap.

The size of the image is given as the number of pixels in the width and then the number of pixels in the height, for example 640 x 480 or 2048 x 1536.

Therefore an image described as 640 x 480 is made up of 307 200 pixels and one described as 2048 x 1536 contains 3145728 pixels.

The following images are made up of different numbers of pixels.

As the number of pixels used to represent the image falls, then so does the resolution (the amount of detail that can be seen).

Tip

Each pixel has its own individual colour and therefore the greater the number of pixels, the greater the detail that can be shown. This is because with fewer pixels a larger area of the image has to be reduced to only one colour.

640 x 420

320 x 210

160 x 110

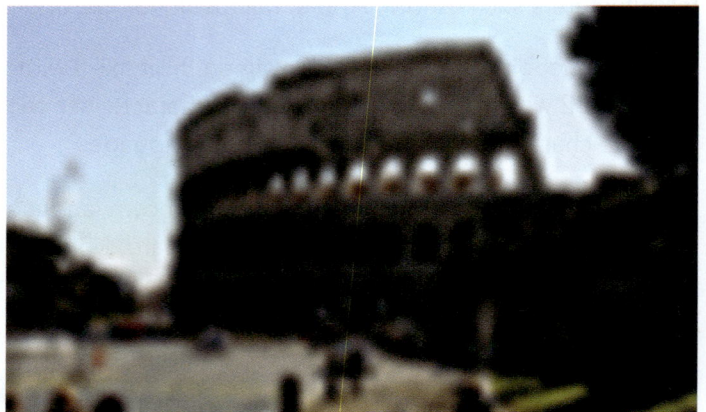

80 x 60

Colour depth

The colour depth is important for the quality of the colours in an image. It is the number of bits used to encode the colour of each pixel.

If one bit is used to encode each pixel, then only two colours can be used (2^1). The 0 represents black and the 1 represents white.

Here is a file encoding a 1-bit graphic. This would encode for the following graphic on an 8-bit grid.

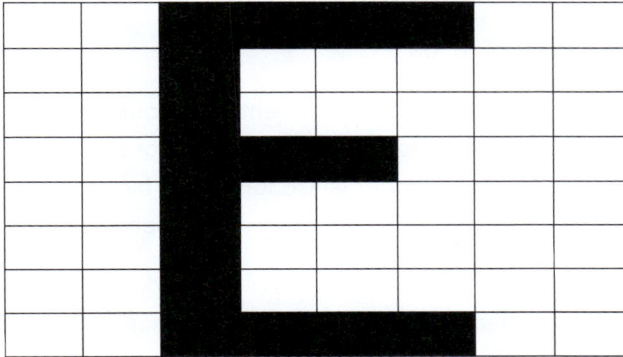

```
11000011
11000011
11011111
11000111
11011111
11011111
11011111
11000011
```

ACTIVITY 8.4

Write the file to encode the following 1-bit graphic.

A colour depth of 3 allows eight colours to be used (2^3).

Black is encoded as 000 and white as 111. The palette contains red, green and blue and their complimentary colours cyan, magenta and yellow.

The present standard most widely used is 24-bit representation. This means that the colour data for each pixel is encoded in 24 bits with 8 bits used for each of the primary colours: red, green and blue. Each colour in the palette is a combination of each of these in different proportions.

Using 8 bits allows 256 different levels of each of red, green and blue. Therefore 256 x 256 x 256 or 16 777 216 different colour variations are possible.

This number of bits produces such a realistic image it is described as being 'true colour'.

Hexadecimal

Entering a colour code in binary for a 24-bit number is very laborious. For example:

The code for black is: 000000000000000000000000

Red is: 111111110000000000000000

These are very easy ones to enter, but the binary code for this shade of purple is more complex.

110001100011000011110100

That string would be far more difficult to enter without making a mistake, which is where hexadecimal comes to the rescue of us error-prone humans. The hexadecimal code for that number is 'C630F4'. It is far easier to remember and enter. That is why programming languages allow users to enter colour codes in hexadecimal.

Remember that hexadecimal codes should have a hash sign in front. Therefore the code entered would be #C630F4.

The following screenshot shows the decimal and hexadecimal codes for the green colour shown.

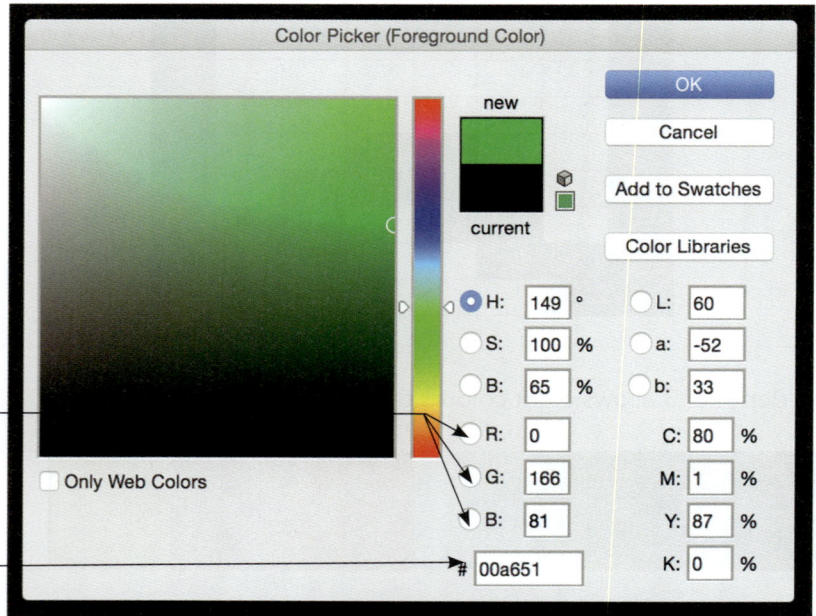

These are the decimal values for the red, green and blue channels.

Convert them to hexadecimal to check if the value shown below is correct.

The hexadecimal code for this colour.

Maths skills

The number of bits is divided by 8 to find the number of bytes.

This is divided by 1000 to find the number in kilobytes.

File sizes

As the number of pixels and the colour depth increases then so will the size of the image file. For a digital image of 2048 x 1536 pixels there is a total of 2048 x 1536 = 3 145 728 pixels. Because 24 bits are used to encode each pixel, the file size will be 3 145 728 x 24 = 75 497 472 bits. This is equal to 75 497 472 / 8 = 9 437 184 bytes or almost 9.5 megabytes.

The file size in bits can therefore be calculated using the following formula:

$$W \times H \times D$$

Where 'W' is width, 'H' is height and 'D' is the colour depth used.

ACTIVITY 8.5

Calculate the file sizes of the following digital images.

1. 4220 x 2641 with a colour depth of 24 bits.

2. 640 x 480 using a 256 colour palette.

The better the image quality, the larger the file size. This can be a problem if the image needs to be transmitted electronically, because it will take a long while to download. In many instances (e.g. sending a holiday photograph to a friend) the image quality will be reduced in order to reduce the file size and therefore the download speed. There is always a compromise between file size and download speed.

> ### Remember
>
> 1. A digital image is made up of picture elements or pixels.
> 2. The greater the number of pixels the greater the clarity of the image.
> 3. The colour data of a pixel are encoded in binary.
> 4. In modern applications 24 bits are used to encode each pixel.
> 5. There are 8 bits for each of the red, green and blue elements (channels) of the pixel.
> 6. The file size of an image can be found using the formula W x H x D.
> 7. Because file sizes can become large there is always a compromise between the quality of the image and the needs for storage and transmission of the image.

Complete Interactive Activity 8b on Cambridge Elevate

Representations of sound

Sound is caused by vibrations travelling through a medium such as air, water or metal. These vibrations compress and then pull apart the air molecules thus causing changes in air pressure.

If these vibrations enter our ears and cause tiny sensory hairs to vibrate, then we can hear the sound.

When we speak, our vocal cords vibrate and cause the air to vibrate. Musical instruments function in the same way: the strings of a guitar, the reed in a clarinet or the air in a flute are all made to vibrate. Vibrations travel out in waves; these are called sound waves.

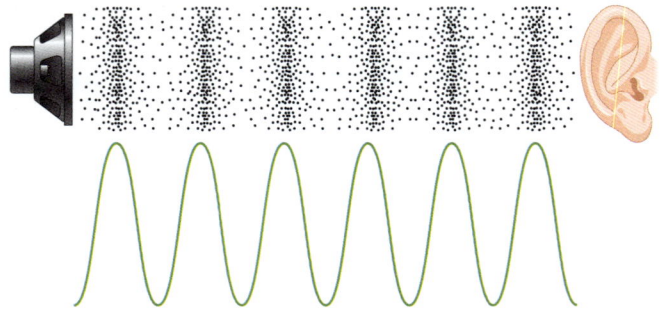

The waves of vibrations produced by the loudspeaker can be represented by the graph plotting the changes in air pressure.

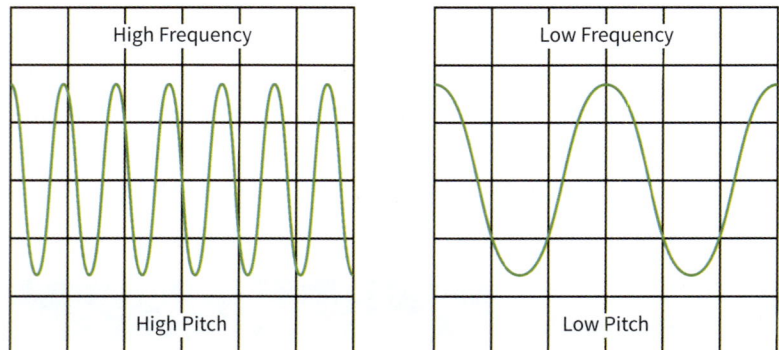

These graphs show the differences between high and low pitched sounds. For the high pitched sound, there are more waves of vibrations every second. They have a high frequency.

The graphs show that there are continuous changes in the air pressure. Recording methods that try to capture this continuous change by converting all of the changes in air pressure to analogous changes in voltage are called analogue recordings. Analogue recordings, such as vinyl albums and audio cassettes, capture completely the continuous changes in air pressure as continuous minute changes in voltage. Contrast this with *digital* recordings, where data can only take values that change in set steps.

Computers are digital. They cannot represent continuous, minute changes in voltage; each transistor is either on or off, with nothing in between.

Because the sound wave cannot be represented as a series of continuous changes on computer, snapshots of it must be taken and then fitted together. This is called sampling.

A digital sound file therefore does not contain all of the total available information that an analogue one does. But there are benefits to digital recordings such as:

- It can be edited and manipulated easily by computer equipment.

- It is more portable; it can be carried on a memory stick or SD card while vinyl records and tapes are not as portable.

- It can be played over and over again without deterioration. LPs and tapes deteriorate.

Key terms

analogue: data which can use any value in a continuous range

sampling: making physical measurements of the amplitude of an electronic representation of the sound wave at set time intervals and then converting the measurements to digital values

Tip

Sampling is similar to creating a visual animation from many still images (snapshots), each slightly different to the next. The smaller the changes between each one and the greater the number used each second, the more realistic the animation will be.

- It can be easily copied to a computer. Expensive equipment is needed to copy vinyl records.

- Digital audio files can be easily emailed, downloaded and streamed by users.

- Equipment to record and process digital sound is relatively cheap.

- It has allowed people to produce their own commercial music at home.

There are two factors that will determine how accurately the digital recording matches the original sound: sample rate and bit depth.

Sampling rate

The sample rate is the number of samples taken each second. The higher the sample rate, the more accurately the analogue sound wave will be represented. For CDs, a sample rate of 44 100 per second (44.1 KHz) is used while a maximum of 192 000 samples per second is used for Blu-ray audio.

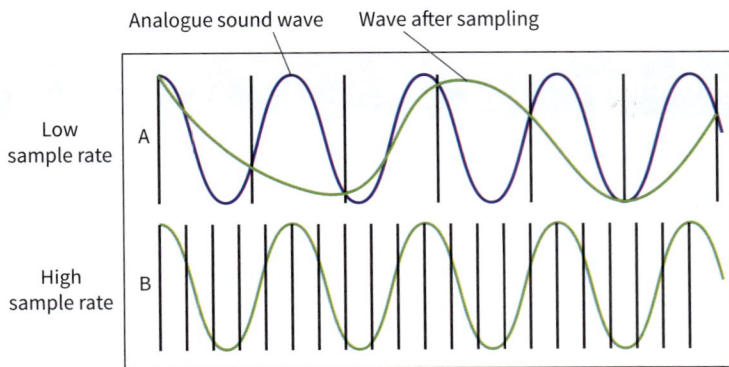

Sample resolution or bit depth

By increasing the number of bits used to encode each sample, the amount of detail contained in each sample is increased.

Using more bits enables the range of the sound to be more accurately represented.

The dynamic range is the range of volumes of sound in the music.

Using 8 bits allows 256 gradations to be measured; 16 bits allows 65 536 and 24 bits allows 16.7 million.

Therefore using more bits allows for much smaller gradations in the volume. For CD recordings, a bit depth of 16 bits is used.

Digital audio file sizes

To calculate the file size for a standard mono sample the following need to be considered:

- sampling rate

- sample resolution or bit depth

- length of the recording.

The size of a three-minute audio file with a sampling rate of 44 100 per second and a bit depth of 16 bits would be: 44 100 (sampling rate) x 16 (bit depth) x 180 (three minutes in seconds) = 127 008 000 bits. This equals 15 876 000 bytes or 15.876 megabytes.

ACTIVITY 8.6

Calculate the size of an audio file for a song lasting five minutes which was sampled at a rate of 41 100 samples per second and a bit depth of 24 bits.

Audio file sizes can become very large and, as with image files, there is always a compromise between file size and the quality of the recording.

If unlimited storage space and powerful computers for processing the audio are available, then file size is not a problem. But if the audio files have to be transmitted electronically or stored on portable devices, then the files need to be as small as possible and this results in a loss of quality.

Remember

1. Sound is caused by waves of vibrations travelling through a medium, usually air.
2. These vibrations cause continuous changes to air pressure.
3. Recording methods that capture the continuous change are called analogue.
4. Recording techniques that just sample the changes at fixed periods are called digital.
5. The quality of a digital recording is determined by the rate of sampling and the number of bits used to encode the data in each sample.
6. Digital file sizes can be calculated by the formula: Sample rate x bit depth x length in seconds.
7. There is always a compromise between storage and transmission requirements and the sound quality.

Compression

Files, especially graphic and audio files, can become very large.

On Facebook more than 200 million images are uploaded each day. On Snapchat, almost 100 000 images are uploaded each minute. It has been estimated that in total over 1.8 billion images are uploaded to social media sites each day! Every day millions of audio and video files are being downloaded.

It is therefore in everyone's interest to make these files as small as possible. Users need upload and download times to be short, and social media sites want to store the files in as small a space as possible.

That is why file **compression** is important. It reduces the file size and gives the following benefits:

- it uses less internet bandwidth when the files are downloaded

- it allows for faster transfer speeds

- it takes up less storage space on the servers of storage providers

- it reduces congestion on the internet through smaller files

- it makes audio and video files suitable for streaming.

Compression algorithms are used to ensure that the file size is as small as possible. If the compressed file can be decompressed to the original without any loss of data, it is called lossless compression. But if the file is compressed by removing some of the data, the original cannot be recovered and it is called lossy compression.

Lossless compression

If a lossless compression algorithm is used to compress the file, then the original can be reconstituted when it is decompressed. Nothing is lost.

The algorithm checks for redundancy: items that do not need to be there.

Look at the following short paragraph:

> *The size of an image file depends on the colour depth and dimensions. The size of an audio file depends on the sample rate and bit depth. The size of an image file and an audio file can be very large.*

This paragraph has 41 words and 200 characters including spaces. Therefore the file size would be 200 bytes if we assume that each 7-bit character is represented in a byte.

But in the paragraph there is significant redundancy: some words are used more than once.

Here is a list of words that appear more than once:

1	the
2	size
3	of
4	an
5	image
6	file
7	depends
8	on
9	and
10	depth
11	audio

This list is a numbered dictionary that can be referred to when the file is being decompressed.

Tip

The size of an image file depends on the colour depth and dimensions. The size of an audio file depends on the sample rate and bit depth. The size of an image file and an audio file can be very large.

Using the dictionary, the file can be written as:

1 2 3 4 5 6 7 8 1 colour 10 9 dimensions. 1 2 3 4 11 6 7 8 1 sample rate 9 bit 10. 1 size 3 4 5 6 9 4 11 6 can be very large.

This version has only 125 characters. The dictionary that would have to be included with the file has 55. The total is 180 and so would have a size of 180 bytes: a saving of 20 bytes.

This saving has been made in only a small file and with a very simple algorithm checking for word redundancy. But imagine if this was done to this book: the same words could be referenced many times and there would be a greater saving of bytes.

Using this method, nothing is lost; the whole paragraph can be rewritten from the compressed file.

Text files are relatively easy to compress in this way as they have lots of repeated items (words) and compression rates of 50 per cent are relatively easy to achieve.

Huffman coding

Huffman coding, also known as 'Huffman encoding' or 'Huffman compression', is an algorithm for lossless compression based on the frequency of the characters or symbols in the file. It ensures that the more common characters have fewer bits to represent them than the less common characters that need more bits to identify them. Therefore the overall size of the file is reduced.

It is therefore called a 'variable-length coding system' because the codes for different characters have different lengths.

During the encoding, a binary tree, called a Huffman tree, is built up.

Key term

binary tree: items of data are stored in *nodes* and the branch points are called *internal nodes*. In a binary tree, each node has at most two branches or *children*

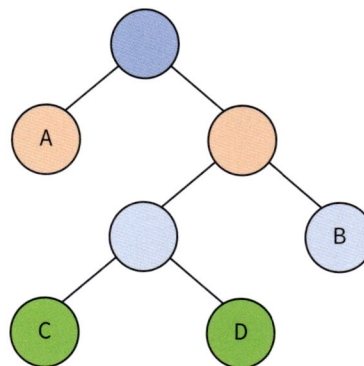

WORKED EXAMPLE

Create a Huffman tree for the following sentence:

She sells sea shells.

1. Scan the sentence and calculate the frequency of the symbols and characters.

Character	Frequency
.	1
S	1
a	1
h	2
space	3
e	4
l	4
s	5

2. These characters are going to form the leaves of the tree and can be placed in a priority queue in order of frequency.

3. The two lowest elements are combined into a node with a frequency that is the sum of their individual frequencies.

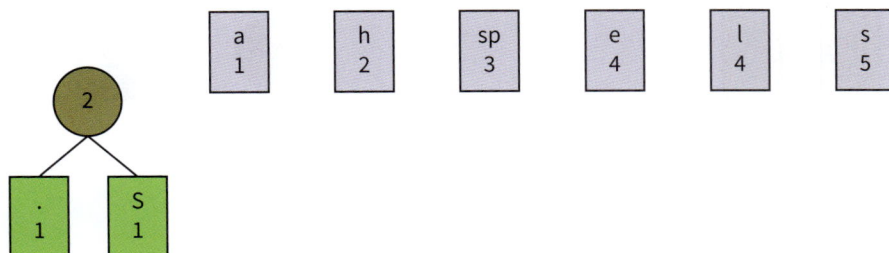

4. The node is then inserted back into the queue at the correct position.

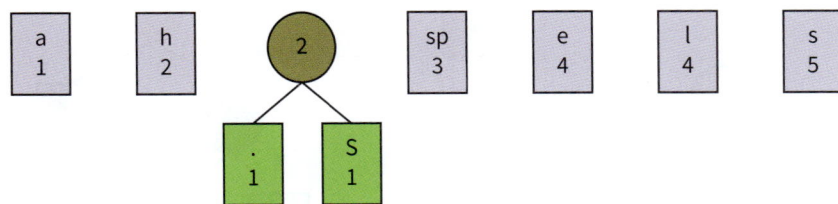

5. This is repeated for the two lowest elements.

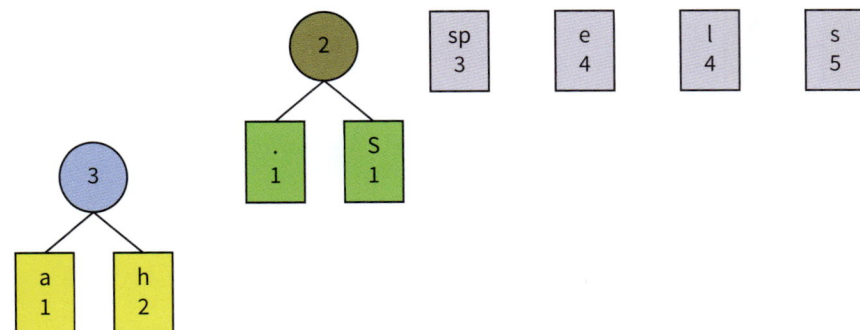

6. This node is then inserted into the queue.

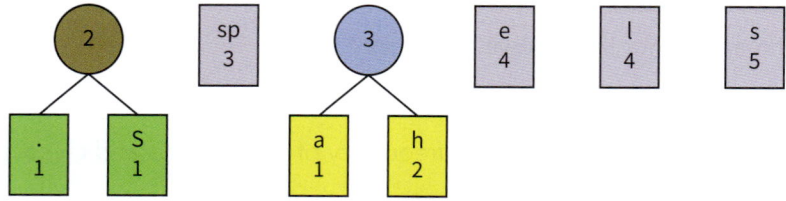

7. The two lowest elements are combined again.

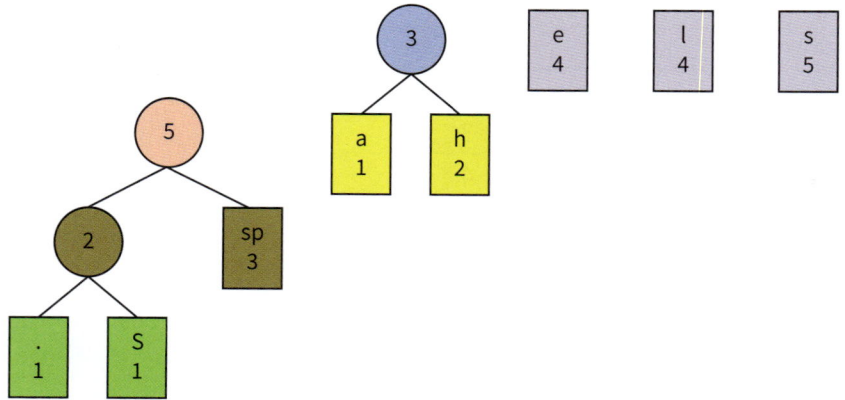

8. The node is then inserted into the queue.

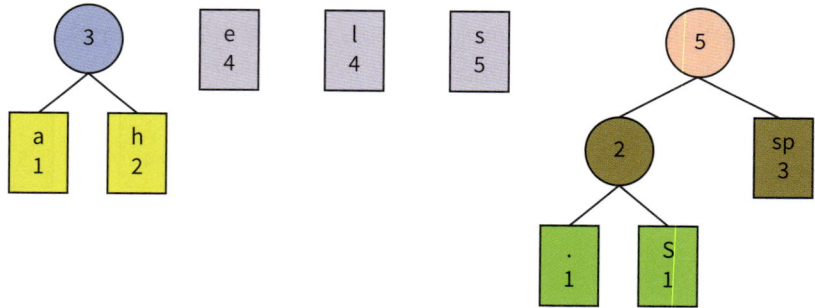

9. And again...

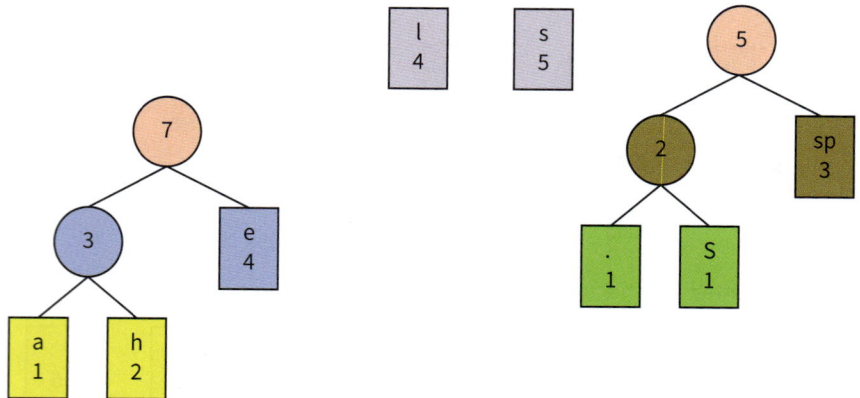

10. It is inserted into the queue.

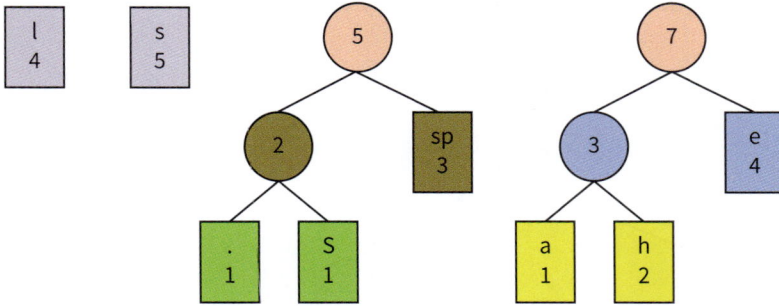

11. The final nodes are now combined and inserted back into the queue.

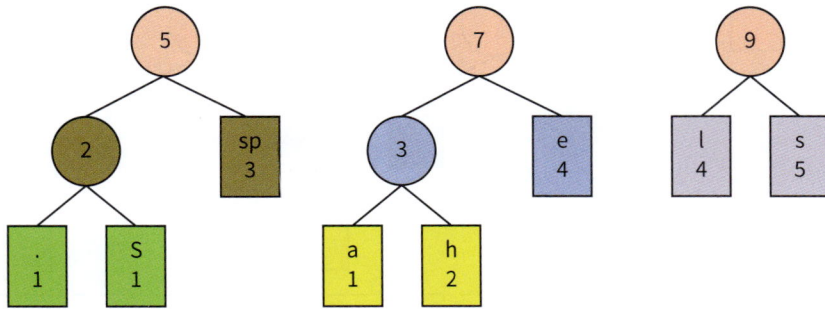

12. The two lowest are again combined and inserted in the queue.

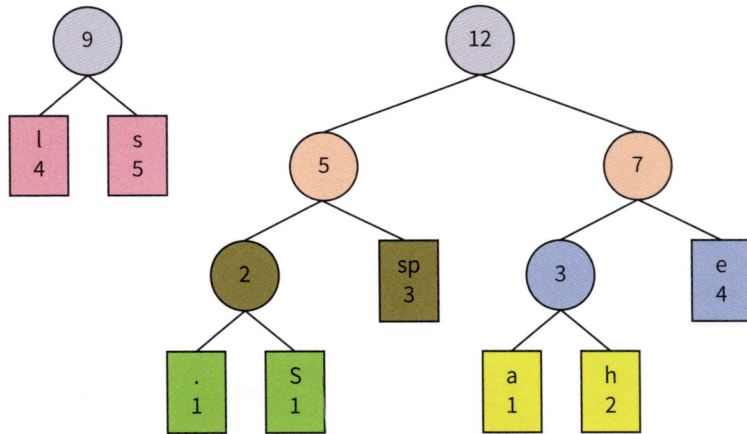

13. The final combination is now made.

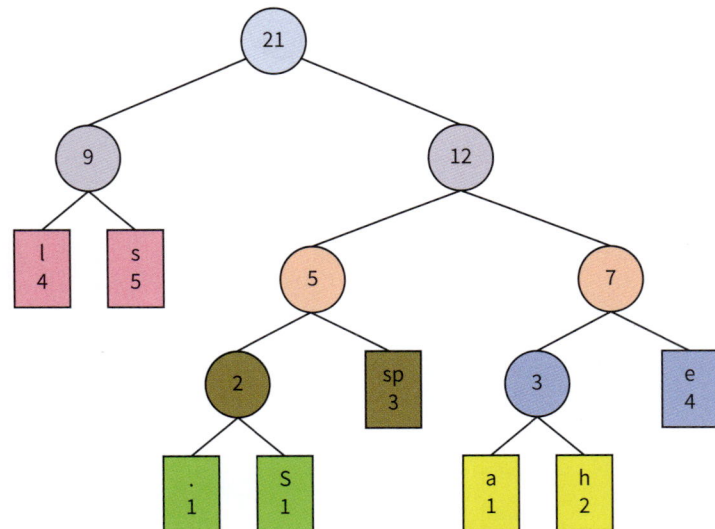

The first or initial node contains the number 21 which is equal to the number of characters in the sentence. The most frequently appearing characters are at the top of the tree.

This Huffman tree can be written as:

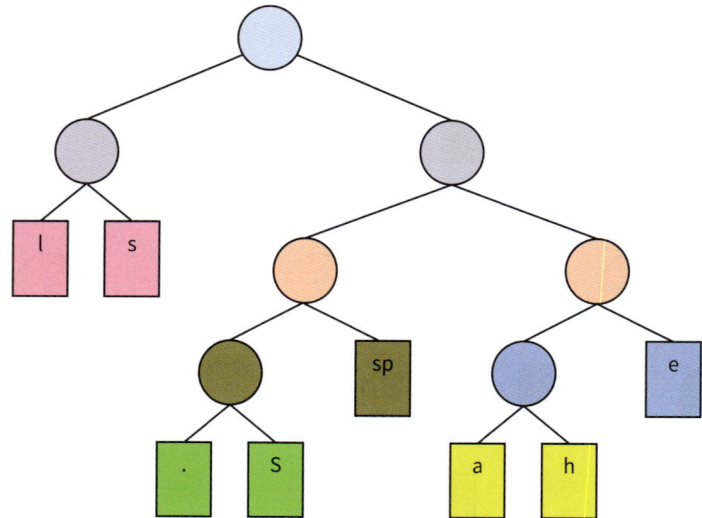

Generating the Huffman code

Once the tree has been created, each character can be given a code by traversing the tree.

0 is used to represent each left branch and 1 for each right branch.

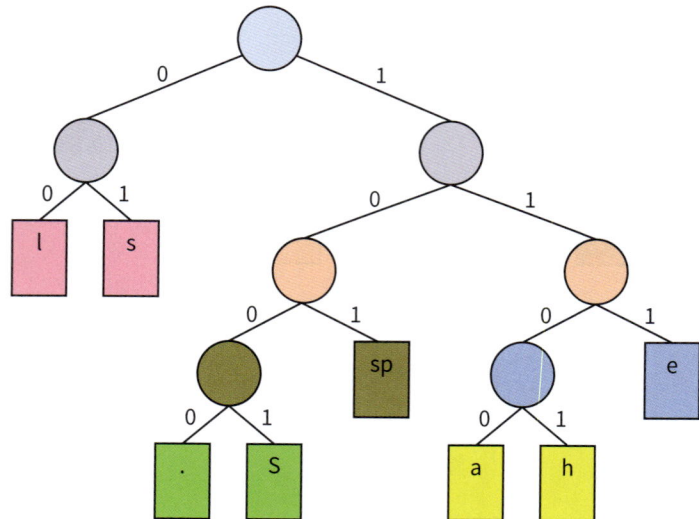

Following the tree, the Huffman codes for the characters would be:

Character	Frequency	Huffman code
.	1	1000
S	1	1001
a	1	1100
h	2	1101
space	3	101
e	4	111
l	4	00
s	5	01

Notice how the more frequently used characters have shorter codes.

The sentence '**She sells sea shells.**' would be represented by the following code:

1001 1101 111 101 01 111 00 00 01 101 01 111 1100 101 01 1101 111 00 00 01 1000

There are 21 characters and symbols. Using 7-bit ASCII code that would equal 7 x 21 = 147 bits.

Using the Huffman codes, only 59 bits are used.

This can be shown in the following table:

Character	Frequency	Bits used in ASCII	Huffman code	Bits used in Huffman code
.	1	7	1000	4
S	1	7	1001	4
a	1	7	1100	4
h	2	14	1101	8
space	3	21	101	9
e	4	28	111	12
l	4	28	00	8
s	5	35	01	10
		147		59

Therefore in one short sentence there is a saving of 88 bits.

Create a Huffman tree for the following character frequencies:

Character	Frequency
A	12
B	2
C	7
D	13
E	14
F	85

State the Huffman coding for each character. Then calculate how many fewer bits will be used than if the characters were stored as ASCII.

A Huffman tree for the text 'the cat sat on the mat' is:

(a) Complete the table to show the Huffman coding for the following characters:

Character	Huffman coding
h	
e	
m	

(b) Complete the table to show the characters from the following Huffman codes:

Character	Huffman coding
	01110
	11000
	0110

Run length encoding

Run length encoding (RLE) works by reducing the physical size of a repeating string of characters. This repeating string, called a run, is encoded into two bytes. The first byte represents the number of characters in the run and the second gives the character.

For example, look at the following string:

aaabbbbbbcccccccccc

This string has a length of 18 bytes.

Using run length encoding, this could be compressed to:

3a6b9c

It could be reduced to 6 bytes.

Run length encoding provides very good compression ratios where there are long runs of a particular character or value. A black and white image, where there are long runs of either black or white, will encode very well. However, a colour photograph, where there are short runs of many different colours, will not encode as well.

We have already looked at this 1-bit graphic:

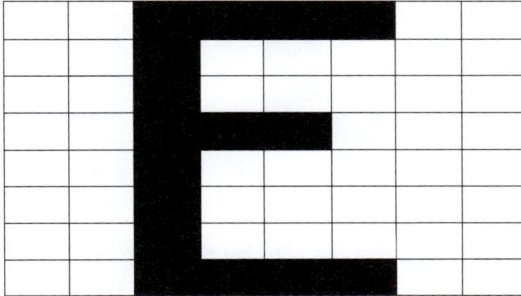

The code for this graphic is:

11000011
11011111
11011111
11000111
11011111
11011111
11011111
11000011

This code represents the colours:

wwbbbww
wwbwwww
wwbwwww
wwbbbww
wwbwwww
wwbwwww
wwbwwww
wwbbbww

When represented by a letter, the size of the file is 64 bytes: 8 bytes per line. Using run length encoding, this size could be reduced:

		Bytes
wwbbbww	2w4b2w	6
wwbwwww	2w1b5w	6
wwbwwww	2w1b5w	6
wwbbbww	2w3b3w	6
wwbwwww	2w1b5w	6
wwbwwww	2w1b5w	6
wwbwwww	2w1b5w	6
wwbbbww	2w4b2w	6
		48

Therefore the file size of this one character can be reduced from 64 bytes to 48 bytes.

Tip

Although lossy compression is not part of the specification and won't be examined, it is useful to know about.

The original (RAW) image

4.25 megabytes

740 kilobytes

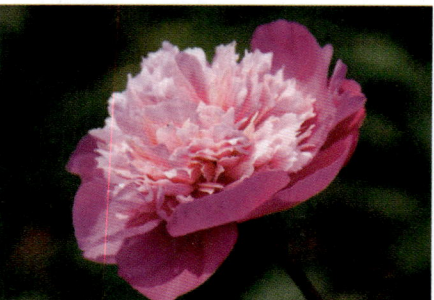

193 kilobytes

ACTIVITY 8.9

Show the result of applying a run length encoding algorithm to the following 1-bit graphic.

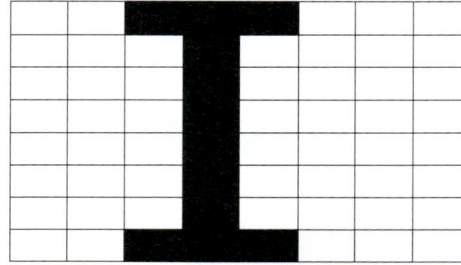

Lossy compression

Lossy compression decreases the file size by throwing out some of the data. Unlike lossless compression, the lossy original can never be reconstituted. It has been irreversibly changed.

That is why it cannot be used for text files or program files: a book with many missing words would be unreadable!

But lossy compression can be used for graphic and audio files as they contain much data that can be discarded.

The most commonly used compression technique for graphic files was developed by the Joint Photographic Experts Group and produces JPEG files with the extension jpg.

Here are three images all made from the same RAW image that had a size of 10.7 megabytes. All have the dimensions of 4288 x 2848. The number of pixels has not been reduced, but pixels with similar colour values have been made the same so that the number of bits needed has been reduced.

There are some differences in detail and colour variations, but even the image with the greatest compression would be acceptable for a web page.

Audio files can be compressed in a similar way. Digital audio files that contain all of the sound data are saved in Waveform Audio (WAV) format. Typically, a three minute recording will have a file size of 30 megabytes. There are frequencies and tones that we cannot hear and slight differences in volume and frequency that we cannot distinguish. These are removed to reduce the size and an MP3 file (a way of compressing audio files into very small files) is usually about a tenth the size of a WAV file. Therefore the 30-megabyte WAV file can be reduced to a 3-megabyte MP3 file.

Remember

1. Files are compressed to reduce transfer speeds and storage space.
2. With lossless compression, the data in the original file are not changed.
3. With lossy compression, original data are permanently deleted.

Complete Interactive Activity 8d on Cambridge Elevate

Download Worksheet 8.3 from Cambridge Elevate

Practice questions

1. Calculate the files sizes (in megabytes) of the following:

   a. A digital image of 2120 x 1320 pixels with a colour depth of 24 bits.

   b. A four-minute sound file with a sample rate of 44 100 and a bit depth of 16 bits.

2. For the following 1-bit graphic state, calculate:

   a. the result of applying a run-length encoding algorithm

   b. the original file size and the size after applying run ength encoding.

Your final challenge

Download Self-assessment 8 worksheet from Cambridge Elevate (this content has not been approved by AQA)

Your challenge is to create algorithms and code programs to compress and decompress files using run length encoding.

a. The first part of the challenge is to create and test a program that will perform run length encoding on a 2-colour file where the bits are given as one continuous string e.g.

   bbwwwbbbbbbbwwwwwwwwwwwwwwwbbbbbbbbbbbbbbwwbb bbbbbbbbbbbwwwwwwwww

   It should take the above string and print:

   2b3w7b14w14b2w13b9w.

b. Now create and test a program that will return the original string from the run length encoded data.

9 Computer systems: hardware

Why computer systems?

The processor is responsible for executing the instructions given to it in a program but the processor is only one part of a computer system.

- The processor relies on other devices:

    - to allow users to input the instructions

    - to store the instructions

    - to transfer the instructions to it so that it can carry them out

    - to carry out the commands it issues, for example to print an essay or display an image.

ENIAC, the first computer, was 8 feet (2.5 metres) high and 100 feet (30.5 metres) long and far less powerful than today's laptops.

Computer systems

The processor is often called the 'brain' of a computer because it is where data are processed, decisions are made and actions are initiated.

However, the brain cannot function independently. It needs things like:

*   sensors, such as eyes and ears, to provide it with data

*   storage, to store data and information

*   muscles, to carry out the actions it decides are necessary

*   bundles of nerves, to transmit messages to and from the muscles and sensors.

The input devices for a human central nervous system are shown in the diagram below.

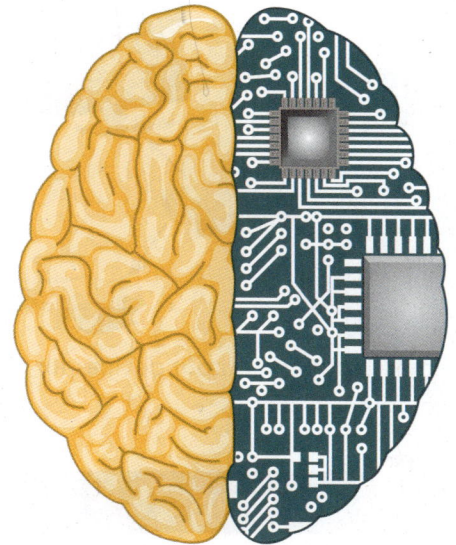

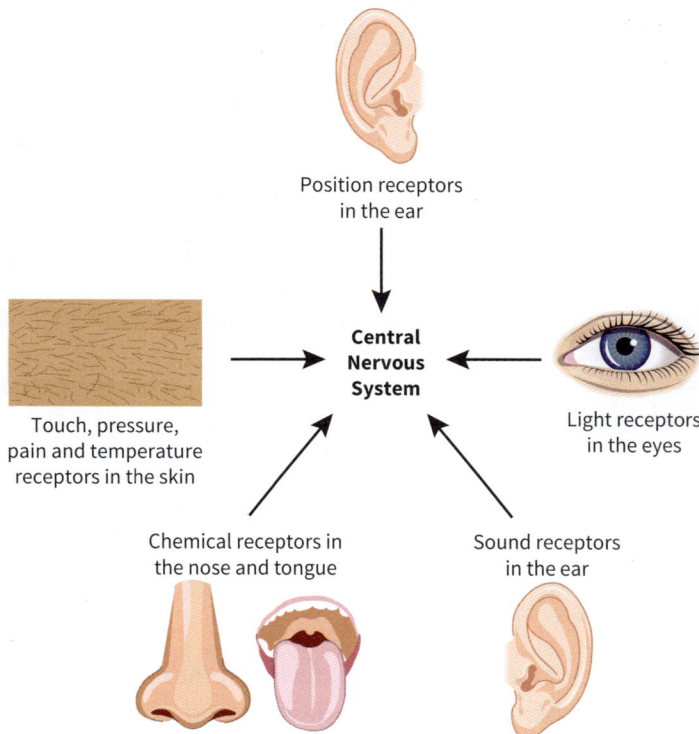

In a similar way, the processor needs other components:

*   input devices, such as a keyboard, a mouse and light sensors, to provide it with data

*   memory, to store the instructions and the results of its processing

*   permanent, long-term memory devices such as hard disk drives

*   output devices, such as monitors, printers and motors, to carry out the results of its processing

*   bundles of wires, called buses, through which data are transmitted from one component to another.

> ### Key term
>
> **bus**: a bundle of wires carrying data from one component to another or a number of tracks on a printed circuit board fulfilling the same function

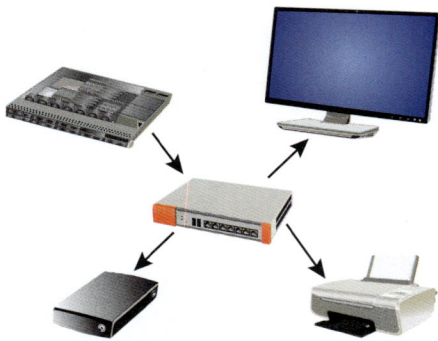

Some input and output devices for a computer system.

Key terms

hardware: the physical components making up the computer and its peripheral devices

system software: software that manages the operation of the computer, tells it what to do, tells it which programs to run, controls what the users see on screen etc.

application software: are end-user programs. Also called 'apps' or 'applications', they are written to be run by users to perform user-identified tasks. For example, for productivity or entertainment. They include word processor, spreadsheet, database, game and image editing software

printed circuit board: the base that supports the wiring and electronic components that are soldered to it or fit into sockets on the board

The components mentioned above are all physical devices and are referred to as **hardware**.

However, there is another vital component, called **software**, which consists of all the programs that a computer system needs in order to function. Software runs on hardware.

Even before a computer system can do anything useful, it needs software called **system software** to 'wake it up' and tell it how to operate. For example, the system software tells the processor how to communicate with some of the other devices (although note that with RAM, for example, communication is completely hardware based).

It can then use the **application software** such as word processors and spreadsheets to do something useful.

Embedded systems

An embedded system is a computer system built within a larger device, such as:

- Washing machines

- Alarm systems

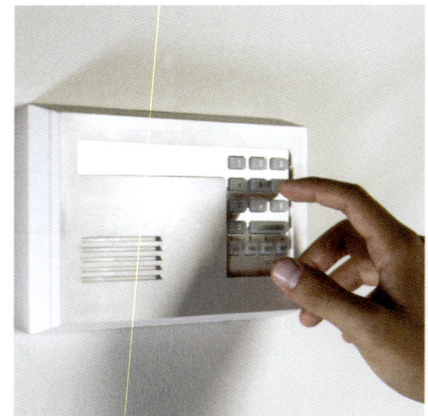

Computer systems are embedded in these devices. Embedded devices are limited to a certain number of tasks, unlike desktop and laptop computers which are general purpose computer systems capable of carrying out many different tasks. Examples of devices with embedded computer systems might be: washing machines, microwave ovens, home entertainment systems, alarm systems, heating controllers etc.

All of the components in an embedded system including processor, memory and input and output interfaces are on a single **printed circuit board** (PCB). The memory contains the program. The board is a component built into a larger device, hence the name 'embedded'.

In an embedded system, resources such as memory are limited and the hardware components are often unique to that system. The programs are often written in assembly language rather than a high level language so that the hardware components can be more easily controlled.

ACTIVITY 9.1

Many modern electronic devices contain embedded systems.

1. Explain what is meant by an 'embedded system'.

2. List three devices that contain embedded systems.

Remember

1. A computer is a machine that can be programmed.
2. All computers contain a processor.
3. A computer system consists of hardware and software.
4. An embedded system is one which is built into a larger device and carries out a limited number of functions.

Systems architecture

The processor is the central processing unit (CPU) of the computer. It is here that the data processing takes place.

The way the CPU is designed and executes (carries out) the program instructions is known as 'von Neumann architecture'. In 1945, John von Neumann proposed his design for a 'stored program' computer where both the program and data were stored in the same memory. His design included a processing unit, a program counter, memory to store data and instructions and external storage and input and output mechanisms.

This diagram shows the components of the central processing unit and how they communicate with each other and with the other computer system components. Take a look at the components; their functions will be described when we look at the way in which program instructions are executed.

Key term

central processing unit: this is the component of the computer that controls the other devices, executes the instructions and processes the data

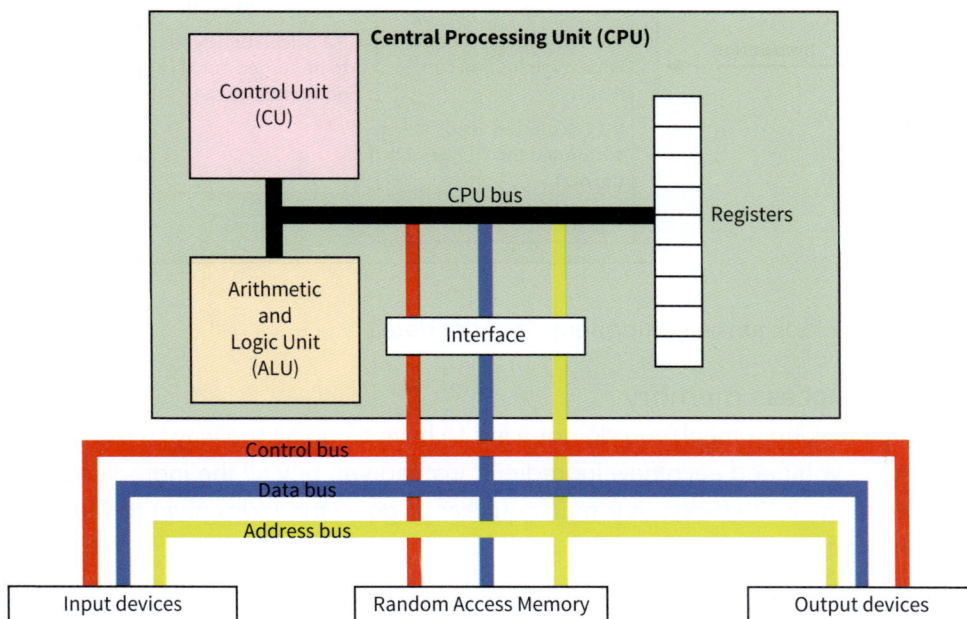

Executing the instructions: the fetch-execute cycle

The way in which the 'von Neumann architecture' executes the program instructions is through the fetch-execute cycle.

The fetch-execute cycle is running from the moment that the computer is switched on.

Watch the fetch-decode-execute cycle animation on Cambridge Elevate

Fetch

In the fetch part of the cycle, the instruction and data are moved from the random access memory to the CPU.

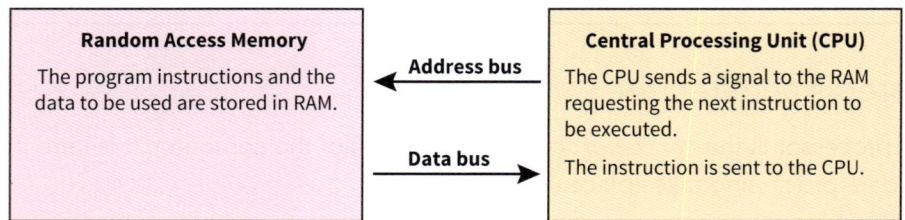

Random Access Memory		Central Processing Unit (CPU)
The program instructions and the data to be used are stored in RAM.	← Address bus	The CPU sends a signal to the RAM requesting the next instruction to be executed.
	Data bus →	The instruction is sent to the CPU.

Decode and execute

In the decode part of the cycle, the control unit interprets the instruction and decides which action to perform. During the execute phase, the instruction is carried out.

This may involve performing calculations such as additions and calculations performed by the ALU or fetching data from memory or writing data to it.

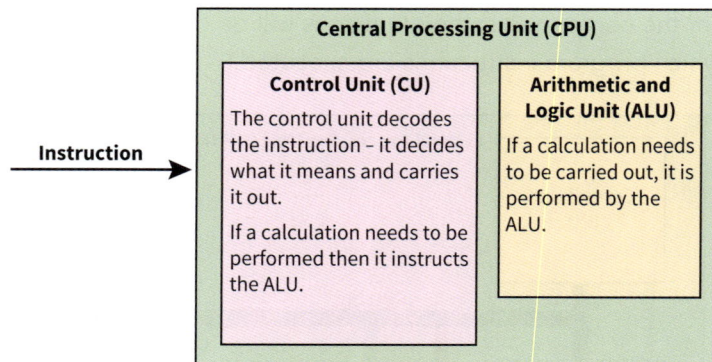

Central Processing Unit (CPU)

Instruction →

Control Unit (CU)	Arithmetic and Logic Unit (ALU)
The control unit decodes the instruction – it decides what it means and carries it out. If a calculation needs to be performed then it instructs the ALU.	If a calculation needs to be carried out, it is performed by the ALU.

We will now look at the components in more detail.

Random access memory

If you are making a meal, you do not want to have to go all the way to the shop every time you need each new ingredient. Instead you buy all the ingredients and put them in the fridge; it is much quicker to go to the fridge than to the supermarket!

It is the same for computers. It can take a long time to fetch data and program instructions from the hard drive. Therefore they are stored in the RAM, a

temporary store of data, so that information can be retrieved quickly by the CPU when required for the program it is running.

Memory can be thought of as consisting of billions of pigeonholes or storage locations. Each storage location can hold a byte of data and each one has an address so that the CPU knows where to store and retrieve the instructions and data.

RAM is said to be 'random access' because each memory location can be accessed in any order if the 'address' of that location is specified. This speeds up data retrieval as the CPU can go to any location and does not have to start each time at the first location and go through them in order until it finds the correct one. That method is called 'serial access'.

RAM is said to be volatile because if there is no electrical power, then the RAM will lose all of its data.

There are different types of RAM: dynamic RAM (DRAM) and static RAM (SRAM). DRAM is slower than SRAM, but it is used as the main memory store because it is cheaper.

	Location 0
	Location 1
	Location 2
	Location 3
	Location 4
	Location 5

ACTIVITY 9.2

Carry out research to find out why DRAM is slower than SRAM.

Read only memory (ROM)

Read only memory (ROM) is also used in computer systems. ROM is an integrated circuit on a chip. It is programmed with specific instructions to perform a particular function when it is manufactured.

The BIOS (Basic input/output system) is stored in ROM. The BIOS controls what happens when the computer is first switched on. The BIOS checks the hardware devices to ensure there are no errors and loads basic software so that it can communicate with the devices. It then locates and passes control to the operating system.

The data can be read but they cannot be changed: the computer cannot write to the chip, unlike RAM.

While RAM is volatile, ROM is not and the data are not lost when power is removed.

ACTIVITY 9.3

1. Describe the functions of RAM and ROM in the operation of a computer.

2. List two basic differences between RAM and ROM.

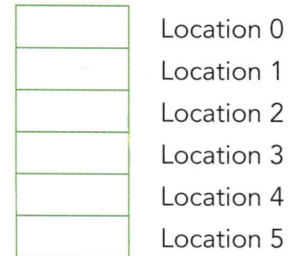

Complete Interactive Activity 9a on Cambridge Elevate

Key terms

storage location: a place in RAM where a single piece of data can be kept until it is needed

address: a number assigned to the storage location so that it can be accessed

volatile: data are permanently lost when power is switched off

main memory: the physical memory that is internal to the computer. The word 'main' is used to distinguish it from storage devices such as hard disk drives. It can be directly accessed by the CPU

Remember

1. RAM acts as a temporary store of program instructions and data.

2. RAM consists of billions of memory locations with unique addresses.

3. The addresses can be accessed in any order.

4. RAM is volatile and can be written to.

5. DRAM is slower than SRAM, but is far cheaper.

6. ROM is used to store basic information and instructions that a computer needs when it is starting up (booting).

7. ROM is non-volatile but cannot be written to.

Buses

A bus is a collection of wires that carry signals or communications between the various components of the computer system. The control unit uses the control bus to send instructions to other components of the computer. The components use a bus to send information back to the CPU as well. The data bus is used for the transfer of data between the CPU and the RAM and the address bus for the CPU to access memory locations in the main memory.

The components of the CPU

Registers

Registers are storage locations within the CPU itself. They can be accessed even more quickly than the RAM described previously.

Some of these registers serve specific functions, but some of them are general purpose registers used for the quick storage of data items.

The arithmetic and logic unit

The arithmetic and logic unit (ALU) performs arithmetic and logical operations. It carries out activities such as:

- addition and subtraction

- multiplication and division

- logical tests using logic gates explained in Chapter 11

- comparisons such as whether one number is greater than another.

The control unit

The control unit coordinates the actions of the computer by sending out control signals to the other parts of the CPU, such as the ALU and registers, and also to the other components of the computer system, such as the input and output devices. Control signals make everything happen inside a CPU.

An important element of the control unit is the decoder. This part of the control unit decodes (works out what they mean) the program instructions that have been brought from the memory and decides what actions should be taken. It then sends control signals to the other components to carry these actions out.

The clock

The clock regulates the timing and speed of all computer functions. Within the clock is a quartz crystal which vibrates at a particular frequency when electricity is applied to it.

Pulses are sent out to the other components to coordinate their activities and ensure instructions are carried out and completed.

One instruction can be carried out with each pulse of the clock, and therefore the higher the clock rate, the faster the CPU will be able to carry out the program instructions.

> **Key terms**
>
> register: a storage location that is inside the CPU itself
>
> control signals: electrical signals that are sent out to all of the devices to check their status and give them instructions

The clock speed is measured in cycles per second. One cycle per second is a rate of 1 hertz.

One megahertz (MHz) equals 1 million cycles per second and one gigahertz (GHz) is 1 000 000 000 cycles per second. Rates of 1 to 3 GHz are common in most home computers.

Buses

In addition to the buses that connect the CPU to other components, internal buses within the CPU are also used to transfer data within it.

Download Worksheet 9.2 from Cambridge Elevate

Complete Interactive Activity 9b on Cambridge Elevate

ACTIVITY 9.4

Name the parts of the CPU that perform the following functions:

1. carry out arithmetic and logical computations

2. store data within the CPU itself

3. coordinate the activities of the CPU and computer.

ACTIVITY 9.5

With the aid of diagrams, describe the events that take place during the fetch-execute cycle.

Processor performance

Everyone wants their computers to work faster and faster and so manufacturers have continued to increase the speeds at which computers work.

Clock speed

The rate at which instructions are processed is controlled by the clock speed. The faster the clock speed, the faster the rate of processing. Or, to put it another way, a new instruction will start processing on a clock tick: the more clock ticks there are, the faster the instruction will be processed. Clock speeds have increased and a rate of 3 GHz is common in modern computer processors. However, increasing the clock speed to increase processing speed has limitations:

- The instructions are processed by transistors and the rate at which they operate is limited.

Remember

1. The CPU consists of the
   a. control unit (CU)
   b. arithmetic and logic unit (ALU)
   c. registers
   d. clock
   e. buses

2. The control unit controls the activities of the CPU by sending out control signals.

3. The ALU carries out arithmetic and logical operations.

4. The registers are memory stores within the CPU.

5. The CPU processes data by carrying out three steps:
   a. Fetch: an instruction is transferred from the memory to the CPU.
   b. Decode: the CPU works out what the instructions mean.
   c. Execute: the control unit carries out the instructions using the ALU for instructions involving logical or mathematical operations.

- The processor generates a large amount of heat and this increases as the clock speed increases. Although the heat is dissipated by a fan and heat sink to prevent it from malfunctioning or even melting, there are limits to the rate of cooling.

- Processors with clock speeds of 9 GHz require cooling by liquid nitrogen.

ACTIVITY 9.6

In order to increase the speed of their computers, users often increase the clock frequency.

1. What is this process called?

2. A user who increased the clock frequency noticed that his computer was now noisier. Explain why this could be caused by increasing the clock frequency.

Multicore processors

Manufacturers introduced multicore processors in 2006 to increase processing speed. A multicore processor has more than one processor core (but only one CPU). The following diagram illustrates the structure of a dual-core processor.

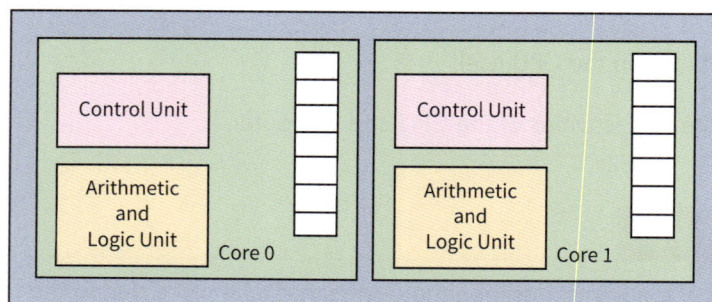

The following table shows the names given to processors having different numbers of cores.

Number of cores	Common name
1	Single-core
2	Dual-core
4	Quad-core
5	Penta-core
8	Octa(o)-core
10	Deca-core

The advantages of multiple core processors over single core processors are:

- the cores can work together on the same program; this is called parallel processing.

- the cores can work on different programs at the same time; this is called multitasking.

However, not all programs will run at twice the speed with a dual-core processor. The tasks required might not be able to be carried out in parallel. They might be sequential so that one task requires output from a previous task and so the second task cannot start until the first has finished.

Cache memory

Bottlenecks occur when one component cannot work as fast as other components and so hinders progress.

In the fetch-execute cycle this bottleneck is caused by the main memory that is used to store the instructions and data.

Although it is far quicker to fetch the instructions from the main memory than from a hard disk drive, the RAM is still far slower than the CPU and then the instructions have to be transferred through the data bus.

The speed of processing will be limited by the RAM which supplies the instructions regardless of how much clock speed is increased or how many cores are used.

The solution to this bottleneck problem is to use faster memory very close to, or even within, the CPU. This memory is used to store recently used data and data likely to be frequently used and is called a cache.

Most CPUs have independent instruction and data caches. The data caches have to be read and written to but the instruction caches just have to be read by the CPU.

The use of caches allows the CPU to check the fast cache for the data it needs. It does not have to wait for it to be fetched from the much slower main memory. The faster SRAM is used for the cache.

The caches are located on the processor chip. The fastest is the Level 1 cache and is smaller than the Level 2 and Level 3 caches.

The L1 cache is checked first followed by the L2 and then L3 caches. In a multi-core processor the cores have their own L1 and L2 caches while the Last Level Cache is usually shared by all the cores. With a larger cache there is a greater probability that the instruction or data item needed to be fetched is in the cache and so the RAM will not need to be accessed. This will speed up processing.

The sizes and positions of the caches are shown in the following diagram.

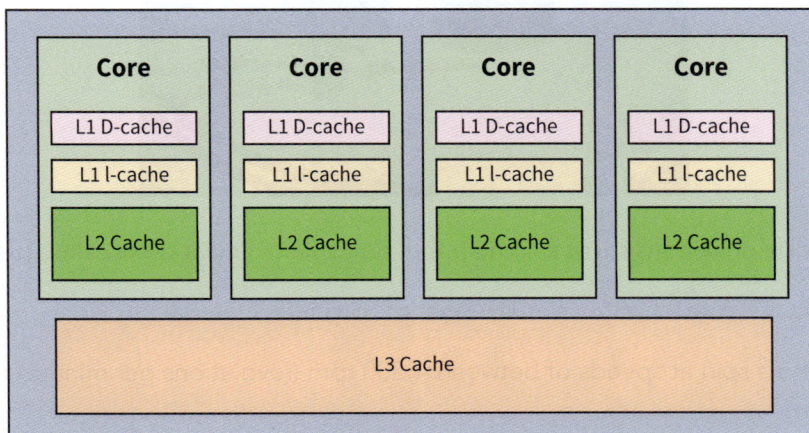

> **Watch the Von Neumann bottleneck animation on Cambridge Elevate**

> **Key term**
>
> cache: a temporary data store so that the data can be accessed very quickly when needed

> **Download Worksheet 9.3 from Cambridge Elevate**

A computer is advertised as being 'quad-core'.

1. Explain what is meant by 'quad-core' and how it improves the performance of the computer.

2. Explain how using cache memory also improves the performance.

Remember

1. The clock speed cannot be increased indefinitely because of the extra heat generated.
2. A processor with several cores is said to be multicore.
3. The processing speed of the CPU is limited by the speed that data can be supplied by the slower RAM.
4. Cache memory stores regularly used items of data so that they can be accessed more quickly.

Complete Interactive Activity 9c on Cambridge Elevate

Key terms

secondary storage devices: devices that store information but which do not lose the data when they are switched off; usually not on the main circuit board (motherboard)

magnetic storage: storing data using magnetic media such as a hard disk drive

optical storage: storing data using optical devices such as CD's and DVD

electrical storage: storing data using devices such as flash memory. This is sometimes called '**solid state**'

Secondary storage devices

Because RAM is volatile, data must be stored on other devices called secondary storage devices so they are not lost when the computer is switched off.

Data on secondary storage devices cannot be accessed directly by the CPU.

Storage devices store data in three different ways – magnetically, optically and electrically (solid state).

Magnetic storage

Magnetic storage devices include *hard disk drives* and magnetic tape.

A hard disk drive consists of a spindle that holds flat, circular disks called platters.

The disks are coated with a shallow layer of magnetic material.

The platters spin at speeds of between 4,200 rpm (revolutions per minute) to 15,000 rpm.

Information is written to and read from a disk as it rotates past a read-write head that is positioned very close to the disk's surface. Each platter usually has its own read-write head. The read-write heads detect and modify the magnetisation of the disk's surface.

Data is stored digitally in the form of tiny magnetized regions on the platter where each region represents a bit. To write a data on the hard disk, a magnetic field is placed on the tiny field in one of these two polarities: either north to south or south to north. An orientation in the one direction can represent the '1' while the opposite orientation represents "0".

This polarity is sensed when the data is being read.

The data is stored on concentric circles on the surfaces known as tracks. Sections within each track are called sectors which can hold 512 bytes of data.

When a data file is stored on a disk it may be split up and saved on different sectors and tracks. The operating system creates an entry in the disk's File Allocation Table (FAT) for the new file that records where each part is located and their sequential order.

Hard disk drives are suitable for the storage and backup of large amounts of data which do not have to be transported.

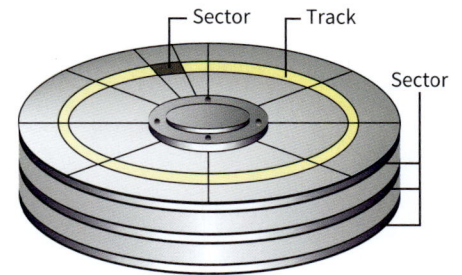

Advantages	Disadvantages
Fast access speeds (but not as fast as solid state storage)	Not very portable.
Random access: data can be read instantly from any part of the disk	Susceptible to physical knocks that might cause the read-write heads to hit the disks and corrupt data
Store large amounts of data: hard disk drives that store terabytes of data are common in most home computers	Fragmentation of files on the disk can seriously slow down access speeds
Low cost	

Optical storage

Optical storage uses light from lasers to read and write data on discs.

Here are some examples:

- Compact discs (CDs) typically store 700MB.

- Digital versatile discs (DVDs) typically store 4.7GB.

- The latest formats of Blu-ray discs can store up to 128GB.

An optical disc has a single spiral track running from the inside to the outside.

The spiral track is over 5 km long.

When CDs are produced digital data is stored along the track by etching pits onto the surface of the disc. The disc between the pits is called a land. When the light from a laser hits the lands it is reflected back to a detector but is scattered away by the pits and no light is detected. These two events represent the digits '0' and '1'.

163

In a recordable CD or CD-R the disc surface is covered in a dye which is translucent and so light passes through it and is reflected by the disc surface. When data is being written to the disc a powerful laser light burns the dye creating black spots that do not reflect. That is why writing data to the disc is called 'burning the disc'. The reflective areas are interpreted as 1s and the black spots as 0s.

A rewritable CD or CD-RW has a layer of a metallic alloy that can exist in two forms – one reflects light and the other doesn't. When data is written, the forms can be changed between reflective and non-reflective. As there is no permanent change, data can be written to the disc many times.

Optical discs are useful for distributing programs, files and images and backing up data which can then be stored at another site.

Advantages	Disadvantages
Cheap	Do not store as much as hard disk drives
Easy to transport from one site to another	Slow access speeds
	Stored data degrade over time
	Disks are fragile and easy to break.

Solid state storage

Data can be stored electrically using flash memory.

Flash memory consists of transistors that keep their charge even when the power is switched off - floating gate transistors. (Normal transistors lose their state when the power is turned off). At first, all transistors are charged (set to 1). But when a save operation begins, current is blocked to some transistors, switching them to 0.

Flash memory was developed from a type of ROM called 'electrically erasable programmable read only memory' (EEPROM) and was introduced in 1984.

EEPROMs had to be completely erased before they could be written to, but flash memory can be written to and read in small blocks.

- Flash memory is used in:

    - SD (Secure Digital) cards (2 to 512GB)

    - Micro SD cards (2 to 512 GB)

    - SDXC (Extended Capacity) cards (2TB)

    - USB flash drives (256GB but can be up to 1TB).

Flash memory is used for data storage in cameras, mobile phones and embedded devices and increasingly as the main secondary storage device in computers, especially in laptops, as solid state drives (SSDs).

The MacBook Air uses a flash memory solid state drive (SSD) for its main secondary storage.

Key term

flash memory: this is memory which can be programmed electrically but then keeps its data when the power is turned off

Flash memory devices are ideal for transporting data as they are light and being solid state have no moving parts which could be damaged.

Advantages	Disadvantages
Very fast access speed; far faster than discs	More expensive than a hard disk drive or DVD
Small, light and easily portable	The storage capacity is less than a hard disk drive
Quiet	There is a limited number of erase/write cycles, up to 100,000 for high quality SSD's and so it cannot be used indefinitely
Flash memory is said to be 'solid state' as it has no moving parts which could be damaged if the device was knocked or dropped and therefore there is less chance of losing data	

Secondary storage media compared

	Hard disk drive	Optical drive	Solid state
Capacity	Very large. 1–2 TB common in home computers	Low. CDs typically store 700 MB. DVDs typically store 4.7 GB. Blu-ray discs can store up to 128 GB	Solid state drives are usually from 128 to 512 GB
Speed	Fast	Slow	Very fast
Portability	Portable but there is the risk damage from physical knocks which may cause the read-write heads to hit the discs and corrupt data	More portable than a hard disk drive but disks are relatively large	Very portable. Small solid state storage devices can be fitted inside cameras and mobile phones
Durability	Very durable	Easily scratched and data can be damaged.	Lower than a hard disk drive. Limited number of erase/write cycles
Reliability	Very reliable	Very reliable if not scratched	Very reliable and data are not affected by magnetic fields as they are in hard disk drives
Cost	Very low	Very low	More expensive than hard disk drives and optical devices

Download Worksheet 9.4 from Cambridge Elevate

Cloud storage

Cloud storage is off-site storage made available to users over a network, usually the internet. Users store and back up their data on storage devices, usually hard disk drives, somewhere that they can access over the internet. Where in the world that 'somewhere' is, they do not know.

There are vast data centres around the world that store all the data that users upload, such as their photographs and images.

Cloud storage uses magnetic and increasingly solid state storage.

The following table shows how cloud storage compares to local storage.

Advantages	Disadvantages
Data will be secure if there is a fire or other problem as the data are being stored at another site.	Needs an internet connection. Download and upload speeds can be affected by the internet connection.
The data can be accessed from anywhere in the world with an internet connection.	The hosting company could be targeted by online hackers.
No need to buy an expensive storage device.	You have less control if the data are held by another company.
Many users can access the data and collaborate with each other from anywhere in the world.	Storing some data online may breach the Data Protection Act as it should be kept secure and confidential.

Complete Interactive Activity 9d on Cambridge Elevate

ACTIVITY 9.8

Suggest, with explanations, suitable storage solutions for the following people:

1. A gap-year student is travelling around the world. She would like to be able to back up the photographs from her camera so that friends at home will be able to see them.

2. The owner of a mail-order company has constantly changing orders and customer information is being processed throughout the day. What would be the best backup medium for this company?

3. A school student needs a method to back up his school work and transfer documents between school and home.

4. The owner of a small business with only one computer and no internet access would like to back up the business data once a week.

Remember

1. Magnetic media: electro magnets in read-write heads read and write data on discs coated with magnetic materials.
2. Optical media: light from lasers read and write data on specially prepared discs.
3. Electrical or solid state storage: data is stored electrically using flash memory.
4. Cloud storage: off-site storage accessed over the internet.

Practice question

1. Catherine has bought a new laptop computer that was advertised as having a 1.6GHz dual-core CPU and 512KB Level 1 cache.
   a. State the purpose of the CPU.
   b. Describe what is meant by:
      i. 1.6GHz CPU
      ii. dual-core CPU
      iii. Level 1 cache.

Your final challenge

Your challenge is to design and code a multiple-choice quiz, based on the contents of this chapter.

The design brief
- There should be at least five questions.
- Each question should have four possible answers, only one of which is correct.
- After taking the quiz the user should be:
  - informed of their score
  - given the correct answers for the questions that they got wrong.
- You should create and then test your quiz.

Extension
Ask the users to enter their names and then save the users' names and their scores in a text file.

Download Self-assessment 9 worksheet from Cambridge Elevate (this content has not been approved by AQA)

10 Computer system: system software

Learning outcomes

By the end of this chapter you should be able to:

- explain what is meant by system software
- explain what is meant by an operating system
- describe the functions of the operating system
- explain what is meant by utility programs
- list some examples of utility software and their functions.

Challenge: to create a program to clean up a hard disk drive

- Over time, the hard disk drive in a computer becomes very messy with parts of files spread around in different locations. This is called 'fragmentation' and leads to a loss of performance as it takes far longer to load and save the files.
- Your challenge is to write a program to put the files back together again in a simulation of defragmentation.

System software manages all the actions of the computer and helps users to organise their programs and data and tell the computer what they want it to do.

Why system software?

- Computer hardware needs to be told what to do. This is the role of the system software.
- The CPU cannot communicate with peripherals without the help of system software.
- If a word processing or spreadsheet program needs something to be displayed on screen or on paper, the system software communicates with the monitor and the printer.
- If several programs are running at the same time, the system software keeps them all running smoothly.
- Utility software helps with maintenance jobs such as defragmenting the hard disk drive, compressing files and improving security.

Software classification

A computer system consists of hardware and software, which includes system software and applications.

The system software includes the BIOS and also the *operating system* and *utility programs*. The BIOS tests the system hardware and loads the operating system. It is specially written for each motherboard and performs any other operations that are needed by that particular motherboard.

See the role of ROM in Chapter 9.

Operating system

An operating system is a set of programs that controls how the user interacts with the hardware and software of a computer system. It has programs that:

- manage all of the hardware devices and software

- control all of the processes running on the computer

- ensure that all hardware and software interact correctly

- ensure the smooth execution of applications by allocating the resources required for them to operate.

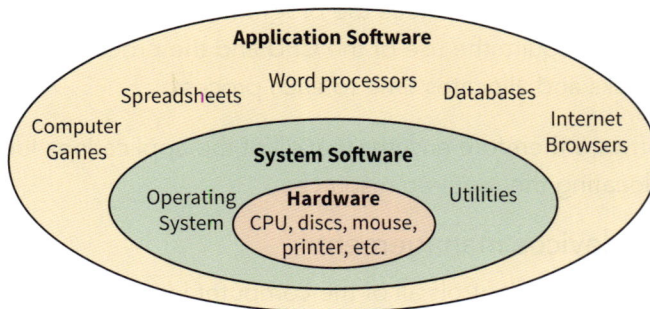

There are many different operating systems in use today including:

- Windows

- OS X

- Linux

- Ubuntu

- Unix

- Android

- iOS.

They all have five basic managers:

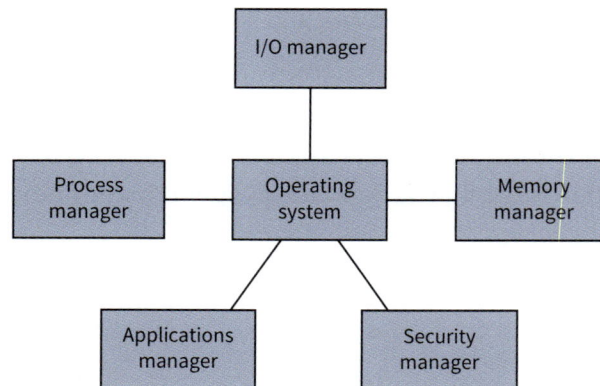

Memory management

The memory manager is in charge of the RAM. Programs often need to use the RAM throughout their operation. Some programs will be large and complex and will use the RAM extensively whereas some very small programs will not need to use it much. The memory manager checks that all requests from programs for memory space are valid and allocates accordingly.

Processor management

In a computer system, many programs will be running at the same time (this is called multitasking) and the activities the programs are performing are called processes. They all require the use of the CPU and the processor manager prioritises the tasks and allocates time to each process.

The system software therefore ensures that all of the applications function correctly by allocating the required resources.

Input/output devices management

The peripheral manager controls all of the computer input and output by managing requests from programs to use devices such as printers, speakers, keyboards and hard disk drives.

The peripheral manager communicates with the devices through software called drivers that translate the instructions sent by the device manager into ones that the devices can understand.

Applications management

As mentioned above, the operating system provides an interface between applications programs and the computer hardware by providing services such as the application program interfaces.

The software makes its requests to the operating system through application program interfaces (APIs), which are standard software routines that developers can build into their software for this purpose.

The operating system loads the application code, assigns memory space and allocates processor time to the application.

Security management

The operating system controls access to the computer by allowing the user to set up login names and passwords.

It also allows file access control: the ability to stipulate which users can access which files and whether they can just read them or can edit or delete them. This is discussed in the section on file management.

Protection against viruses and other malware is discussed in the section on utility programs.

The operating system is also responsible for the following:

User interfaces

Users interact with the operating system through a user interface provided by the operating system. The user interface is a system which converts what the user inputs to a form that the computer can understand and vice versa.

Utility programs

Utility programs perform specific tasks related to computer functions, resources, files and security. They help to configure the system, analyse how it is working and optimise it to improve its efficiency. Some examples are security programs and system optimisation programs.

Security programs can include:

- anti-virus software scans for and removes malicious files

- encryption software uses an algorithm to encrypt (scramble) a file according to the key which is used; the key is needed to decrypt the file back to its original form

- a firewall prevents unwanted access to a computer over a network, for example a local network or the internet

- spyware detectors block and remove programs designed to collect personal information and transmit it to another user.

System optimisation programs can include:

- system clean-up tools to search for and remove files that are no longer needed

- disk defragmentation tools used to rearrange the parts of files on the disk drive. When a file is saved to disk, parts of the file might be saved in different areas of the disk; these tools try to move all the parts to the same area for quicker access

- file compression software to make files smaller so that they take up less storage space and can be transmitted to other users more easily.

Key term

user interface: the way in which a user interacts with a computer system

Complete Interactive Activity 10a on Cambridge Elevate

Download Worksheet 10.1 from Cambridge Elevate

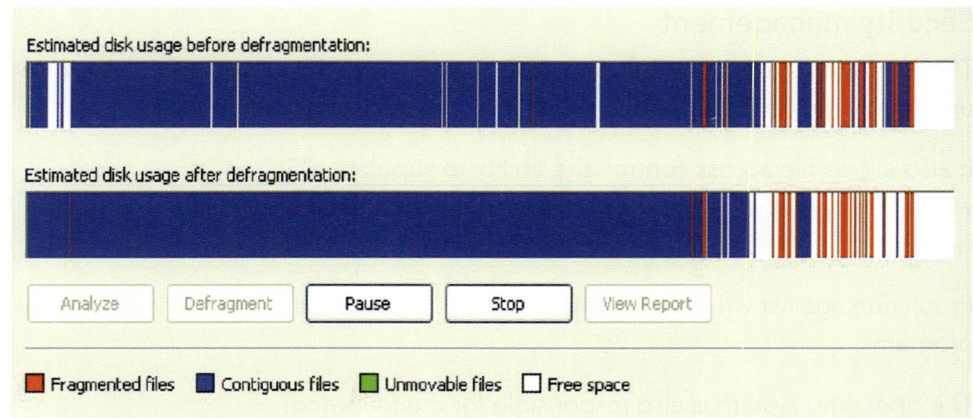

Estimated disk usage before defragmentation:

Estimated disk usage after defragmentation:

Analyze | Defragment | Pause | Stop | View Report

■ Fragmented files ■ Contiguous files ■ Unmovable files □ Free space

This image shows the fragmented files on the hard disk drive and how they will be arranged after defragmentation.

Complete Interactive Activity 10b on Cambridge Elevate

Download Worksheet 10.2 from Cambridge Elevate

Remember

1. The operating system:
   a. is a collection of software and forms part of the system software
   b. manages:
      - processor(s)
      - memory
      - I/O devices
      - applications
      - security.
2. Utility programs:
   a. perform specific functions to maintain and optimise the computer operations and ensure the security of the system
   b. include:
      - system clean-up and update tools
      - disk defragmentation tools
      - anti-virus programs
      - file compression tools.

Practice question

1. One of the functions of an operating system is multitasking.
   a. Explain one reason why multitasking is needed in an operating system.
   b. State two other functions of an operating system.

Your final challenge

- As files are saved, edited, enlarged and resaved they can become fragmented so that different parts of the file are located at different positions on the hard disk drive. This fragmentation means that it takes longer to open and save the files.

- In the following example, there are three (A, B and C) files spread across the drive. After defragmentation, they are all placed in order on the drive.

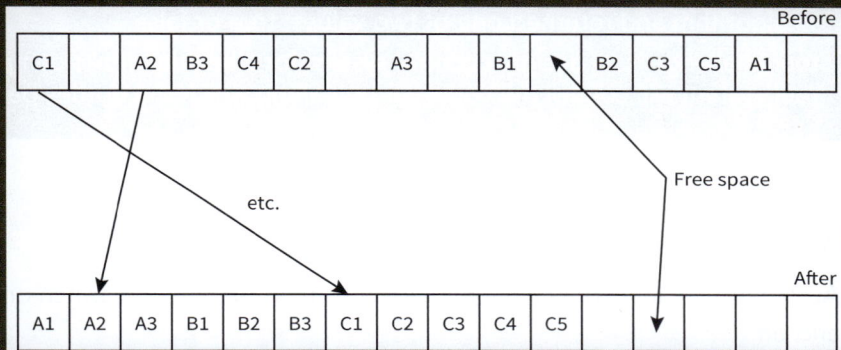

- Your challenge is to create an algorithm, and to code and test a program, that will rearrange the file segments as shown.

Tip

Using a two-dimensional array will help with the solution.

Download Self-assessment 10 worksheet from Cambridge Elevate (this content has not been approved by AQA)

11 Boolean logic

Challenge: design logic circuits to solve a control problem

- In Chapter 1, we looked at Boolean operators using the keywords AND, OR and NOT. We saw how these could be combined to create logic in an algorithm and returned one of two values: true or false.
- Your challenge is to design a control system for a healthy drinks company. Your system will control the conveyor belt along which the bottles pass.

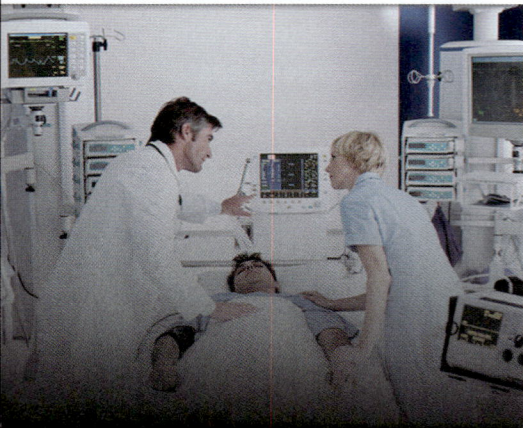

Why Boolean logic?

- Automatic security lights rely on logic gates to know when to switch on and off.
- Sensors used with logic gates can trigger actions, for example windows shut automatically when it rains.
- Boolean logic is used to evaluate whether a condition is true or false.

Boolean logic

Boolean logic is very important to computer science because of the way in which computers work.

Computers operate as digital devices using transistors that are either on or off. The transistors either transmit an electric current (on) or they do not (off). These two states of on or off can be used to represent the two conditions of true (on) or false (off). The two states are also represented by the digits 1 and 0.

Compound statements

Transistors can be combined into logic circuits in order to solve problems using Boolean logic. When multiple Boolean operators are used in a statement (a compound statement), it can be tricky to work out if the condition for the statement as a whole is true or false.

Logic gates can make a difference between life and death as they help to monitor patients and trigger YES/NO alarms if there is a problem.

For example, if we wanted to select red or blue, medium-sized T-shirts from a shop no more than 10 miles away we could write the statement as:

Code ————————————————————————————

```
IF (colour = "red" OR colour = "blue") AND size = "M" AND
distance <= 10 THEN…
```

This is a compound statement. In this instance, if all of the above specifications are met, then the condition is true and if they are not, then the condition is false. But if we wanted any colour except pink, the statement would read:

Code ————————————————————————————

```
IF (NOT colour = "pink") AND size = "M" AND distance <= 10
THEN…
```

This makes it more difficult to work out at a glance whether the statement is true or false.

Truth tables can help as they show all the possible results of each sub-statement (true or false) and the combined results for the whole statement.

Truth tables

The way in which Boolean operators reach their decision about whether statements are true or false can be shown using truth tables.

WORKED EXAMPLE

Look at the following 'IF' statement:

```
IF X = 3 AND Y = 6 THEN

    OUTPUT "They are correct."

ENDIF
```

In order for the message to be printed, X **must** equal 3 and Y **must** equal 6.

For the compound statement to be true **both** sub-statements **must** be true.

This can be shown in a truth table.

Inputs		Outputs
X = 3	Y = 6	X = 3 AND Y = 6
F	F	F
F	T	F
T	F	F
T	T	T

Now let's use a truth table for a real-life example.

Boolean logic is used in burglar alarm systems.

Tip

There are four possible combinations for the two values. Using the AND operator, both must be true for the compound statement to be true.

We only want the alarm to sound if:

We have turned the alarm on **AND** the door is open.

The truth table will look like this:

Inputs		Outputs
Turned on	Door open	Alarm sounds
F	F	F
F	T	F
T	F	F
T	T	T

So the 'alarm sounds' is true only if both of the other statements are true.

WORKED EXAMPLE

Now look at the following compound 'IF' statement where the two simple 'IF' statements are joined by the 'OR' operator:

```
IF X = 3 OR Y = 6 THEN

    OUTPUT "That is OK."

ENDIF
```

In this case, if only one of them is true, the statement will be true and the message will be printed.

The truth table will look like this:

Inputs		Outputs
X = 3	Y = 6	X = 3 OR Y = 6
F	F	F
F	T	T
T	F	T
T	T	T

WORKED EXAMPLE

In the following 'IF' statement, the 'NOT' operator has been used.

```
IF NOT (X = 3 AND Y = 6) THEN

    OUTPUT "Conditions are met."

ENDIF
```

The 'NOT' negates or reverses the statement in brackets. So the statement will be printed whenever X does not equal 3 AND Y does not equal 6, that is whenever they are not both true at the same time.

Tip

Remember from Chapter 1 that = means 'equals to'.

Tip

There are four possible combinations for the two values. Using the 'OR' operator, at least one must be true for the compound statement to be true.

Tip

Using the 'NOT' with the 'AND' operator reverses the logic of the 'AND' statement.

If the 'AND' statement is false then the 'NOT AND' statement will be true and vice versa.

The truth table will look like this:

Inputs		Outputs
X = 3	Y = 6	NOT (X = 3 AND Y = 6)
F	F	T
F	T	T
T	F	T
T	T	F

Using the 'NOT' with the 'AND' operator reverses the logic of the 'AND' statement.

If the 'AND' statement is false, then the 'NOT AND' statement will be true and vice versa.

ACTIVITY 11.1

Create the truth table for the following 'IF' statement.

```
IF NOT (X = 3 OR Y = 6) THEN

    OUTPUT "Conditions are met."

ENDIF
```

Complete Interactive Activity 11a on Cambridge Elevate

Logic gates

We can use our brains to work out the results of logical operations and use truth tables for assistance. The microprocessors in computers, however, are physical, digital devices without brains and they use transistors operating as electrical switches to calculate whether complex conditions are true or false.

These transistors can be wired together to form logic gates.

Key term

logic gate: an electronic component that either produces or does not produce an output depending on the inputs it receives and the logic rule it is designed to apply

Each logic gate has one or more *inputs* and an *output*. An electric current that is output represents the binary digit 1 (or true) and a low or no current at all represents 0 (or false).

Watch the logic gates animation on Cambridge Elevate

Logic gates are switches that perform a logical function on one or more logical inputs and produce an output if the conditions are true or false.

'AND' gate

The 'AND' gate has two inputs, A and B and one output, Q. It has the same results as the truth table for the 'AND' operator presented previously. Here is the truth table for the 'AND' gate:

Inputs		Outputs
A	B	Q
0	0	0
0	1	0
1	0	0
1	1	1

An 'AND' gate would be used in alarm systems to ensure that the alarm would sound only if the alarm was switched on AND the door was open.

'OR' gate

The 'OR' gate has two inputs, A and B and one output, Q. Here is the truth table for the 'OR' gate:

Inputs		Outputs
A	B	Q
0	0	0
0	1	1
1	0	1
1	1	1

In order for the gate to produce an output, there must be a current at either or both inputs.

'OR' gates would be used in a fire alarm system so that the alarm could be triggered from any call point, for example from the one in the hall OR the one in the kitchen OR the one in the living room.

'NOT' gate

> **Tip**
>
> In the truth table, we are using the digits 1 and 0. The digit 1 indicates that there is an electric current and 0 that there is no current. So 1 is used to represent 'on' and 0 to represent 'off'.

This 'NOT' gate has one input A, and one output, Q. Here is the truth table for the 'NOT' gate:

Inputs	Outputs
A	Q
0	1
1	0

If the input is 1 the output is 0 and vice versa.

A 'NOT' gate would be used in a microwave. If the door is open, then the microwave will not turn on. If the first condition is true, then the second condition will be false.

Download Worksheet 11.1 from Cambridge Elevate

Logic circuits

The gates can be combined to produce logic circuits. A logic circuit is designed with multiple logic gates so that it can take a variety of inputs (sometimes many hundreds) and process them to allow decisions to be made according to the various inputs. The inputs might be, for example, sensors on a motor car, or a plane, or at different points in a production line in a factory.

Key term

logic circuit: a combination of standard logic gates used to perform complex logic operations where the outputs of some gates act as the inputs to others

WORKED EXAMPLE

A student is setting up an automatic watering system for the greenhouse while she and her family are on holiday. She has a light sensor that is on and will emit a signal during the day, and a moisture sensor which is on and will emit a signal when the soil is wet. But she only wants the watering system to turn on at night and then only when the soil is dry, that is when there is NO light and when there is NO moisture. She chooses to use two 'NOT' and one 'AND' gates.

We can use letters to represent the inputs and outputs:

A = light (1) or dark (0) condition.

B = wet (1) or dry (0) condition.

Q = output to indicate whether the control system is to be active (1) or inactive (0).

So we can write:

Q = NOT(A) AND NOT(B)

So the watering system will turn on only if both conditions are false, that is it must be dark AND the soil must be dry. The following gates will be required:

Tip

The numbers in brackets indicate whether 0 or 1 applies to a particular status (light, dark, wet, dry etc.).

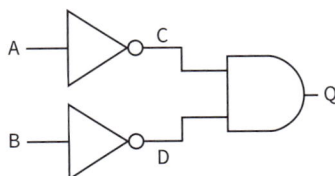

The inputs from the two sensors (A and B) feed into 'NOT' gates that then feed into an 'AND' gate. The outputs from 'NOT' gates (C and D) provide the inputs for the 'AND' gate. If the inputs into the 'NOT' gates are 1 then the outputs at C and D will be 0. So if the light and moisture sensors are supplying electric currents, they will be stopped by the 'NOT' gates. If sensors are not supplying a current, then the 'NOT' gates will transmit a current at C and D.

The truth table will be as follows:

Inputs		Intermediate Values		Output
A	B	C	D	Q
0	0	1	1	1
0	1	1	0	0
1	0	0	1	0
1	1	0	0	0

The watering system will be turned on only if it is dark AND there is no moisture.

Download Worksheet 11.2 from Cambridge Elevate

ACTIVITY 11.2

Give the logic circuit and the truth table for the following statement:

Q = NOT (A OR B)

WORKED EXAMPLE

An alarm system uses three switches: A, B and C. The following combination of switches determines whether an alarm, X, sounds:

If switch A OR switch B are in the ON position AND if switch C is in the OFF position, then a signal to sound an alarm, X, is produced.

This can be written as:

```
IF (A = 1 OR B = 1) AND NOT (C = 1) THEN

    X ← 1

ENDIF
```

This can be represented by the following logic circuit:

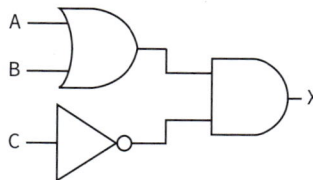

The truth table would be:

Inputs			Output
A	B	C	X
0	0	0	0
0	0	1	0
0	1	0	1
0	1	1	0
1	0	0	1
1	0	1	0
1	1	0	1
1	1	1	0

Complete Interactive Activity 11b on Cambridge Elevate

Download Worksheet 11.3 from Cambridge Elevate

Interpreting truth tables

You should be able to look at truth tables, or logic circuits with their truth tables, and explain their logic – what they are doing.

WORKED EXAMPLE

Create a truth table for the following logic circuit and explain how it functions.

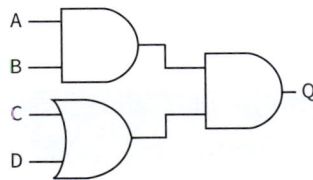

Inputs				Output
A	B	C	D	Q
0	0	0	0	0
0	0	0	1	0
0	0	1	0	0
0	0	1	1	0
0	1	0	0	0
0	1	0	1	0
0	1	1	0	0
0	1	1	1	0
1	0	0	0	0
1	0	0	1	0
1	0	1	0	0
1	0	1	1	0
1	1	0	0	0
1	1	0	1	1
1	1	1	0	1
1	1	1	1	1

The logic circuit will output 1 if inputs A and B are both 1 in combination with either C or D (or C and D) having an input of 1.

This can be written as:

Q = (A AND B) AND (C OR D)

ACTIVITY 11.3

Create a truth table and explain the following circuit.

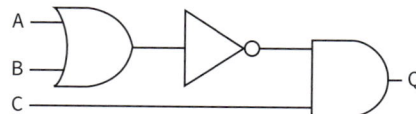

ACTIVITY 11.4

Create a truth table and explain the following circuit.

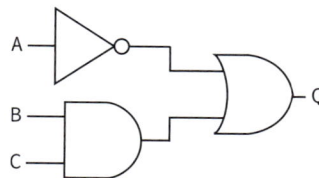

Complete Interactive Activity 11c on Cambridge Elevate

Practice questions

1. The following logic circuit can be written as: **P = (NOT A) AND B**.

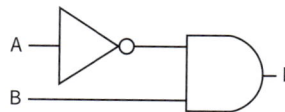

Complete the truth table for this logic circuit.

Inputs		Output
A	B	P
0	0	0
0	1	

2. Write the correct values for the missing inputs and outputs for each of the following gates.

   The first one has been done for you.

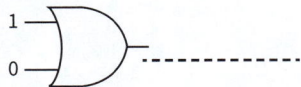

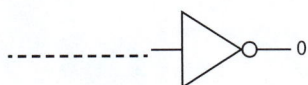

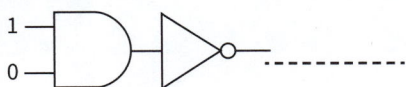

Your final challenge

- A healthy drinks company uses a conveyor belt in the factory.
- Before use, the bottles must be sterilised. They are moved along a conveyor belt which can be switched on by two switches, A and B, but only after the supervisor operates the master switch C.
- Draw the logic circuit and truth table to demonstrate to the designers of the system how it should work.

Download Self-assessment 11 worksheet from Cambridge Elevate (this content has not been approved by AQA)

12 Programming languages

Learning outcomes

By the end of this chapter you should be able to:

- explain the difference between low- and high-level languages
- explain the advantages of using high-level languages
- explain how program instructions are encoded in low-level languages
- explain why high-level languages need to be translated
- explain the characteristics and use of:
  - an assembler
  - a compiler
  - an interpreter.

★ Challenge: write programs using a low-level language

- Programs may be written in assembly language.
- These programs can be checked with a program called a computer simulator.
- Computer simulators mimic the actions of a real computer.
- Your challenge is to write programs in assembly language and check them using a computer simulator.

Ada Lovelace, the daughter of the poet Lord Byron, is credited with writing the first computer program in 1842.

Why programming languages?

- Programming languages are used to give instructions to computers: to tell them what to do!

- Programming languages evolve over time (just like living organisms) as users make improvements or add new features. Gradually they become so different to the original that they are a new language.

- Just like evolution in the living world where changes to the environment stimulate the evolution of new types of animals and plants, changes in technology lead to the development of new computer languages. For example, Java was created to develop applets for the World Wide Web (WWW) and portable electronic devices. Without the WWW or tablets, there would probably be no Java.

- Different languages have strengths and weaknesses in different areas. For example JavaScript for building web-based applications, Ruby for developing mobile apps, SQL for querying databases, C++ for games development, R for data analysis and Python as a general purpose language.

- But whatever the language used, the code still has to be converted into strings of 1s and 0s: the only language that computers can understand.

Popular programming languages

Programming languages, such as Python, Java, C and Visual Basic, all provide instructions for the microprocessor to carry out or execute.

For example, the following simple program written in the Python programming language will instruct the microprocessor to ask for two inputs and then to calculate the area and perimeter of a rectangle.

Code

```
def rectangle(leng, wid):

    ar = leng * wid

    per = (leng*2) + (wid*2)

    return (ar, per)

length = int(input("Please enter the length"))

width = int(input("Please enter the width"))

area, perimeter = rectangle(length, width)

print(area, perimeter)
```

It uses words and symbols like '=' and '*' that we can easily understand. But, unfortunately, written in this way, the microprocessor would not be able to understand it.

A microprocessor cannot understand English. It can only understand binary (strings of 1s and 0s).

Machine code

The commands that the microprocessor executes, represented as strings of 1s and 0s, are called machine code or machine language.

Just as combinations of 1s and 0s are used to encode characters in the ASCII code, similar combinations are used to encode the instructions that have to be carried out. The microprocessor interprets the strings of binary digits as instructions. Each type of microprocessor has a fixed number of commands that it can understand. These make up the microprocessor's instruction set and they are different for the different types of microprocessor.

For example, this string '0010' could be used as an instruction in one type of microprocessor to add one number to another.

Machine code is a low-level language as it uses the computer's actual instruction set.

The instructions for the microprocessor have two parts or 'fields'. The two fields are the opcode and the operand.

- The opcode specifies the operation that is to be performed, for example add numbers or store data in a memory location.

185

- The operand represents the data that are to be used, or the memory location in which the data can be found or have to be stored. For example:

$$0001 \quad 1101$$

opcode   operand

Assembly language

As it is difficult for humans to think and write programs in pure machine code using 1s and 0s (just imagine trying to debug a program consisting of millions of 1s and 0s), programmers often use assembly language.

Instead of writing opcodes in binary, in assembly language mnemonics are used.

Translation

An assembler translates the mnemonics of assembly language programs into machine language instructions for the microprocessor to execute. As assembly language is very similar to machine code, there is one assembly language instruction per machine code instruction.

Because the assembly language instructions are very similar to those in machine language, assembly language is referred to as a low-level language.

ACTIVITY 12.1

The following table shows part of the instruction set of a particular microprocessor that uses 4 bits for opcode and 8 bits for the operand.

Opcode	Mnemonic	Explanation
0000	STO	Store data at memory location indicated by the operand.
0001	LOAD	Load the number located in the operand
0010	LOAD	Load the number found at the memory location indicated by the operand.
0100	ADD	Add the number located in the operand.
1000	ADD	Add the number found at the memory location indicated by the operand.

The opcode and operand for the command 'Load the number 13' would be: 000100001101

As 0001 is the opcode for 'Load' and 00001101 is 13 in binary.

Give the opcodes and operands for the following:

a. Load the number found at memory location 6.

b. Add the number 113.

c. i. Load the number 10, add the number 21 and store the result at memory location 30.

   ii. State the data that would be found at memory location 30.

Download Worksheet 12.1 from Cambridge Elevate

ACTIVITY 12.2

For a taste of programming in assembly language, investigate The Little Man Computer that can be accessed at www.cambridge.org/links/kase4001. This 'computer' has a limited instruction set and the site provides some tutorials for you to work through.

Assembly language is often used in the programs used by embedded systems. An embedded system is a computer system built within a larger device such as a washing machine or camera. These are discussed in Chapter 9.

High-level languages

Programming in assembly language is more user-friendly than using machine code, but it is still more difficult than writing programs in a high-level language using statements like 'IF…THEN', 'DO…UNTIL' and 'WHILE'.

High-level languages are programming languages that are machine independent and resemble human languages. A vast number of different high-level languages are available and most programs are written in high-level languages.

They are at a higher level of abstraction from the actual computer hardware and focus more on the programming logic rather than using the underlying hardware components such as memory addressing.

High-level languages provide built-in data structures and constructs, such as selection and iteration, and have libraries of functions that programmers can use instead of having to write them all themselves.

The vast majority of software is developed in a high-level language because of the many advantages that they provide to the programmer.

The commands still need to be translated into machine language before they can be executed by the microprocessor. There are two ways of doing this: using a compiler or an interpreter.

Compiler

A compiler reads the whole high-level code (the source code) and, if there are no errors, translates it into a complete machine code program (the object code) which is output as a new file and can be saved.

Advantages	Disadvantages
The translation is done once only and as a separate process.	If it encounters any errors, it carries on trying to compile the program and reports the errors at the end. The programmers then have to use the error messages to identify and remove the bugs.
The program that is run is already translated into machine code so is much faster in execution.	You cannot change the program without going back to the original source code, editing that and recompiling.
It protects the software from competitors who might otherwise be able to see how it is designed and built.	

Key terms

compiler: a program that converts high-level programs into low-level programs

intrepreter: a program which will run a high-level program directly, interpreting the instructions and converting them, without them needing to be in the machine code of a computer

Interpreter

An interpreter reads the source code one instruction or line at a time, converts this line and executes it. The next line is read and translated and so on. This has to be done each time the program is run.

Advantages	Disadvantages
When an error is found, the interpreter reports it and stops so the programmer knows where the error has occurred.	Every line has to be translated every time it is executed and therefore it is slower.
The program can be easily edited as it always exists as source code.	The user has to have the interpreter as well as the source code.

Advantages of using high-level languages

The advantages of using high-level language are:

- Faster program development: it is less time consuming to write and then test the program.

- It is not necessary to remember the registers of the CPU and mnemonic instructions.

- Portability of a program from one machine to other: each assembly language is specific to a particular type of CPU, but most high-level languages are generally portable across different CPUs.

Advantages of using low-level languages

The advantages of using low-level language are:

- Programs written in low-level languages require less memory and execution time.

- They allow the programmer to directly control system hardware and are used extensively for programming embedded systems.

Download Worksheet 12.2 from Cambridge Elevate

Remember

1. The microprocessor can only execute commands given in machine code (machine language).
2. Each instruction consists of an opcode and an operand.
3. Assembly language uses mnemonics to make it easier for humans to remember and write the opcodes.
4. An assembler converts the assembly instructions into machine code.
5. High-level languages are more like human languages.
6. High-level languages have to be converted to machine code by compilers or interpreters.
7. Low-level languages include both machine code and assembly languages.

Complete Interactive Activity 12a on Cambridge Elevate

Watch the Branches and Little Man Computer animation on Cambridge Elevate

Practice question

1. A developer is writing a program.

    a. The program is written in a high-level language and it is then translated into machine code. Describe two differences between high-level language and machine code.
    b. One type of translator is an interpreter.
        i.   Describe how an interpreter translates high-level language programs into machine code.
        ii. State the name of a different type of translator that can be used to translate high-level code into machine code.

Your final challenge

Your final challenge is to write and test programs using the Little Man Computer simulator at www.cambridge.org/links/kase4001. Write programs in assembly language to carry out the following:

*   Input two numbers and output them in numerical order.
*   Input two numbers and multiply them together.

Download the Self-assessment 12 worksheet from Cambridge Elevate (this content has not been approved by AQA)

13 Computer networks

⭐ **Challenge: act as a consultant for network design**

- You have to give professional advice to organisations on the setting up of networks.
- Your challenge is to give accurate, professional-sounding advice to your clients.

Thanks to networks we can tell the world what we are thinking and feeling by publishing our photos, videos and thoughts online.

Why networks?

The networking of computing devices has had a profound impact on our lives and the ways in which we work, communicate with each other, buy products and services and find out information in our daily lives.

- Networks allow us to live in a connected world.

- Worldwide communication is possible for everyone.

- Our personal devices can be networked so that they can communicate with each other.

- Our laptops can be networked with our mobile phone, printers, mouse, speakers and headphones.

- The internet is a huge network of networks and the World Wide Web allows us to connect and communicate with people and services throughout the world.

- Thanks to networks we can tell the world what we are thinking and feeling by publishing our photos, videos and thoughts online.

Computer networks

A computer network allows computers and devices to be connected together to share data. This includes:

- computer to computer communication

- computers communicating with devices such as printers, a mouse and a keyboard

- mobile phone networks

- smart televisions

- tablets and media players downloading videos and music and playing them through external devices such as speakers and digital projectors.

We live in a networked world where people and things are interconnected.

There are different types of networking. Some of these are outlined below:

Personal area network (PAN)

A personal area network (PAN) is a network communicating up to 10 metres between computer devices such as laptops, mobile phones, tablets, media players, speakers and printers. They may be devices belonging to one person or to several.

> **Key term**
>
> personal area network (PAN): network used for data transmission over short distances by devices such as laptops, mobile phones, tablets, media players, speakers and printers

The PAN may just connect the local devices or allow them to connect to other networks such as the internet. The devices usually communicate wirelessly over distances up to 10 metres by radio waves using a technology called Bluetooth.

Local area network (LAN)

Computers in a site such as an office building use a local area network (LAN) to connect with each other.

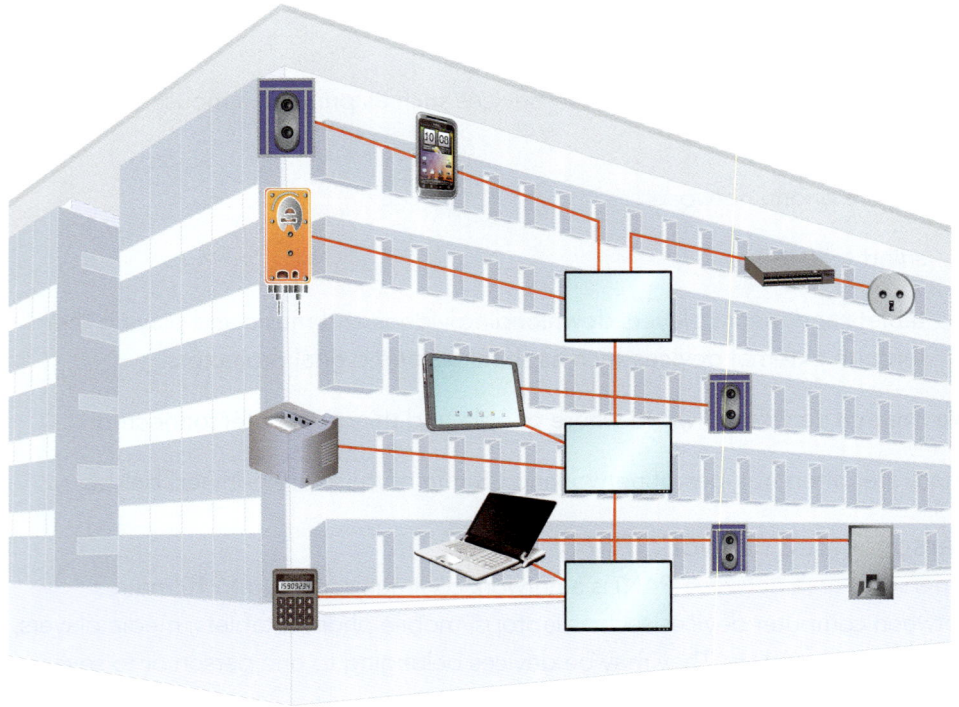

A local area network is a computer network within a small geographical area such as a home, a school, an office building or a group of buildings on a local site. It is usually owned and managed by a single organisation, for example a school or business.

Wide area network (WAN)

A wide area network (WAN) is a network that connects separate LANs over a large geographical area. This ensures that computers in one location can communicate with computers and users in other locations.

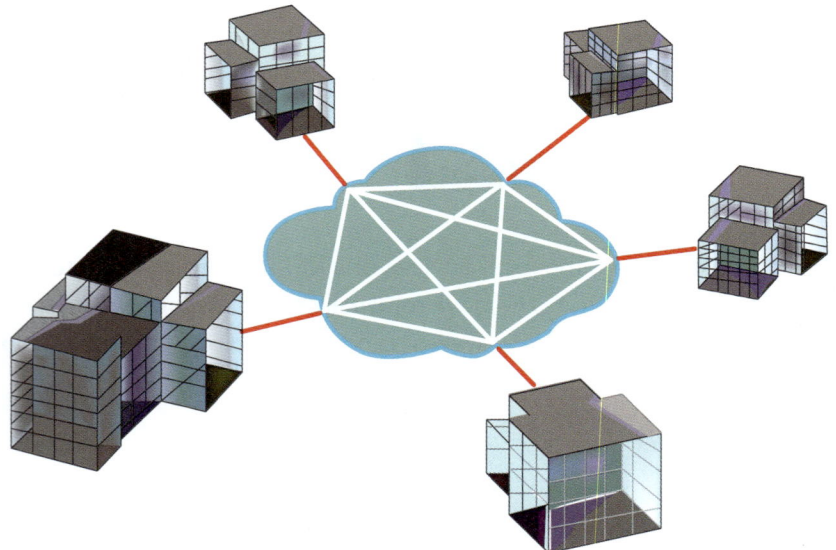

The LANs at different sites of a multinational company can communicate with each other. The WAN will therefore be managed by several different people or parts of an organisation working together (collective ownership) or each LAN could be managed independently (distributed ownership).

The internet is a global system of interconnected computer networks that serves billions of users worldwide. The internet is therefore an example of a huge WAN. This is explained in a later section on the internet.

Benefits and risks of computer networks

Networking provides many benefits because of the ability to communicate between users and devices, but there are also risks.

Benefits	Risks
Devices such as printers can be shared and therefore each user does not need their own device connected directly to their computer.	Extra hardware and infrastructure are needed which might be expensive and therefore not cost effective.
Files can be shared with other users across the network and the users can work collaboratively on the same documents. The files do not have to be saved to a storage medium, for example CD, DVD or USB memory stick.	Technical knowledge is needed to set up and manage the network.
Users can communicate with each other using electronic messaging.	When sharing an internet connection, some users might use too much bandwidth and cause problems for other users.
Users can share the same internet connection using a router which directs traffic to the correct users.	Networking can lead to computer viruses spreading more rapidly.
Users are given greater flexibility and can access their personal files from any computer on the network.	If all data are stored centrally, then it is more at risk from hackers because the hackers do not have to search for the data on individual, stand-alone computers.
If all data are stored centrally, then it is easier to back it up without having to back up each computer individually.	If data are stored on a central file server and the file server malfunctions, then they will be unavailable until it is fixed.
There is greater security as users can be given usernames and passwords. The activity of the users can also be monitored.	
Software management is easier as it can be installed centrally and then copied to all computers over the network. This also increases security as the installation of illegal software by users can be prevented.	

Complete Interactive Activity 13a on Cambridge Elevate

1. Describe the characteristics of:

   a. a personal area network

   b. a local area network

   c. a wide area network.

2. Describe three benefits and three risks for a school using networked rather than stand-alone computers.

Key terms

cables: a way of connecting computers using cables and sockets

microwaves: electromagnetic waves which can be used to carry data between computers

protocols: agreed rules for requesting and sending data across networks

How do computers connect to a network?

In order to connect to a network, a computer needs some hardware and also some software that allows it to communicate with the other computers. Devices can be connected using cables. The most commonly used are 'twisted pair' cables in which pairs of copper wires are twisted together and carry electrical signals, and optical fibre cables which are made of glass. As optical fibre cables transmit information encoded in beams of light, the data transmission is much faster. The connection can also be radio waves, including microwaves.

A network interface card or network adaptor

A network interface card (NIC) or network adaptor is a component that connects a computer to a network. It formats the data sent from the computer into a required format according to the protocols (rules) of the network.

Originally, the adapters for desktop PCs were on 'cards' that were installed in the computer but they are now usually built into the motherboard. Network interface cards and adapters now support both wired and wireless network connections.

Every NIC is created with a hardware number permanently 'burned' into it. This permanent hardware number is known as the media access control (MAC) address. MAC addresses are 48 bits in length and are usually displayed as a 12-digit hexadecimal number.

Every MAC address is unique so that all data on a network can be sent to the correct component, just like letters delivered to the correct house or text messages and voice calls to the correct phone.

Remember

1. There are different types of network: PAN, LAN, WAN.
2. There are benefits and risks to individuals and organisations when networking computers.
3. Computers need a network adapter to connect to a network.
4. Cables and radio waves can be used to carry the data.

Transmission media

The two main ways that devices use to communicate over a network are by cable or radiowaves; in other words, 'wired' and 'wireless'.

Cable

The traditional method is to connect the computers using cables. In large networks, there is usually a combination of twisted pair copper wire and fibre optic cable.

Copper wire carries the data as electric currents while in fibre optic cable data are transmitted as pulses of light generated by a light emitting diode (LED) or a laser.

Fibre optic cables have a far greater bandwidth and can carry signals faster than copper cables. The signals can also travel over greater distances without needing to be boosted.

Copper wire would be suitable for a small network with relatively few devices, for example a small office or a classroom. For large LANs with many users, fibre optic cables should be used, for example a large office building or for a school site.

In order to transmit data over the cables there are rules, called protocols, concerning how the data are packaged and how collisions are detected or prevented. The most widely used standard is Ethernet.

Microwave

Microwaves consist of electromagnetic radiation travelling in waves with a frequency higher than 1 gigahertz (GHz; 1 GHz to 300 GHz per second). Microwaves are a type of radiowave and they are used to transmit data across networks in frequencies of between 2.4 and 5 GHz.

A wireless access point and a router (explained below) can be used to connect wired and wireless networks.

Wireless access points

Wireless access points allow wireless devices to connect to a wired network using Wi-Fi.

- They convert data they receive through cables into a wireless signal and vice versa.

- They are commonly used in public buildings to provide internet hotspots.

- Unlike routers, they cannot send data down a particular pathway or route.

A WLAN or wireless local area network allows computers to communicate within a network using radio waves.

The most commonly used standard of data transmission using radio waves is Wi-Fi.

Others include GSM, for example 3G and 4G (Global System for Mobile communications: used for mobile phones), Bluetooth and Wi-Fi direct.

Tip

Bandwidth is the amount of data that can pass through the transmission medium per second. It is often called the bit-rate. It does not measure how fast the bits are travelling, only how many can get through a particular point in a second. Bandwidth is measured in bits per second (bps) or megabits per second (Mbps). (Note: bandwidth is measured in mega**bits** and not mega**bytes**.)

Key terms

Ethernet: a set of rules or protocols for computers to follow when communicating data over a network

frequency: the number of waves produced per second

Wi-Fi: consists of the protocols needed for communication over a wireless network. It is the wireless version of wired Ethernet protocols

Comparison of wired and wireless networks

	Wired	Wireless
Bandwidth	Very high bandwidth up to 100Gbps.	Far lower bandwidth. The latest version of Wi-Fi can offer speeds from 433Mbps to 2 or 3Gbps.
Installation	Setting up is more difficult. Cables have to be run all over the site.	Easy. All that is needed are wireless access points.
Cost	Cost of cables and hardware can be expensive. Also cost of work done to install cables.	Cheap. Just the cost of wireless access point.
Security	Security is good. A user has to physically plug their computer into the network using a cable.	Security is poor. Anyone within range can see the network and connect to it and use it. The access point must be secured with a security password. Some form of encryption must be set up.
Interference	There is usually no interference with the signal on a network cable.	The signal can be affected by walls and electronic equipment such as microwave ovens. It is also affected by distance from the access point and the number of connected computers.
Mobility	Not very mobile. You have to plug the computer into a wall socket and cannot use it in a room without one. Contact is lost as soon as it is unplugged if you want to move to another room.	Very mobile. Users can access the network from anywhere on the site. Can move from room to room and remain connected.

Key term

bandwidth: the amount of data that can pass through the transmission medium per second. It is often called the bit-rate

ACTIVITY 13.2

Discuss the benefits and drawbacks of setting up either a wired or wireless network in the home.

Complete Interactive Activity 13b on Cambridge Elevate

Network topologies

A network **topology** describes how all of the parts of a network are arranged and connected together. The topology includes the **nodes** (e.g. computers, printers, modems) and the connecting lines (cables).

Bus topology

Each machine is connected to a long, single cable which acts as a backbone to link all the devices in a network. Each computer or server is connected to the single bus cable through a connector called a T-piece. A terminator is required at each end of the bus cable to prevent the signal from bouncing back and forth on the bus cable.

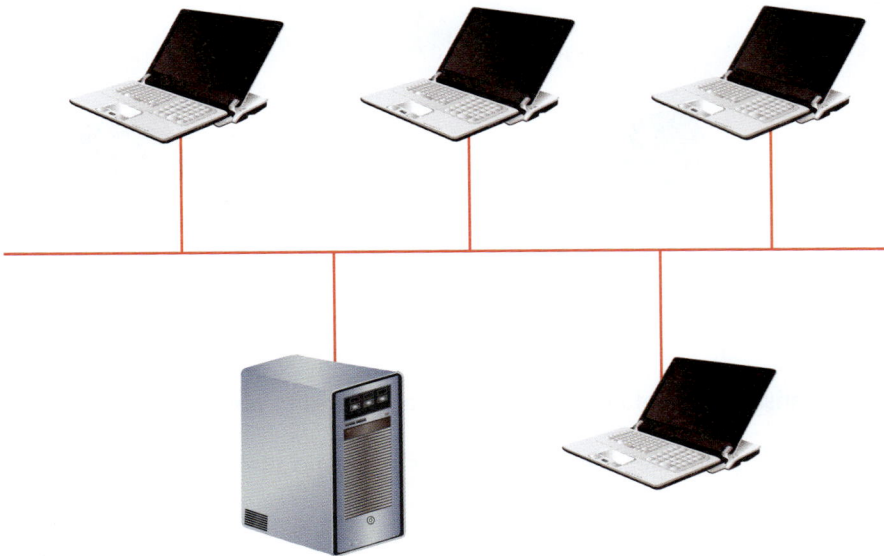

Advantages

- Requires less cable length than star topology.

- A bus topology could be used to quickly set up a small network without the need for any other equipment such as hubs or routers.

Disadvantages

- The cable length is limited. This limits the number of network nodes that can be connected.

- Each device on the network 'sees' all the data being transmitted, thus posing a security risk.

- If the network cable breaks, the entire network will be down.

Control area networks (CANs) are used to allow microcontrollers and devices to communicate with each other in the control systems of cars and railway and aerospace devices.

Key terms

topology: the structure of the network

node: places on the network where there are items of equipment

Star topology

Each computer is individually connected to a central point that can be a file server or switch. The central point that is used is usually a switch.

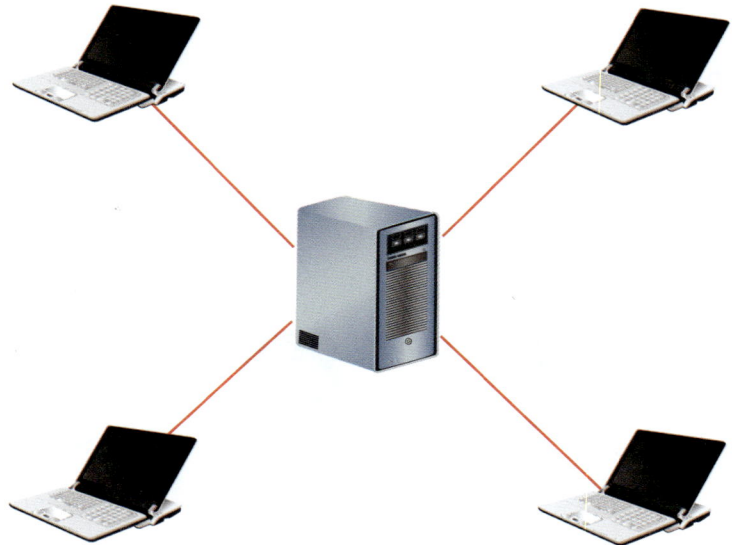

Switches

- All of the computers on the network plug into a port on the switch using a cable.

- They transmit the data being sent from one node to another.

- They can read the destination addresses and send them to only the intended computers.

- They can do this because they build up a table of all of the MAC addresses on the network.

Advantages

- Data packets can be directed to the intended node directly without having to pass along the complete network. This lowers overall network traffic and improves security as data is not being transmitted to every node on the network.

- There will be less network traffic and fewer collisions.

- If one link fails, all the other devices will continue to operate.

Disadvantages

- Network operation depends on the functioning of the central component (file server or switch) and if this fails, then so will the entire network.

- It requires more cable length than a simple bus topology where the computers are connected in a line and so it will be more expensive.

Remember

1. Data can be transmitted in networks by cables and radio waves.
2. The most widely used standards for transmission are Ethernet for wired and Wi-Fi for wireless.
3. Topology is the arrangement of the computers and other devices in the network, and how they are connected together.
4. There are several topologies including bus and star.

Complete Interactive Activity 13c on Cambridge Elevate

ACTIVITY 13.3

A small business uses a star topology for its local area network. List three benefits of using a star topology.

The internet

The internet is a global system of interconnected computer networks that serves billions of users worldwide and is therefore a wide area network. The internet provides many services including email and the World Wide Web.

The internet is often called a 'network of networks' because it consists of millions of private, public, academic, business and government networks that are linked by different networking technologies.

The World Wide Web was first proposed by the British scientist Tim Berners-Lee in 1989. He created the first website in 1990.

Hosts

A host is a computer that can be accessed by users working at remote locations using networks including the internet. Web hosting companies rent space on their servers where people can develop their own websites that can be accessed by users all over the world using the World Wide Web.

In 1969, there were four host computer systems and today there are tens of millions. The Internet Society was established in 1992 to oversee the policies and protocols that define how we use and interact with the internet.

There is a huge infrastructure of cables forming the backbone of the internet. These cables are provided and maintained by large corporations such as IBM and AT&T and they charge for access.

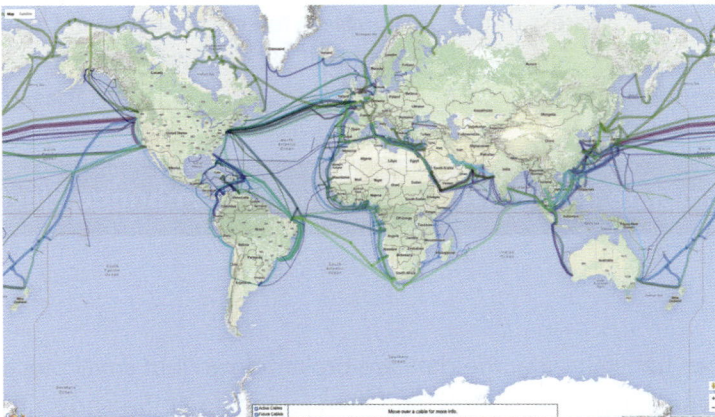

Connecting to the internet

To connect to the internet, computers require hardware:

Hardware	A network adaptor as described in the networking section. A modem.
Access to cable infrastructure	Large organisations can negotiate their own access with the corporations which control the infrastructure, but smaller organisations and individual users will require the services of an Internet Service Provider (ISP) who organises that access. They also provide storage space for the websites of their users. This is called *hosting*.
An address	Every computer needs a unique software address in order to communicate over the internet. This is provided by the IP address (see the section on IP addresses for more details). IP stands for Internet Protocol; the set of procedures used by computers accessing the internet. Every computer accessing the internet must have a unique identifier and this is the computer's IP address.

IP addresses

An IP address is a set of numbers that are used to identify one particular computer.

The IP address is like a postal address and it will allow internet data and messages to be sent to the correct computer. IP addresses originally consisted of four 8-bit numbers for version 4 addresses (IPv4), for example 216.27.61.137. This provided only 4 billion unique addresses, so IPv6 was introduced. IPv6 uses 128 binary bits to create a single unique address on the network. An IPv6 address is expressed by eight groups of hexadecimal numbers separated by colons, as in 2001:cdba:0000:0000:0000:0000:3257:9652. Note that 128 bits provide 3.4×10^{38} unique addresses.

Domain names

Domain names are used to identify one or more IP addresses. They are more convenient to use and easier to remember than the four octets of binary numbers, for example, the IP address of the URL (uniform resource locator) of Cambridge University Press (www.cambridge.org) is 174.35.68.38. cambridge.org is the domain name part of the URL. The .org refers to the top level domain (TLD) it belongs to.

Complete Interactive Activity 13d on Cambridge Elevate

Packets

When devices transmit data, the data are broken down into small pieces called packets. These are sent separately, and then joined up at the end so that the message is complete.

Rules are needed so that all of the computers on the network work together. For example, how will the receiving computer know when the message is complete or if there has been a transmission error?

A packet consists of:

- A header containing the source and destination addresses and the position of this packet in the complete message or file.

- The body containing part of the complete message data (also known as the payload).

- A footer (also known as the trailer) that informs the receiving device that it has reached the end of the packet and can also be used for error checking to ensure the complete packet has been delivered intact.

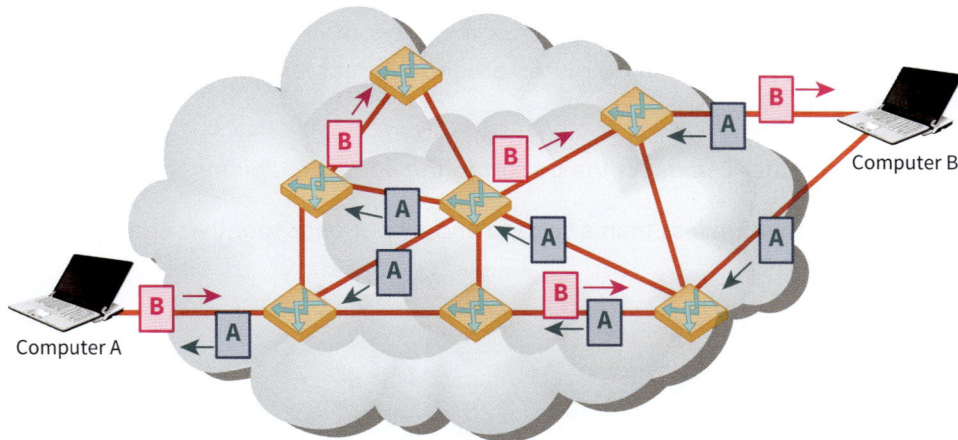

The packets are then sent out on their various journeys to the recipient computer. They do not all follow the same route. In fact, they do not all necessarily arrive in the correct order, but because they are labelled the receiving computer can put the packets back together in the correct order.

The delivery of the packets is accomplished by devices called routers.

Routers
Routers connect different networks together.

- They are similar to switches in that they read the address information and forward the messages to the correct network. A switch does this within a single network, but a router does this across several networks.

- Routers are commonly used in the home to allow many computers to share an internet connection. The router links the home network to a much larger one: the internet.

- Routers can have both cable and Wi-Fi connections.

The router will transmit the incoming web pages, streamed audio, etc. to the correct computer on the network.

The journey of the packets across a large network like the internet is extraordinary. They could be travelling from the east coast of America to your bedroom! Here's how it works:

- The source computer splits the file into packets and addresses them with the recipient's IP address.

- These packets are then sent onto the network using cables or microwaves as in a wireless network.

- Routers on the network inspect each packet and decide the most efficient path for the packet to take on the next stage of its journey.

- In order to do this each router has a configuration table containing information about which connections lead to particular groups of addresses.

- The routers can balance the load across the network on a millisecond-by-millisecond basis.

- If there is a problem with one part of the network while a message is being transferred, packets can be routed around the problem, ensuring the delivery of the entire message.

- The final router can direct the packet to the correct recipient.

Thousands of miles in less than a second and all put back together again!

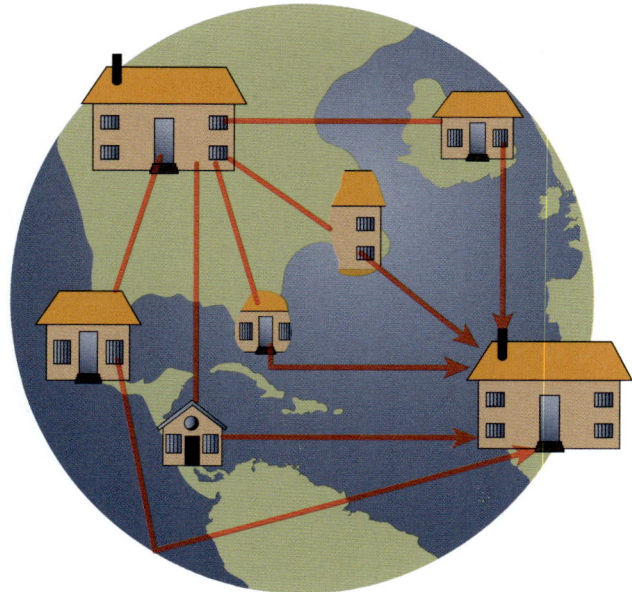

Key term

packet switching: a method of data transmission in which a message is broken into a number of parts which are sent independently over the most suitable routes. The message is reassembled at the destination

This method of data communication shown in the above diagram is called packet switching. It is efficient because it means that there does not have to be a dedicated line between the two communicating devices. Compare this with making a telephone call on a landline where there is a dedicated line between the two telephones. That method is called circuit switching.

In packet switching, the same line can carry parts of billions of communications at the same time and if there is a problem or the line is full, then another route can be quickly found.

Download Worksheet 13.2 from Cambridge Elevate

Protocols

There must be rules so that computers on all networks can communicate with each other when they are requesting and providing data and services. With as complicated a process as sending data packets, rules, called protocols, are essential.

The two suites of protocols for communication over a network, Ethernet and Wi-Fi, have already been discussed. Other protocols needed for the internet are explained below.

TCP/IP stands for transmission control protocol / internet protocol. It is actually a suite or set of protocols arranged in four layers. Data to be transmitted (or to be received) must pass through the layers where packaging data are added or read.

The four layers are:

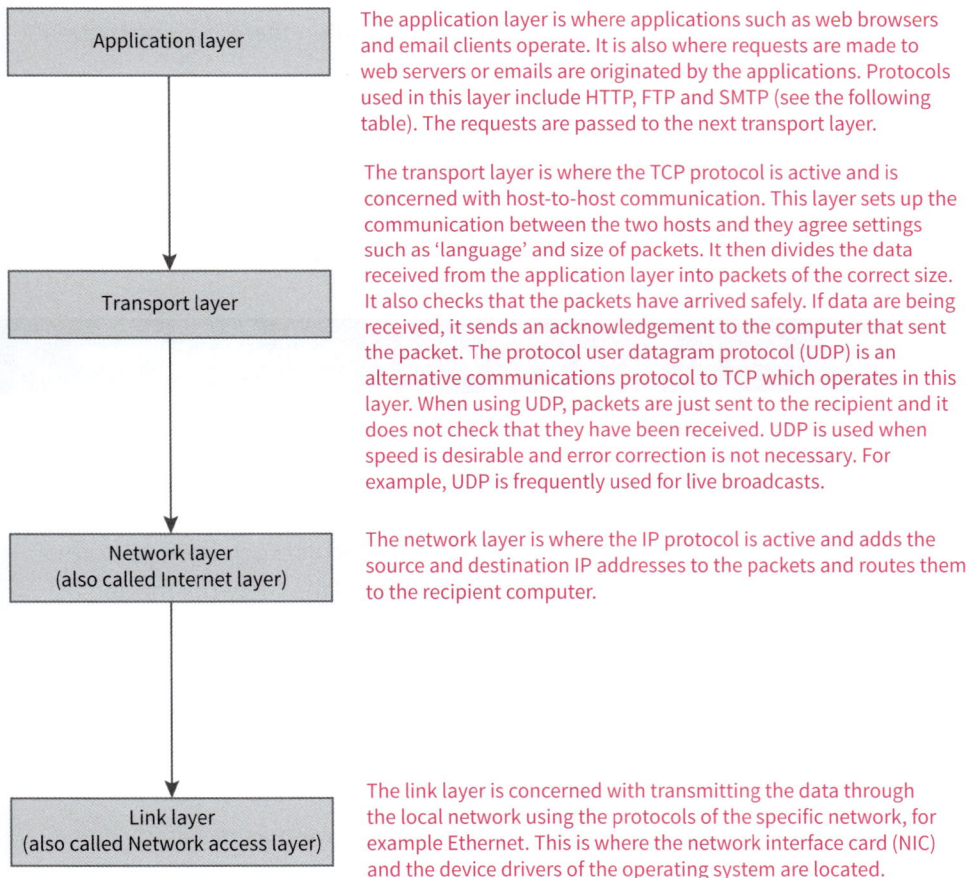

Application layer	The application layer is where applications such as web browsers and email clients operate. It is also where requests are made to web servers or emails are originated by the applications. Protocols used in this layer include HTTP, FTP and SMTP (see the following table). The requests are passed to the next transport layer.
Transport layer	The transport layer is where the TCP protocol is active and is concerned with host-to-host communication. This layer sets up the communication between the two hosts and they agree settings such as 'language' and size of packets. It then divides the data received from the application layer into packets of the correct size. It also checks that the packets have arrived safely. If data are being received, it sends an acknowledgement to the computer that sent the packet. The protocol user datagram protocol (UDP) is an alternative communications protocol to TCP which operates in this layer. When using UDP, packets are just sent to the recipient and it does not check that they have been received. UDP is used when speed is desirable and error correction is not necessary. For example, UDP is frequently used for live broadcasts.
Network layer (also called Internet layer)	The network layer is where the IP protocol is active and adds the source and destination IP addresses to the packets and routes them to the recipient computer.
Link layer (also called Network access layer)	The link layer is concerned with transmitting the data through the local network using the protocols of the specific network, for example Ethernet. This is where the network interface card (NIC) and the device drivers of the operating system are located.

Protocols of the application layer

The table shows some of the protocols of the application layer.

FTP	File Transfer Protocol; the rules to be followed when files are being transmitted between computers.
HTTP	Hypertext Transfer Protocol; the rules to be followed by a web server and a web browser when supplying and requesting information. HTTP is used for sending requests from a web client (a browser) to a web server and returning web content from the server back to the client.
HTTPS	Secure HTTP; allows for communications between a host and client to be secure by ensuring that all communication between them is encrypted.
SMTP	Simple Mail Transfer Protocol; the protocol for sending email messages from client to server and then from server to server until the email message reaches its destination.
POP	Post Office Protocol; used by a client to retrieve emails from a mail server. All of the emails are downloaded when there is a connection between client and server.
IMAP	Internet Message Access protocol; unlike POP, the messages do not have to be downloaded. They can be read and stored on the message server. This is better for users with many different devices as they can be read from each rather than being downloaded to just one.

Complete Interactive Activity 13e on Cambridge Elevate

Benefits of using networking layers

Networking technologies are separated or compartmentalised into layers, each one containing specific hardware and software protocols. Each layer performs specific tasks and interacts with the adjacent layers in the 'network model'.

The benefits of this approach are:

- It simplifies the overall model by dividing it into functional parts.

- Each layer is specialised to perform a particular function.

- The different layers can be combined in different ways as required.

- One layer can be developed or changed without affecting the other layers.

- It makes it easier to identify and correct networking errors and problems.

- It provides a universal standard for hardware and software manufacturers to follow so that they will be able to communicate with each other.

Download Worksheet 13.3 from Cambridge Elevate

ℹ️ Remember

1. The internet is a huge network of networks.
2. To connect to the internet, a user needs a network adapter and a modem.
3. Protocols are the rules computers use for communicating on networks.
4. An ISP provides access to the internet infrastructure for the users.
5. A computer needs an IP address.
6. IP addresses can be associated with domain names, which are easier to remember.
7. DNS resolves the names back into IP addresses.
8. TCP/IP is a suite of these protocols.
9. The TCP/IP protocols have four layers:
   a. the application layer
   b. the transport layer
   c. the network layer (also called the internet layer)
   d. the link layer (also called the network access layer).

✏️ Practice questions

1. Protocols are used by computers communicating over networks.
   a. Explain what is meant by a 'protocol'.
2. TCP/IP is a collection of network protocols acting in layers.
   a. With the aid of a diagram, give examples of protocols operating in each layer and their roles in network communication.
   b. List three benefits of arranging the protocols in layers.

⭐ Your final challenge

You have two clients.

1. 'Smith and Brown' are a small firm of solicitors. There are two solicitors and they also have a general office with two clerical workers. They would like a network so that they can share facilities and work collaboratively.
2. 'The Academy' is a secondary school with two main buildings and 50 classrooms, two of which are computer rooms. They would like a network so that all the students can log in using their laptops wherever they are in the school.

Your task is to give the clients advice such as:

- The type of network that is best suited to them.
- The hardware they will require to network their computers.
- Any software needed to set up the network.
- The infrastructure they will need.

You can present your advice as a written report or a presentation.

⬇️ Download

Self-assessment 13 worksheet from Cambridge Elevate (this content has not been approved by AQA)

14 Cyber security

Learning outcomes

By the end of this chapter you should be able to:

- explain the need for and importance of cyber security
- describe the different strategies that criminals use to attack computer networks
- explain how people are the greatest security risks to networks
- describe the threats posed to networks
- explain how these threats can be identified, prevented and combatted.

⭐ Challenge: design and code an information point

- Information points are useful places where users can seek information about security threats. They can be placed in strategic places such as libraries, etc.
- Your challenge is to design and code an information point that will allow users to use a menu system to select information about security threats and how they can be prevented and combatted.

Hackers have remotely disrupted internet-enabled cars, adjusting the temperature, windscreen wipers and wiper fluid, and even disabled the brakes and taking over the steering.

Why cyber security?

Everyone takes the security of their homes and possessions seriously, but they often never take any precautions to protect their personal data from online hackers. Everyone needs to take precautions to protect their cyber security.

- Networks are always at risk from unauthorised access especially from online hackers.

- Sometimes banks or large companies are targeted. But individuals are at risk too.

- Any individual with an internet connection and an email address is likely to be targeted, often having their personal details and credit card numbers stolen. This is known as identity theft.

- There were 34 151 confirmed instances of identity fraud recorded in the first three months of 2015!

🔑 Key term

cyber security: the use of technology, working practices and precautions designed to protect networks, computers, programs and data from attack, damage or unauthorised access

Social engineering

There are many threats to network security. Most target the computers and communications software, but many target far weaker links: the people who use them.

A study released in 2015 found that human error was the root cause of 52 per cent of all security breaches to networks. The greatest problems were failure to follow general policies and procedures, general carelessness and a lack of knowledge of threats.

Some of the methods used to breach network security need no knowledge of programming or computers. They are low-tech 'con-tricks', referred to as social engineering, aimed at enticing vulnerable people to disclose their personal information.

Examples of social engineering are blagging, phishing, pharming and shouldering.

Blagging

This is sometimes called pretexting and can be done face-to-face, by telephone or by computer. The criminal invents a scenario to try to get the victim to divulge information, for example pretending to be a charity or an official such as a police officer, bank employee or an insurance claims investigator.

Phishing

This is when fraudsters send emails claiming to be from a bank or building society e-commerce site in order to find out your personal and financial details.

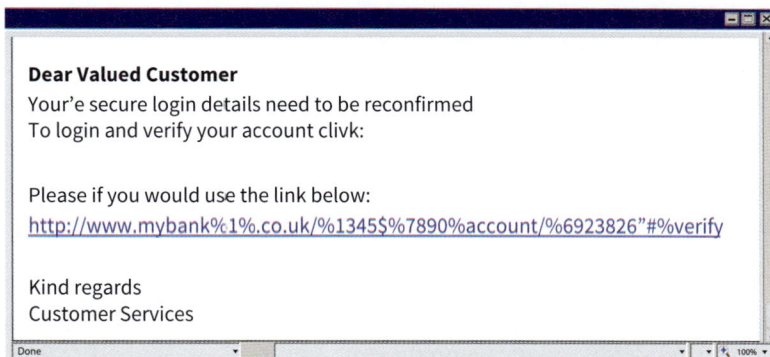

Key term

social engineering: psychologically tricking people into divulging their secret information or doing things that they would not otherwise do

---

Dear Valued Customer
Your'e secure login details need to be reconfirmed
To login and verify your account clivk:

Please if you would use the link below:
http://www.mybank%1%.co.uk/%1345$%7890%account/%6923826"#%verify

Kind regards
Customer Services

Done   100%

Phishing emails can often be recognised by:

- **Urgency:** they want you to respond quickly, without thinking, for example to supply your bank details before the account is suspended.

- **Careless use of language:** they often contain spelling errors and a careless writing style.

- **Impersonality:** you may not be addressed personally but only as 'Dear Customer'. However, as the criminals become more sophisticated they are able to find your personal details from various sources such as social networking sites.

- **False links:** you are asked to click on a link which leads to a website controlled by the criminals.

- **Attachments:** sometimes you are asked to open programs or documents sent with the email; these attachments may contain spyware.

The term 'phishing' comes from 'fishing': bait is spread across the internet in the hope that people will bite. 'Spear phishing' is where individuals or particular groups who might have specialist information are targeted. It has been estimated that over one billion pounds a year is being stolen through phishing scams.

Pharming

In Chapter 13, we saw that domain names are used to represent IP addresses and how they are translated back into the IP address when you enter the name in your browser. If you have visited the site before, then this IP address will be stored on your computer (in the DNS cache) and your browser will connect without using the DNS. Malware that you may have received in an email can change the IP address of the domain name to a bogus one that you will then visit instead.

Malware can also infect the DNS servers themselves so that everybody is directed to the bogus site!

To prevent pharming users should:

- Check that the http address of the site is the one you intended to visit.

- Check that there is a secure connection (http**s**) if you have to enter sensitive information.

- Check the site's security certificate.

- Install the latest security updates.

- Install antivirus software.

> **Key term**
>
> antivirus software: software designed to prevent, detect and remove malware

Shouldering

This is sometimes referred to as 'shoulder-surfing' and it involves finding login names, passwords, credit card and PIN (personal information numbers) details by direct observation, such as:

- someone in an office watching others entering passwords

- watching someone enter their PIN at a cash machine (ATM)

- an employee at a shop or petrol station watching a PIN being entered

- criminals using binoculars or closed circuit television to watch from a distance or record users entering sensitive information.

To prevent shoulder surfing, shield the keypad from view by using your body or cupping your hand over the keypad. When working on a laptop, keep your back to a wall with no open sides. Extra care should be taken when entering a password.

ACTIVITY 14.1

Catherine has just received the following email:

> **Dear customer**
> As we have updated the system we need you to check you're details as soon possible.
>
> Please if you would use the link below:
> http://onlinecustomer.thebank.com/account/login
>
> You will be asked to enter details of your password and card details.
> If you do not respond within 24 hours your account is terminated.

a. What is the name given to this type of email?

b. State three clues that might suggest that it is a bogus email.

Malware

Malware is short for **mal**icious soft**ware** and includes any software designed to:

- disrupt the functioning of a computer system
- gain unauthorised access to a computer system
- gather information from the users without their knowledge.

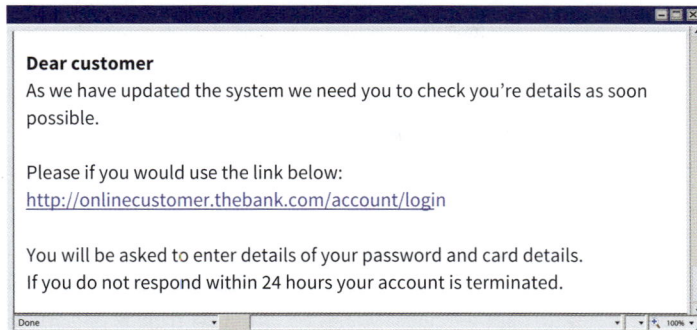

Types of malware include:

- virus
- worm
- Trojan (or Trojan horse)
- spyware
- adware.

Key terms

malware: software designed to gain unauthorised access to a computer system in order to disrupt its functioning or collect information without the user's knowledge

Trojan horse: a phrase used to describe unintentionally accepting a hidden enemy attack; from an ancient Greek myth where a large wooden horse (in which enemy soldiers were hidden) was left as a gift for the city of Troy, and the people took it into the city, sealing their fate

Malware	Explanation	Precautions

Virus	A virus is a computer program that is hidden within another program or file. It can replicate itself into other programs or files which are then often passed by a user to other computers. Viruses usually have a harmful effect, for example corrupting or deleting data on a disk.	• Install a firewall to ensure software is not downloaded without your knowledge (see later in this chapter).
		• Ensure that the operating system is up to date.
		• Install the latest security updates or set to automatic update.
		• Install antivirus software and ensure that it is constantly updated or set to automatic update.
		• Ensure that the antivirus software can scan emails.
		• Use adware removal software.
		• Install anti-spyware protection software that removes or blocks spyware.
		• Avoid opening emails and attachments from unknown sources.
		• Surf and download more safely:
		  • Only download programs from trusted websites.
		  • Read all security warnings, licence agreements and privacy statements
		  • Never click 'Agree' or 'OK' to close a window. Instead, click the red 'x' in the corner of the window.
		  • Be wary of popular 'free' music and movie file-sharing programs.

Worm	A worm is different to a virus in that: • It has an independent existence: it does not have to exist inside another program or file. • It does not need human action to spread it: it can travel unaided to other computers, for example through a network or by sending itself in emails to everyone in a user's address book. As the worm is making thousands of copies of itself it will use the computer's resources and cause other programs to run slowly. On a network, it will consume bandwidth and affect performance. Some worms cause damage by deleting data or by creating a 'back door' so that the hacker can take over the infected computer with potentially catastrophic consequences.	
Trojan or Trojan horse	A Trojan does not replicate or attach itself to other files. It must be installed by a computer user who thinks they are installing legitimate software or by opening an email attachment (that is why they are called Trojan horses). • Trojans can just be annoying, for example by changing the desktop and adding new icons. • They can also be malicious, for example by deleting files and destroying system information. • They can also create 'back doors' to computer systems so allowing criminals to access your personal data, for example they can transmit your key presses or screen shots across the internet to the criminal's computer.	
Spyware	Spyware similar to Trojans in that it 'spies' on the computer and sends information to a criminal. The difference is that it comes packaged with other software, for example free software that you download so that the user does not know they are installing it.	
Adware	Adware is the name given to programs that are designed to: • display advertisements on the computer • redirect search requests to advertising websites • collect marketing-type data about users, for example the types of websites that they visit, so that customised adverts can be displayed. When this is done without a user's consent it is considered to be malware. Adware is often bundled with freeware and shareware programs or a computer can be infected by visiting a malicious website. Adware can also be used to refer to free programs that have adverts within them. The user can often register the program and pay a fee to have the adverts removed.	

ACTIVITY 14.2

1. Describe the differences between a virus and a Trojan horse.

2. Describe the precautions that users should take to prevent infections by viruses and Trojan horses.

ℹ Remember

1. Malware describes software intended to prevent a computer functioning correctly, to corrupt or destroy data, or to collect user information without users' knowledge.
2. Malware includes viruses, worms, Trojan horses, spyware and adware.
3. Users can protect their computer systems and use software to destroy malware.

> **Complete Interactive Activity 14b on Cambridge Elevate**

Methods of attack

When criminals are targeting large organisations, there are various methods of attack.

Type of attack	Description of attack
Brute force attacks	This is a general attack on a network and requires no specialist knowledge of the individuals or the organisation. It is a trial-and-error method of obtaining login names and passwords to allow the hacker to access the network. For example, automated software can be used to generate and try millions of login names and passwords. Success is based on computing power and the number of combinations tried rather than an ingenious algorithm. That is why it is called 'brute force'.
Denial of service (DoS) attacks 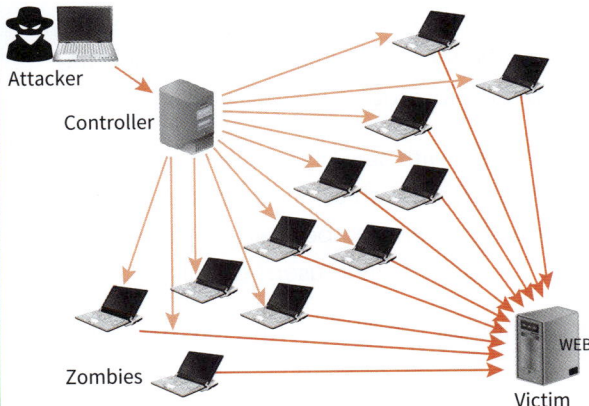 Attacker Controller Zombies WEB Victim	This type of attack is designed to make a network or website grind to a halt by flooding it with useless network communications such as repeated login requests. The criminals may use malware to take control of lots of computers ('zombies') that all send login and information requests at the same time. The criminals may use these attacks to extort money from the company to stop the attacks. They may offer their services to a rival company to 'take out' the competition. They may be used by activists (known as 'hacktivists') to punish a company that they deem to be unethical.
Data interception and theft	In Chapter 13, we saw that data travel across all networks, including the internet, in packets. This data traffic can be intercepted. The criminals use packet analysers or 'packet sniffers' to intercept the packets which are then analysed and their data are decoded. The criminals can therefore steal sensitive data such as logins, passwords, credit card numbers and PINs.

Type of attack	Description of attack
SQL injection	Websites, for example social networking sites and online banking sites, use databases to store users' details. In order to query these databases and search for information, structured query language or SQL may have to be used. When a user enters their username and password, SQL is used to check if these are correct and stored in the database. Criminals can input specially created commands instead of a username or password. These commands can bypass the login requirements and gain access to the database so that the criminals have access to the data, for example names, addresses and credit card details. Organisations must carefully check the data entered to filter out these dangerous commands. This is called input sanitisation.
Zero-day attacks	Before new software is released it is tested as much as possible, but there may be a security fault, unknown to the developers, that allows illegal access. This security hole can then be accessed by hackers who may then be able to gain network access. The day that the flaw is discovered is known as 'day zero' and then there is a race between the hackers who want to exploit the flaw and the developers who want to fix it.

Key term

input sanitisation: when any inputs from users that could be harmful to its systems are filtered out and removed

Download Worksheet 14.2 from Cambridge Elevate

Securing a network

There are many methods that can be taken to counteract these threats and preserve network security.

Physical security

The first line of defence is to prevent unauthorised people from entering the buildings where the network equipment is located.

- Keep access doors locked and fit them with security recognition measures, for example keypads or biometric systems such as fingerprint pads or iris scanners. Biometric security recognition can also be used on mobile devices to authenticate users. Use swipe cards containing users' details.

- Install closed circuit television to monitor the exterior and interior of the building.

- Install burglar alarms and monitors in all rooms.

- Fit radio frequency identification (RFID) chips to all equipment so that an alarm will sound if the equipment is taken out of the building.

- Use chains and locks to attach equipment to work benches.

Network policies should cover the use of removable media such as USB flash drives, smartphones, CDs, DVDs, MP3 players and even digital cameras.

These devices pose a threat as malware can be introduced to the network and data can be removed and stolen.

Even if data is removed for work reasons, the company may be sued if this data is covered by the Data Protection Act and there is the risk of the devices being lost or stolen.

The policy will probably state that the connection of such devices is prohibited unless the user has made a request for their use.

The policy will probably state that only devices provided by the company can be used.

Often employees transport documents containing unencrypted sensitive information on these devices which are easily lost or stolen.

User security

People are the weakest points in any system causing the greatest security risks. The following methods can be used to minimise the risks:

- Network access control: a user's access rights can be set, for example:
  - they may not be able to see certain folders and files
  - they may be able to read the folders and files, but be unable to edit or delete them.

Threats to networks are often caused by incorrect access rights. They may have been configured incorrectly so that unauthorised people gain access to files.

- Authentication: all users should have to log in to the network using login names and passwords. Weak passwords are a major security risk. A weak password is one that is easy and quick to detect by humans and computers. Hackers often use 'brute force techniques' employing software that will try every single combination of letters, numbers and symbols until it finds the correct combination. The greater the length and variation in the characters, the longer it will take.

> **Key term**
>
> **authentication**: the process of determining whether someone trying to log into the network is who they declare to be

Default passwords are often supplied when a user account is first set up and the user should be made to change them as the same one is often used for most or all accounts.

Hardware devices such as routers are often supplied with a default password too, such as 'password'. If the default password was not changed then a hacker who knew the make of the router could guess what the password was.

Hackers can also find out users' details such as their dates of birth or names of relatives, items which are used in weak passwords. Passwords should:

- be at least 8 characters long
- contain both numbers and letters
- contain both upper and lower case letters
- contain at least one non-alphanumeric character (!, $, ?, etc.)
- never contain a user's identifiable information such as name, date of birth, phone number, postcode, car registration, etc.

- be changed regularly

- not reuse previous passwords

- never be written down

- never be shared with other users.

Many users expect to be able to use removable media devices such as USB flash drives, smartphones, CDs, DVDs, MP3 players and even digital cameras.

These devices pose a serious security threat:

- Data can be stolen by unauthorised copying.

- Users can copy or install unauthorised data and applications onto an organisations servers and client computers.

- Malware can be introduced onto the system through removable devices.

- Users can install device unauthorised drivers for devices.

Organisations should have policies in place to cover the use of authorised removable devices and the transfer of data for work purposes as devices can be lost or stolen. There have been many news reports of sensitive data that has been lost or stolen from the removable devices of Government employees.

Encryption

All data that is transmitted or stored on a network must be considered at risk of being read by unauthorised personnel. It should therefore be converted into a form that they cannot understand.

- Encryption is the scrambling of data into a form that cannot be understood by unauthorised recipients.

- The encrypted data must be decrypted back to its original form.

- The encryption is carried out using a 'cipher'.

- A common method is the use of a 'public' and a 'private' key.

- The public key is freely available to anyone, but the private key is only known to the owner.

- Messages encrypted by a particular public key can only be decrypted with the corresponding private key.

Firewalls

Firewalls are either software or hardware devices that protect against unauthorised access to a network, and are primarily used to prevent unauthorised access from the Internet. They can be configured to prevent communications from entering the network and also to prevent programs and users from accessing the Internet from the network. For example, a firewall can inspect the incoming packets and reject those that are from an IP address not on a trusted list or block communication to certain external IP addresses.

Download Worksheet 14.3 from Cambridge Elevate

MAC address filtering

In Chapter 13, it was stated that every network adaptor is created with a hardware number permanently 'burned' into it. This permanent hardware number is known as the media access control (MAC) address.

Every MAC address is unique so that all data on a network can be sent to the correct component.

MAC address filtering allows network administrators to list allowed MAC addresses in a table thus ensuring that only specified devices can connect to the network. This filters devices, not users. This method is not very effective in wireless networks as a hacker using a wireless network analyser will be able to see the MAC addresses of every allowed device, and can change their computer's MAC address to match one that is in the table of allowed addresses (although this is tricky to do).

Network policies

Network administrators should also have procedures in place to prevent problems occurring, as well as plans to follow if there is a problem. It is essential that good procedures are rigorously applied.

These can include an acceptable use policy consisting of rules that users should adhere to.

Identifying vulnerabilities

The security of a network should be constantly tested to see if it is vulnerable to attacks by hackers. This is called 'penetration testing'. Penetration testing is the testing of a computer system, network or web application to find vulnerabilities that an attacker could exploit. The test then indicates how those vulnerabilities could be exploited to demonstrate the havoc that could be caused.

The main objective is to determine security weaknesses. It can also be used to test an organisation's security policy, the security awareness of the users, and the organisation's ability to identify and respond to security incidents.

A penetration test asks: 'How effective are our current security controls'?

White-box penetration testing

This penetration test simulates hacking by 'insiders'; people who have full knowledge of the network. It is also called 'full disclosure' testing as the testers are given details of items such as IP addresses, source code, network protocols and even login names and passwords.

Key term

penetration test: tests a computer system or network to find vulnerabilities that an attacker could exploit

Black-box penetration testing

This is also called 'blind testing' because testers are given very little or no information prior to the penetration test. The testers have to find their own way into the network without any knowledge of usernames, passwords and other normal means of access. Black-box testing is more realistic to everyday penetration attacks and will produce more accurate results, giving the most realistic indication of potential threats to the network.

Personal security

There are several methods used to improve a user's personal security and to prevent others from creating or changing the details of an online account in their name or accessing their mobile devices.

Email confirmations

When a user is creating or updating an online account, they are often sent an email to their registered address with a link to access before their account changes are actioned.

This is to confirm the identity of the person requesting the changes.

CAPTCHA

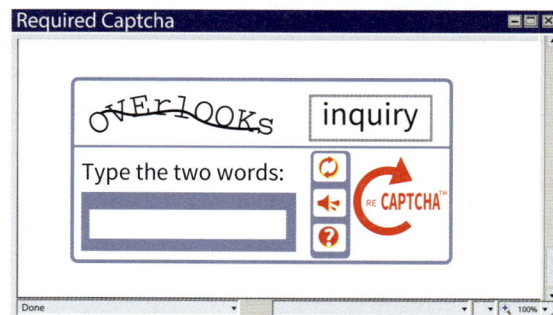

The name CAPTCHA stands for **C**ompletely **A**utomated **P**ublic **T**uring test to tell **C**omputers and **H**umans **A**part. It is intended to ensure that the user attempting to gain access to a network is a human and not a computer that would be unable to read the distorted characters given in the test. The CAPTCHA test is intended to protect online networks from access by malicious bots.

Bots can be used for malicious purposes such as harvesting email addresses from internet sites and cause denial of service attacks.

The CAPTCHA should prevent the bots from accessing a site.

Biometric authentication

Biometric authentication is becoming common on mobile devices such as smartphones and tablets where the most common method is fingerprint scanning.

Automatic software updates

The producers of programs such as web browsers, email programs, image viewers, instant messaging software and media players are continually identifying security flaws in their software that can be exploited by hackers.

To counter the risk they produce updates or 'patches' which should be applied to the software to counteract the threats.

Key terms

bot: (also known as an internet bot or WWW bot) is software that runs repetitive automated tasks over the internet

biometric authentication: a process that validates the identity of a user who wishes to sign into a system by measuring some unique, physical characteristic of that user such as fingerprints, eye scans, face recognition and voice prints

patch: software designed to update a computer program in order to fix or improve it

Unpatched software is a major security flaw. Users can download these patches and apply them themselves, but many manufacturers offer automatic software updates. If the user agrees to these, they are downloaded and applied without the user having to do it themselves so that the software is always up to date.

Complete Interactive Activity 14c on Cambridge Elevate

Remember

1. There are many ways in which criminals can attack network systems and steal data.
2. Methods include brute force, DoS, SQL injection and zero-day attacks.
3. Networks must be kept as secure as possible using methods such as
   a. access control
   b. user security
   c. firewalls
   d. encryption.
4. Organisations should have network policies in place to detect and withstand attacks and recover if their security is breached.
5. Penetration testing involves carrying out controlled attacks using all of the methods that criminals would use to test the safeguards in place.

Practice question

1. A mail-order company stores thousands of customers' details, including debit and credit card details, on its computer network. The company is concerned about the security of this information.
   a. Explain three measures that the company could take to prevent unauthorised access to their computer system.
   b. Describe a measure that the company could take to prevent employees from accessing information that they are not permitted to view.
   c. Explain how penetration testing can assist the company in improving its security.

Your final challenge

Your final challenge is to design, code in the programming language you are studying, and test an information point for people searching for information about computer security.

It should:
- have a menu and sub-menu system so that users can select the options they need
- have details about all of the risks faced by computer users
- provide information about how these threats can be avoided and combatted.

Download Self-assessment 14 worksheet from Cambridge Elevate (this content has not been approved by AQA)

15 Ethical, legal and environmental impacts of digital technology on wider society

Learning outcomes

By the end of this chapter you should be able to:

- investigate and discuss the following issues in relation to the development and impact of digital technologies:
  - environmental
  - ethical
  - legal
  - cultural
- discuss issues of data collection and privacy
- describe the legislation relevant to digital technology.

★ Challenge: design and code an online test

- An increasing number of examinations are now taken online using a computer rather than pen and paper.
- From the driving theory test to school tests and examinations, greater use is being made of computerised testing and marking systems.
- Your challenge is to design and code an online test which can be taken on and marked by a computer, based on the issues raised in this chapter.

Digital technology can allow people who have lower limb paralysis to walk again using their own muscles by transmitting nervous impulses from their brains.

Why digital technology?

Digital technology provides huge benefits in all areas of people's lives.

Impact of digital technologies

Here are two examples of how things were in the past:

- Portable music players looked like this 50 years ago. They had very short battery life, the records could get scratched and they could have terrible sound quality.

- Typewriters were mechanical machines for writing text. They were heavy, the text was difficult to correct, and there was no spell checker! It was also difficult to make multiple copies of the documents.

If you wanted to make copies of your typing, you put two pieces of paper in the typewriter at the same time with a piece of special paper, called carbon paper, between them to make a 'carbon copy' (this is why we write 'cc' on an email when we want to copy someone in).

Digital technologies have had a huge impact on everyone in the world. Even if people do not personally have access to them, or choose not to use them, they cannot escape their consequences.

Now, we should consider the impact of technologies on our world.

Environmental impact

The impact of digital technology on the environment has been both positive and negative.

Negative impact: energy consumption

All electronic devices use electricity in order to work. Even if they use solar cells to provide the electricity, they are still using energy, and the production and disposal of solar cells has some environmental impact.

- All electronic equipment consumes electricity when it is working and also when it is recycled.

- In the production of computer equipment, huge quantities of electricity are used in addition to non-renewable and in some cases, dangerous materials.

- As more people are using computers, tablets and smartphones then more electricity is required and electricity production has harmful effects on the environment.

- Social networking makes the problem worse as all those tweets, status updates and selfies have to be stored somewhere. They are stored on servers in huge data centres; in 2011 it was calculated that there were half a million worldwide. Data centres consume vast amounts of electricity for the running of the stacks of servers and more importantly for cooling them down.

In 2012 data centres in the USA consumed electricity equivalent to 30 nuclear power stations. By 2030, about 40 per cent of the world's energy consumption will be due to the use of digital devices.

Negative impact: e-waste

Many people do not dispose of digital devices properly. 'E-waste' is any waste created by electronic devices that have been thrown away, as well as waste substances created in the manufacture and use of electronic devices.

- Landfill sites take up areas of land that could be used for other purposes.

- Toxic substances, such as lead, mercury and cobalt, can get into the soil and the water supply from the landfills and cause health problems.

- Some companies illegally send e-waste to developing countries. Ghana in Africa has become a huge dumping ground for e-waste from developed countries.

- Computers from British firms, universities and colleges and even from government departments have been found in tips in developing countries.

- As a result, people in these countries are exposed to toxic substances either when trying to extract the toxic substances from the e-waste or when the huge piles are buried or burned.

E-waste can be disposed of safely:

- Many firms and organisations pay private companies to recycle their old computers safely.

- Councils also pay these companies to recycle electronic items collected at their household waste recycling centres.

- Another solution is to donate the equipment to charities who distribute it to people who need it but cannot afford to buy it.

Positive impact: monitoring climate change

Digital technology can be used to monitor the environment and transmit and analyse the data.

Digital devices are used to monitor climate change and transmit and analyse the data.

Computers use the data to build complex models that are used to understand the factors affecting climate change and make predictions for the future.

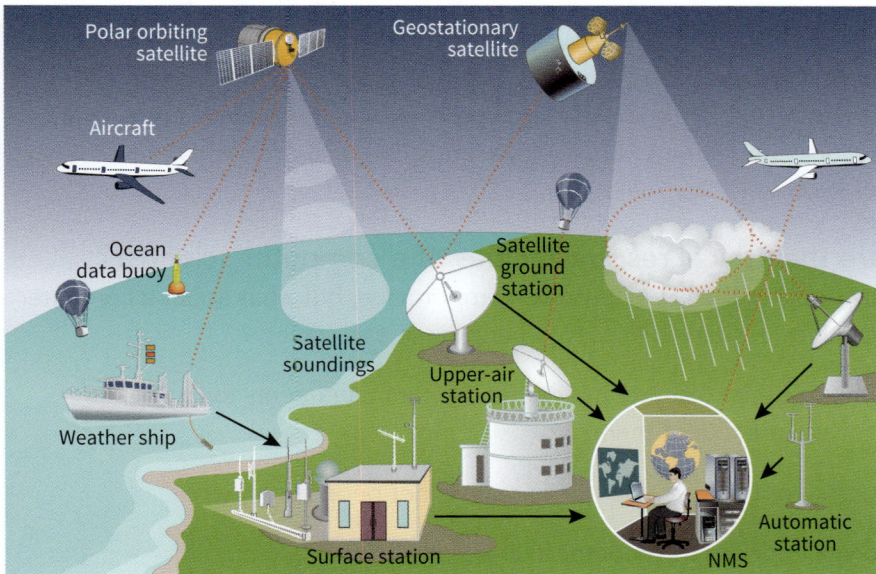

Positive impact: conservation

Digital tracking devices can be attached to animals to study their behaviour.

Conservationists use digital tracking devices with GPS and digital maps to track and study the lives of endangered species. The results are analysed by computers to help improve conservation strategies.

Mobile phone apps are also used by environmental groups to share information and educate people about the consequences of their actions.

Positive impact: energy production

Computer software is used to design efficient devices to produce electricity from wind and wave power. The designs can then be tested using computer models without having to first build the models and then modify them in the light of the results. Computer software is also involved in their production and installation.

Wind turbines and tidal energy technologies are designed and tested using digital technology.

ACTIVITY 15.1

'Computer scientists have a role to play in combating global climate change.' Discuss this statement.

Remember

1. Digital technology has detrimental effects such as:
   a. use of electricity in production and functioning
   b. disposal in landfill sites
   c. release of toxic chemicals when burned or buried in landfills.
2. Digital technology has environmental benefits such as:
   a. monitoring and modelling of climate change
   b. use in animal conservation
   c. design and development of 'green energy' sources.

Download Worksheet 15.1 from Cambridge Elevate

Complete Interactive Activity 15a on Cambridge Elevate

Ethical issues

There are several laws that govern the use of computer systems and data. However, ethics is about good practice and behaving in a morally correct way. Ethical actions are different from lawful actions. Sometimes actions can be legal, but are they ethical?

What are the ethical responsibilities of a computer scientist?

Obviously obeying the law is of primary importance, but what about a computer scientist's ethical responsibilities to other people and society?

The Computer Ethics Institute has written 10 commandments for computer scientists. Here are four of them:

1. Thou shalt not use a computer to harm other people.

2. Thou shalt not use a computer to steal.

3. Thou shalt think about the social consequences of the program you are designing.

4. Thou shalt always use a computer in ways that ensure consideration and respect for your fellow humans.

These commandments stress that a computer scientist must always consider how their work can affect other people.

Ensuring that their programs are correct and are fully tested, especially when failure can lead to fatal consequences, is important for points 1 and 4 above.

Have a look at this example.

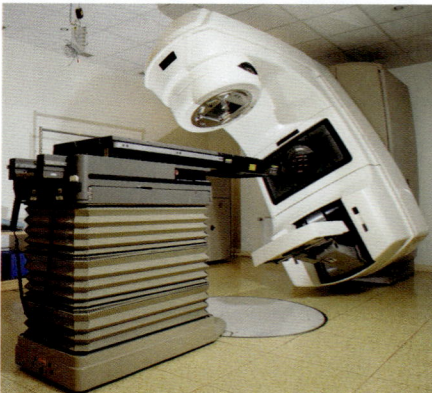

The Therac-25 was a radiotherapy machine used to treat patients with cancer by directing beams of electrons or X-rays at tumours. Between 1985 and 1987, there were six accidents where patients were given massive overdoses of radiation resulting in severe injury or death.

The previous model, the Therac-20, used electronic control systems to prevent overdoses, but it was decided to use software control in the Therac-25. The software was developed by one person and was not properly documented or tested.

The programmer obviously failed in his responsibilities to the users of the device and his software. But was the programmer aware of this? Had he received proper training from the company? Should the software have been developed by a team? Should it have been independently reviewed?

ACTIVITY 15.2

Carry out research into the Therac-25 case and report your findings, discussing the causes and the ethical responsibilities of both the computer scientist and the company.

Surveillance cameras

Computer scientists have been involved in the development of software for cameras and surveillance systems. They have developed number plate and face recognition systems so that every individual person in a city like London can be tracked.

Obviously there are benefits in doing this, such as crime prevention, but should computer scientists consider the possible misuse of these systems? Have they given the authorities too much power in being able to track their citizens 24 hours a day, secretly?

Cracking and hacking

A hacker (originally referred to as a computer expert) was a person who enjoyed learning programming languages and computer systems and was an expert in their use. As illegal access to computer systems became more common the term was also used to cover those individuals with criminal intent. The original hackers insisted that all their hacking activities did no harm and that the new term of 'cracker' should be used and their actions should be described as cracking.

Hackers and crackers obviously have extensive computer knowledge and might work as computer scientists. Hackers might illegally access a computer system or network site to promote a social cause and they are referred to as hacktivists. Hacktivists claim to use computers and computer networks to promote political ends, chiefly free speech, human rights and ethical behaviour.

But is this ethical? Can someone commit a criminal act and claim it is ethical? Do the ends justify the means?

Social consequences

One of the Computer Ethics Institute's commandments states 'Thou shalt think about the social consequences of the program you are designing.'

The pictures show two developments resulting from software created by computer scientists: ATMs (Automated Teller Machines) that allow people to withdraw cash from their accounts and the use of robots in manufacturing processes.

Both developments have led to people losing their jobs in the manufacturing and banking industries. Should computer scientists have considered this when creating the software?

> ### 🔑 Key terms
>
> **hacking:** the unauthorised access to a computer system and the data it contains
> **cracking:** gaining unauthorised access to computer systems, often on a network, by bypassing internet security systems with the intent of committing a crime or with malicious intent

223

ACTIVITY 15.3

Technological developments that cause social change, such as those of the industrial revolution, are often resisted if they are not managed correctly. The term 'Luddite' is often used as meaning anyone who resists all new technology but the original 'Luddites' were not fighting against the new technology (most of them were actually using it). They were fighting against the effects it had on their livelihoods and living conditions because the new technology allowed employers to pay them less and as a result many were starving.

What is your opinion? Is it justified to use new technology to enrich yourself even if it leads to other people starving?

Carry out research on the original 'Luddites'.

Drones

It is now possible to fire missiles at people and drop bombs on them thousands of miles away using drones, making it easier to kill thousands of people.

Computer scientists developed the control and guidance software to allow this to happen, but the same software has had other, beneficial uses for ship and commercial airline safety. What is your opinion on the ethics of developing this software?

ACTIVITY 15.4

Robots have rapidly evolved from being human controlled to being automated and now they are becoming fully autonomous.

Autonomous robots are designed to make their own decisions without human involvement or guidance. Who is responsible for their actions?

Discuss the ethical issues raised for computer scientists developing these systems.

ACTIVITY 15.5

A computer scientist develops and programs systems for various companies, both large and small.

Inevitably, as her programs are used, bugs are discovered and enhancements are requested.

There are more bugs to fix and enhancements to be made than she can cope with and she has to prioritise her work.

She has an ethical dilemma. Should she:

- drop everything and fix each bug as it appears?
- fix the bugs of the larger companies first as they pay more money?
- decide which bugs are the most serious and fix them first?

Key term

autonomous: the ability to act on their own without human input

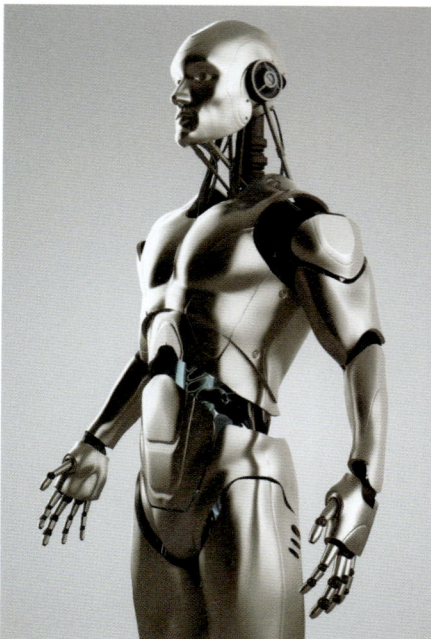

How can she decide which bug is more serious than another or how much harm it will do?

Discuss what she should do in order to act in an ethical way.

Security and privacy

Everyone who owns a mobile phone is being tracked by mobile phone masts around the world.

The service providers keep records of locations, calls, texts and websites visited.

This data is useful for marketing and targeting adverts at particular users.

Internet service providers keep similar records of all online activity.

What we do online using computers and phones during every minute of every day is recorded!

Under the **Regulation of Investigatory Powers Act 2000 (RIPA)** data can be handed over without a warrant or any other safeguards to the police and security services to prevent terrorism and organised crime. The data are handed over as part of surveillance methods that can also include footage from surveillance cameras and having police officers actually following people around.

Most people would accept this intrusion on their privacy to prevent terrorism, but what if it was used for other purposes such as checking if a family put their bins out on the wrong day? Using the data for a purpose other than for which they were intended is called 'mission creep'.

> ### Key term
>
> **Regulation of Investigatory Powers Act 2000**: this is a law that regulates the behaviour of officers who are investigating crime; it covers surveillance, listening to phone calls, obtaining information from internet service providers, mobile phone providers etc.

ACTIVITY 15.6

Local councils have used data collected under RIPA in the following circumstances:

1. to check on families to make sure they were not cheating on school catchment area regulations

2. to check if people are putting out their bins on the correct day.

Thinking about the original reason that the law was passed, what are your views on extending its scope in these ways?

Impact on culture and society

Digital technologies have had a profound effect on the ways in which people live, work and relate to each other.

Mobile phones have had a huge impact on societies and cultures around the world. As well as improving communications in areas where there are no cables and infrastructure, they have allowed everyone to record and report on what is happening. This has been especially important in countries where there are repressive governments who prevent free speech. The use of mobile phones and social media has assisted with many popular revolutions.

Digital technology has led to improvements in medicine.

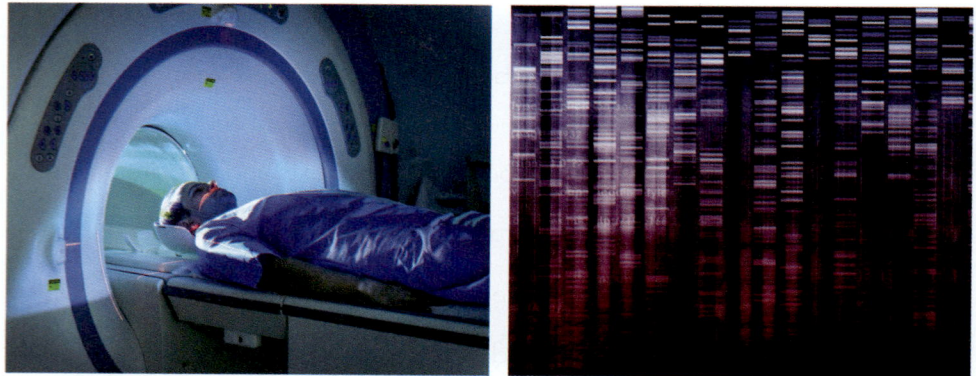

Full body scanners assist in the early diagnosis of cancer, cardiac disease and other abnormalities.

Computers are used in medical research such as the analysis of DNA.

They are also used to store patient records and enable easy access to the records in emergencies.

Computer-based implants

The Verichip, first produced in 2004 but discontinued in 2010, was a chip that could be implanted beneath a person's skin and its unique 16-digit number could be used for authentication when scanned. It was discontinued for security reasons as hackers could read the chips and create duplicates: an example of identity theft.

Modern research is concentrating on computer-based implants in the brain and spinal cord to interface with person's nervous impulses and help paralysed people to walk again.

Wearable technologies

A smartwatch can communicate with a smartphone and be used for messaging and viewing notifications. Some technologies can be worn and are referred to as wearable technologies.

They include wearable headsets, smartwatches, health and fitness trackers, glasses and clothing that can communicate with a smartphone app and be made to change colour or display a video.

Digital rings allow users to control devices through finger movements.

Wearable technology is predicted to have a huge beneficial effect on health.

Key term

wearable technology: includes clothing or electronic devices that can be carried or attached to the body

Smartwatches already allow people to monitor their daily activity and heart rate but specialist devices are being developed for specific purposes such as the monitoring of asthma symptoms. The wearable device can communicate with an app running on a smartphone.

Devices attached to people with back problems can transmit data to an app which then analyses it and suggest how the person should modify their posture.

There is even a smart wearable device to help people to stop smoking. It senses changes in the body and delivers medication to prevent the craving for nicotine.

Wearable technology can also be used to increase efficiency. A large supermarket issued warehouse staff with armbands to scan stock that they were moving and delivering so that they did not need to use pencil and paper or scanners. This technology was also used to monitor the staff and awarded points according to how hard they were working. Understandably, this has been considered as a misuse of the technology.

Modern cars use computer control through an electronic control unit (ECU) for their engine management systems. Problems are diagnosed and fine tuning is done by computer. Gone are the days when a mechanic 'tinkered' with the engine to set the timing or ensured there was a correct mixture of petrol and air.

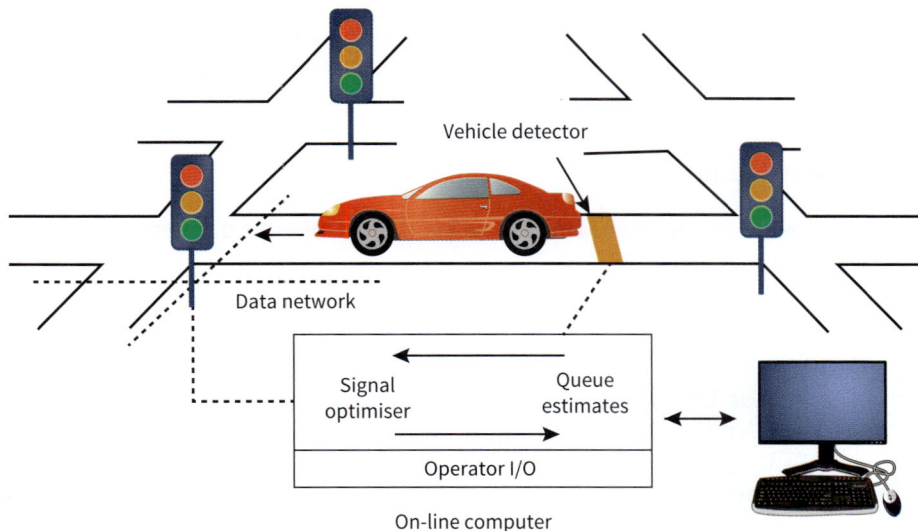

All of the traffic lights in a town or city are computer controlled and centrally coordinated using wireless networks. However, that can be a problem if the networks are not secure. Read this article about commuters who hacked into the system to ensure they had green lights all the way to work: www.cambridge.org/links/kase4002

Computers have had an impact on education and the way information is presented and used. Now most classrooms have an interactive whiteboard that can be used like a large, touch-screen laptop.

The computer games market is huge and is expected to reach 103 billion dollars by 2017. Over 70 per cent of people in the United Kingdom played a computer

game in 2014 with women making up 52 per cent. The largest group is aged over 44 with young people and teenagers making up 22 per cent. The most successful entertainment product of all time, beating blockbuster films, is a British game. Can you discover which game it is? It took over 1 billion dollars worldwide in just three days.

ACTIVITY 15.7

The use of digital technology has had an impact on some of these areas of society and culture.

For each one, give **three** examples of that impact:

a.   the ways in which people interact with each other

b.   work and employment

c.   education

d.   leisure.

The digital divide

People without access to technology, or who do not know know how to use technology, are at a disadvantage to those who do. This is known as the digital divide. There is a digital divide between countries and also between individuals within the same country. For example, in England, there are areas without high speed internet access.

The digital divide can have a huge impact on people who have little or limited access to digital technologies.

- Having low IT literacy can lead to low-paid employment or even being unemployed.

- The Office for National Statistics has calculated that in 2015 over 3.5 million households in the UK had no internet access. In 2013, it was estimated by the charity Age UK that it costs households without internet access an extra £276 per year because they cannot shop or pay bills online.

- Thirty-eight per cent of those who are not online are also unemployed but:

  - from 2013 they have had to prove that they are actively searching for jobs **online** using the government's Universal Jobmatch website

  - If they do not do this, their benefits can be stopped. Therefore they have to travel to libraries for access.

ACTIVITY 15.8

What is your opinion? Should people be penalised if they cannot afford to pay for internet access? Is it ethical to force unemployed people to travel miles to access a government website? Are they being punished for being unemployed? Is that the type of society you want to live in?

> ## ℹ️ Remember
>
> 1. Being ethical means behaving in a morally acceptable way by doing things that society recognises as good.
> 2. Actions can be legal but not ethical and vice versa.
> 3. Using digital devices, such as mobile phones and the internet, enables organisations to track people's movements and daily activity.
> 4. There is a digital divide between those who have access to IT and digital devices and those who do not.

Legislation

The increased use of computerised systems and digital communications has led to the enactment of new laws to control that usage.

Personal data about everyone, including financial information, is held online. The Data Protection Act 1998 was introduced to protect this personal data. It tells organisations who collect and store this information exactly how they can and cannot use it. It also gives people whose data is stored the right to access and change it.

The act imposes conditions on organisations that collect and store data and gives rights to those whose data is stored: the data subjects.

Legal responsibilities of data holders	Rights of data subjects
Data must be processed fairly.	A right of access to a copy of the information comprised in their personal data.
Data can only be used for the purpose for which they were collected.	A right to object to processing that is likely to cause or is causing damage or distress.
Only data that are actually needed should be held.	A right to prevent processing for direct marketing.
Data must be accurate and up to date.	A right in certain circumstances to have inaccurate personal data rectified, blocked, erased or destroyed.
Data must not be held longer than they are needed for.	A right to claim compensation for damages caused by a breach of the Data Protection Act.
Data will be used in accordance with the rights of the data subjects.	
Data will be kept safe.	
Data will not be transferred to any country where they do not have similar data protection laws.	

⬇ Download Worksheet 15.2 from Cambridge Elevate

The Data Protection Act was a response to people's concerns about the storage of personal details online.

a. List **five** reasons why online storage is less secure than paper-based storage.

b. List **five** advantages of online storage over paper-based storage.

The Computer Misuse Act 1990 was enacted to counteract hacking.

It lists three types of offence:

1. Unauthorised access to computer material: using a computer to attempt to access a program or data which you know you are not authorised to access. Just trying to access the information is an offence, even if you are not actually successful in doing so.

2. Unauthorised access with intent to commit further offences: to attempt to access a computer system with the intention of committing a further offence. For example, this could include trying to access personal details with the intention of committing identity theft.

3. Intentional and unauthorised destruction of software or data: to gain unauthorised access to a computer with the intention to change the data or impair the running of the computer, for example by planting a virus.

ACTIVITY 15.10

Identify which of the three crimes in the Computer Misuse Act is being committed in the following examples:

a. A user sees that another user has left their computer unattended and alters and deletes files from their personal area.

b. A user accesses a computer to find out a person's credit card number and security code so they can use them to buy goods online.

c. A student tries to guess the password of a class member and then tries to log into the network as that person.

The Freedom of Information Act 2000 was passed to end a culture of secrecy in government. Before its introduction, the UK had no legislation obliging the public sector to make information available to the general public.

The Act creates a right of access to information held by public authorities which includes central and local government, the health service, schools, colleges and universities, the police and courts.

The person requesting the information does not have to give a reason, but the holder does have to give a reason if they refuse a request. The requester can then appeal to the Information Commissioner.

There have been many disclosures of information in the press enabled by the Freedom of Information Act, including, in May 2015, details of expense claims made by leading politicians.

Copyright Design and Patents Act

Computer scientists like artists, authors, photographers and musicians earn their money by charging people to use their work, for example to use their software, listen to their songs or read their books. They own the copyright to their work so nobody can use it without paying for it, or asking them first.

For example, only the creator of an artistic work has the right to make copies or perform the work in public or give other people permission to do so. This is covered by the Copyright Designs and Patents Act 1988.

Sometimes people try to copy other's work. Copying software such as games and applications, scanning books, downloading pirate tracks, etc. means the creators of these works are not paid. This is illegal and unethical. The increased use of digital technology and the internet has made piracy easier.

This has a significant impact on computer scientists, artists, musicians, photographers and writer, who cannot continue their work if they are not paid. It has been estimated 50 per cent of jobs in the music and film industries will be lost in the next few years owing to illegal copying and downloading.

Even in pre-digital, analogue, times there were infringements when people copied vinyl records onto tape cassettes.

Oracle, the company that owns the patents and rights to the Java programming language, has sued Google for using Java APIs (application programming interfaces) in its Android operating system. Initially the courts found in favour of Google but on appeal Oracle won the case. A group of eminent computer scientists have now asked the courts to declare that APIs should not be covered by copyright laws.

Patent wars

Some companies have been fighting for years in the American courts over software and technology used in mobile phones and who owns the rights to special features. Eventually, one such company was ordered to pay another company a significant amount of money in compensation.

Several major companies formed a coalition to assist in claiming that the design patents covered only minor features and if the court upheld the judgment and forced damages to be paid, it would harm consumer choice and damage companies spending billions of dollars a year on research and development.

🔑 Key terms

copyright: the legal right of the person who created a work to use that work exclusively or to grant permission to others to use it

patent: a permission granted by a government to a person for a set period of time to stop other people from making use of their inventions without their permission

ACTIVITY 15.11

Can you find any examples on the internet of cases challenging patents and leading to these patent wars?

Creative Commons licencing

Creative Commons is an organisation that provides licences allowing the creators of copyright works to give the public permission to share and use this work under certain conditions. They give people the right to share, use, and even build upon a work that an artist, musician or writer has created.

There are several levels including:

- public domain: there are no restrictions. The work can be used without permission or attribution for any purpose.

- attribution licence: the work can be used, distributed and copied as long as the creator is given credit for having created it.

- attribution-non-commercial licence: as above but only if the work is used for non-commercial purposes.

Complete Interactive Activity 15b on Cambridge Elevate

Download Worksheet 15.3 from Cambridge Elevate

Remember

1. Legislation includes:
    a. Data Protection Act 1988
    b. Computer Misuse Act 1990
    c. Copyright Designs and Patents Act 1988
    d. Freedom of Information Act 2000.
2. Creative Commons licences allow creators of copyright works to give permission to others to share and use the works.

Practice question

Discuss the ethical and economical arguments surrounding software piracy.

Download Self-assessment 15 worksheet from Cambridge Elevate (this content has not been approved by AQA)

Your final challenge

Your final challenge is to design and code a program to test students' knowledge of the topics covered in this chapter.
The program should:
- include questions covering all of the items in the chapter
- be text based or have a graphical user interface.

The questions can be of any type, for example multiple choice, text entry, yes/no response or drag and drop. The users should be given their final score and told which questions are incorrect.

Non-exam assessment

The programming project contributes 20% of the marks for the GCSE award.

It allows you to demonstrate your computational thinking skills in creating an algorithm to solve a problem, and then to code and develop the solution through testing and by resolving any problems that you find.

You may use any of the following programming languages for the solution:

C#

Java

Pascal/Delphi

Python

VB.Net

The report

You must produce a report detailing all of the stages you have gone through to solve the problem and to create and refine your solution. This report is important because it provides evidence of the methods you have used to solve the problem you have been set.

You will be awarded marks for:

- designing the solution   maximum of 9 marks
- creating the solution   maximum of 30 marks
- testing the solution   maximum of 21 marks
- potential enhancements and refinements   maximum of 10 marks
- overall quality of the report   maximum of 10 marks

An example problem illustrating the following methodology is given in Chapter 7.

Before you start

It is important that you fully understand what the task is asking and what you will have to do, so you could do the following:

- Read it and reread it.
- Highlight important points.
- Make notes.
- Use a spider diagram or mind map to help you visualise all of the sub-problems and the components you will need for the solution; this will help you to identify the inputs, outputs and processing that will be required.

You should use your skills in decomposition, abstraction and pattern recognition to fully inspect the problem, break it down into its component parts and resolve what has to be done to solve it.

As you are getting to know the task you could be thinking ahead about the programming techniques and constructs that you will need to use (e.g. conditional statements and iteration).

The assessment scheme is set out to reflect the formal method for creating a solution: design; creating the solution or implementation; testing; and suggesting enhancements and refinements.

The quality of the report is also assessed and it should be as complete as possible with relevant content and consistent structure.

Designing the solution (9 marks)

This section of the report could explain the designs for the sub-tasks and requirements you have identified.

In the design section there could be full algorithms for solving all of the sub-tasks displayed as flow diagrams and/or pseudo-code. The algorithms could contain all of the variables and validation techniques identified in the analysis. You may also want to consider the data structures and text file/database structures.

The pseudo-code should be fully commented to describe how the subroutines (functions and procedures) are called by the main program and why they are included. The design should clearly show that the solution is modular and makes use of functions and/or procedures.

The design could contain features to ensure that you have taken account of:

- possible areas for misuse (e.g. entering erroneous data or selecting inappropriate options)

- validation and authentication.

There could be a consideration of a suitable user interface explaining how the user will interact with the system.

Consider whether your design is complete enough for another competent person to use it to code a successful solution.

Creating the solution (30 marks)

Your report could include a full description and explanation of the coding of the solution.

Consider including the following:

- explanations of how you have made it robust by including routines to counteract user misuse and to validate all of the data that are entered
- explanations of testing you have carried out on the subroutines as you have developed them
- changes you have made in the light of your testing
- lists of the resources you have used (e.g. function libraries or program add-ins for developing a graphical user interface).

As a reminder, your code could:

- be modular, using functions and procedures so that it is well organised
- use meaningful variable names, all written in the same way (e.g. as camel case)
- be fully commented so that each section is fully explained.

Your solution will also be assessed for your coding skills and use of appropriate programming techniques.

Solving the problem with 20 lines of clear, concise code is more elegant than solving it with 100 lines of code containing unnecessary variables and constructs.

Elegant code is the result of a careful analysis and thoughtful algorithms.

An elegant solution will make someone say: 'Wow! Why didn't I think of that?'

As you are developing your code you might like to consider issues such as modularity, commenting, appropriate use of techniques, validation and error handling.

Tip

The assessment scheme in the specification has a list of indicative coding skills required. It is worth looking at this!

Remember

Solving the problem with 20 lines of clear, concise code is more elegant than solving it with 100 lines of code containing unnecessary variables and constructs.

Testing the solution (21 marks)

Your report could show how you have thoroughly tested all aspects of your solution.

You could include a test plan listing all of the tests that will be carried out, the reason for carrying out each test and the expected results.

The following shows an example test plan:

Test number	Purpose of test	Test data	Expected result	Actual result	Purpose of test
1	to test the validation routines for data entry	3	9	9	**valid** or **in range** test of data input
2	to test the validation routines for data entry	1	data will be accepted	data were accepted	boundary test
3	to test the validation routines for data entry	10	data will be accepted	data were accepted	boundary test
4	to test the validation routines for data entry	12	message stating that the number should be between 1 and 10	message displayed as expected	**erroneous** or **out of range** test

The tests should show that you are aware of all the problems that could arise when the program is used by another user. For example, it could check that data have actually been entered and that they are within the expected range.

You could do the following:

- Ensure that it lists the test data to be used, plus the expected and the actual outcomes (you can show the actual examples with screen prints).
- Explain how you took remedial action to solve any errors you found that were highlighted by your tests.
- Explain how any unresolved issues could be solved given more time.

- Present evidence of carefully selected samples to show that thorough testing has been carried out.
- Explain how the evidence demonstrates the robustness of your solution and shows that the requirements of the problem have been achieved.

Potential enhancements and refinements (10 marks)

You may want to discuss the efficiency and robustness of the solution, and suggest ways in which it could be improved.

Think about critically evaluating your solution – no solution is perfect and you can demonstrate your ability by thinking of ways in which it could be improved.

Overall quality of the report (10 marks)

Finally you should thoroughly check your report to ensure that it is presented to a high standard in a structured way with all of the sections clearly labelled.

It is worth checking the assessment scheme in the specification to identify what is required for the report.

However, in general it is good practice, when writing any report, to ensure the following:

- It is complete.
- The grammar and spellings are correct.
- All of the content is relevant to the task.
- A range of technical terms have been used accurately.
- All sections are structured consistently.

Ways that you could make the structure of your report clear include using:

- a table of contents
- numbered sections and subsections
- numbered captions for diagrams and screenshots
- references to any sources used.

A good way to ensure that your report covers all of the required items is to create a check list and tick off each item when you are sure that it is covered adequately.

Glossary

A

abstraction: the process of removing unnecessary details so that only the main, important points remain

address: a number assigned to the storage location so that it can be accessed

adjacent items: items of data that are next to each other

alpha testing: testing done by the programmer

analogue: data which can use any value in a continuous range

antivirus software: software designed to prevent, detect and remove malware

applet: a small application or program created in the Java programming language that can be sent to a user along with the web page they have requested (e.g. applets of animations, word processors and games)

application software: are end-user programs. Also called 'apps' or 'applications', they are written to be run by users to perform user-identified tasks. For example, for productivity or entertainment. They include word processor, spreadsheet, database, game and image editing software

argument: the name for the data that is passed to a subroutine by the main program

array: a structure that contains many items of data of the same type. The data are indexed so that a particular item of data can be easily found

assembler: a program which translates assembly language into machine code

assigning: giving a variable a value

authenticate: confirm that a user's password has been entered correctly

authentication: the process of determining whether someone trying to log into the network is who they declare to be

autonomous: the ability to act on their own without human input

B

bandwidth: the amount of data that can pass through the transmission medium per second. It is often called the bit-rate

base 2: a base 2 number system represents numbers using two different symbols. Each place value is two times bigger than the place to its right

base 10: a base 10 number system represents numbers using ten different symbols. Each place value is ten times bigger than the place to its right

beta testing: testing done by a selected group of individuals to receive their feedback about how well the program works

bitmap image: A set of bits that represents a graphic image, with each bit or group of bits corresponding to a pixel in the image.

binary digits: computers can only communicate directly in 0s and 1s; series of 0s and 1s represent the codes for various instructions and data

binary tree: items of data are stored in *leaves* and the branch points are called *internal nodes*. In a binary tree, each node has at most two branches or *children*

biometric authentication: a process that validates the identity of a user who wishes to sign into a system by measuring some unique, physical characteristic of that user such as fingerprints, eye scans, face recognition and voice prints

BIOS: the Basic Input/Output System controls the computer when it is first switched on

bot: (also known as an internet bot or WWW bot) is software that runs repetitive automated tasks over the internet

boundary test: where the highest or lowest acceptable numbers and those just inside or outside the acceptable range are entered; these check any logical errors that might have been introduced using the <= and >= operators

bus: a bundle of wires carrying data from one component to another or a number of tracks on a printed circuit board fulfilling the same function

byte: a group of eight bits

C

cables: a way of connecting computers using cables and sockets

cache: a temporary data store so that the data can be accessed very quickly when needed

called: subroutines are 'called' by the main program: this means that they are started up, given data, run and then the output is collected by the main program (if required)

casting: converting one data type to another data type

central processing unit: this is the component of the computer that controls the other devices, executes the instructions and processes the data

character: often abbreviated to 'char', it is a variable that holds one letter, number or symbol

character set: the list of binary codes that can be recognised by computers as being usable characters

closed: when the computer has finished using the file, closing it saves it safely on to the disk for permanent retention

colour depth: the number of bits used to encode the colour of each pixel

comment: a piece of information for the programmer. It does not form part of the program and is not executed by the computer. It is for information only

compare: assess how items of data are similar or different to each other, to help decide which order they should go in

compiler: a program that converts high-level programs into low-level programs

compound statement: a statement where Boolean operators are combined and work together to examine if several conditions are true or false

compression: reducing the size of a file so that it takes up less storage space or bandwidth when it is transmitted

concatenation: the placing together of two separate objects so that they can be treated as one, for example a string variable can be

joined end-to-end to produce a larger string

constant: a value that does not change while the program is running

control signals: electrical signals that are sent out to all of the devices to check their status and give them instructions

copyright: the legal right of the person who created a work to use that work exclusively or to grant permission to others to use it

cracking: gaining unauthorised access to computer systems, often on a network, by bypassing internet security systems with the intent of committing a crime or with malicious intent

cyber security: the use of technology, working practices and precautions designed to protect networks, computers, programs and data from attack, damage or unauthorised access

D

decision: when a question is asked (as in selection) the answer will lead to one or more varied alternative actions

decomposition: breaking a problem down into smaller, more manageable parts which are then easier to solve

domain name: this is part of the URL for a resource on the internet. When the domain name is used, it will be converted to the correct IP address by the Domain Name Service (DNS) and the contact will take place

driver: a program called by a peripheral manager to operate any device, for example printers, the screen and mouse, when they are called by the main program

dry run: the program is run on paper and each stage is carefully analysed to see what values the various variables, inputs and outputs have. At this stage, a computer is not being used

dynamic array: an array that has not had its size defined and can change as data are appended

E

efficiency: efficiency can be assessed by: How long it takes a program to generate a result. How much code has been written to generate the result. How much memory it uses

electrical storage: storing data using devices such as flash memory. This is sometimes called 'solid state'

entity: something recognised as being capable of an independent existence, which can be uniquely identified, and about which data can be stored. It can be a physical object, for example a car, person, student or book. It can also be a concept, for example a customer transaction

erroneous test: data that should be rejected are deliberately input to check that validation routines are functioning as expected (sometimes called an 'out-of-range test')

Ethernet: a set of rules or protocols for computers to follow when communicating data over a network

ethics: a system of moral principles, often shown by doing things that society recognises as being good or by acting in ways that individuals and societies believe reflects good values

execute: to run a computer program or process

execution: when a program or part of a program is run by the computer

F

field: one item of information. For example, the make, model and maximum speed of a car are all fields

file handle: a label that is assigned to a resource needed by the program. It can only access the file through the computer's operating system

flash memory: this is memory which can be programmed electrically but then keeps its data when the power is turned off

frequency: the number of waves produced per second

G

global variable: a variable that is used in the main program. It can be used by any of the commands or subroutines in the program

H

hacking: the unauthorised access to a computer system and the data it contains

hardware: the physical components making up the computer and its peripheral devices

heat sink: a metal device, glued to the CPU chip with thermally conducting paste, to transfer the heat away from the chip

HTML: hypertext markup language (HTML) is used to write web pages for the internet as well as for ebooks, PDF documents, etc.

I

identifier: the 'name' given to a variable

index: a number that identifies each element of an array or string

input sanitisation: when any inputs from users that could be harmful to its systems are filtered out and removed

instruction: an instruction to a microprocessor to perform a specific task

instruction set: the set of instructions for a particular processor which it will understand and be able to process

integer: a whole number without decimals (can be positive or negative)

interpreter: a program which will run a high-level program directly, interpreting the instructions and converting them, without them needing to be in the machine code of a computer

IP address: a unique software address used to communicate over the internet

iteration: a procedure or a set of statements or commands is repeated either for a set number of times or until there is a desired outcome

L

legal: abiding by the laws and rules of a particular country or jurisdiction

local area network: network used for data transmission by computing devices within one building or site, such as an office building , a school or university campus. It is usually owned and managed by a single organisation, for example a school or business

local variable: a variable that is used only within a subroutine. When the subroutine has completed its work, the local variable is discarded

logic circuit: a combination of standard logic gates used to perform complex logic operations where the outputs of some gates act as the inputs to others

logical error: a problem in the design of the algorithm

logic gate: an electronic component that either produces or does not produce an output depending on the inputs it receives and the logic rule it is designed to apply

logical operator: operators such as 'AND', 'OR' and 'NOT' that perform a Boolean operation on some inputs

loop: part of a program where the same activity is repeated over and over again for a fixed number of times or until a condition is met. Usually the condition is stated within the loop itself

lossless compression: no data are lost and the file can be decompressed with all of its information intact

lossy compression: data are lost in the compression process and when the file is decompressed it will not contain all of the original material

low-level language: a computer language that provides instructions that are the same as or very similar to a computer's instruction set

M

machine code: the instructions in a form that the processor can execute; strings of 0s and 1s

magnetic storage: storing data using magnetic media such as a hard disk drive

main memory: the physical memory that is internal to the computer. The word 'main' is used to distinguish it from storage devices such as hard disk drives. It can be directly accessed by the CPU

malware: software designed to gain unauthorised access to a computer system in order to disrupt its functioning or collect information without the user's knowledge

menu: a set of options to help a user find information or use a program function

microwaves: electromagnetic waves which can be used to carry data between computers

mnemonic: a tool or technique designed to help a person's memory (e.g. 'Richard of York gave battle in vain' used to help remember the order of the colours of the spectrum: red, orange, yellow, green, blue, indigo and violet)

modem: short for 'modulator-demodulator'; modulates and demodulates signals (converts them from digital to analogue and vice versa) sent from and received by a computer over a communications network

motherboard: the main printed circuit board of the computer; it has connectors that other circuit boards can be slotted into

multitasking: when a computer is running several programs at the same time

N

nibble: half a byte

node: places on the network where there are items of equipment

normal test: ensures that the correct result will be produced with the expected data (sometimes called an 'in-range test')

O

opcode: the code for the instruction being given

operand: the data that might be attached to the opcode and that the instruction might need to work with

operator: the symbol that tells the computer what to do

optical storage: storing data using optical devices such as CDs and DVDs

ordered: the data in the list are stored in order

overflow error: when a calculation produces a result that is greater than the computer can deal with or store in the available number of bits

overwritten: if a file exists on the computer and a new file is created with the same name, the new file is kept and the old file is written over and lost

P

packet: a small block of data that is transmitted from one computer to another

packet switching: a method of data transmission in which a message is broken into a number of parts which are sent independently over the most suitable routes. The message is reassembled at the destination

parallel processing: when the processor cores work on different parts of the same program

parameter: the names of the variables that are used in the subroutine to store the data

passed from the main program as arguments

parentheses: brackets

patch: software designed to update a computer program in order to fix or improve it

patent: a permission granted by a government to a person for a set period of time to stop other people from making use of their inventions without their permission

penetration test: tests a computer system or network to find vulnerabilities that an attacker could exploit

permission: a rule that is set up for a particular file to control who can edit, read or write on the file

personal area network: network used for data transmission over short distances by devices such as laptops, mobile phones, tablets, media players, speakers and printers

pixel: the smallest possible dot on a computer screen which can have its colour set independently; images are made up of pixels

place value: the value that a digit's position in a number gives it, for example (for decimal) in the number 356, the digit 5 has a value of 50 whereas in the number 3560, the digit 5 has a value of 500

printed circuit board: the base that supports the wiring and electronic components that are soldered to it or fit into sockets on the board

process: an activity that a computer program is performing

property: one of the characteristics of attributes of a data type, for example one of the properties of a string variable is its length, that is the number of characters it contains

protocols: agreed rules for requesting and sending data across networks

pseudo-code: a language that is similar to a real programming language but is easier for humans to use and understand when they are developing algorithms. Although it doesn't actually run on a computer it can easily be converted to a regular programming language

R

RAM: (also known as random access memory) memory that can be used by computer programs to store data and instructions, but all of its data is lost when the computer is switched off

read mode: the file is opened in such a way as to allow the data to be used by the program but not to allow the program to write any data to the file. Using read mode protects the data file from being accidentally changed by the program

real: a numeric variable which can have a fractional value; it can have digits on either side of a decimal point. Commonly used to store currency values, for example 1.5 for £1.50

redundancy: the number of items of data in a file which are repeated

register: a storage location that is inside the CPU itself

Regulation of Investigatory Powers Act 2000: this is a law that regulates the behaviour of officers who are investigating crime; it covers surveillance, listening to phone calls, obtaining information from internet service providers, mobile phone providers etc.

relational operator: an operator which compares two items of data, for example <, >, =

resolution: the number of pixels per square inch on the computer screen. The higher the resolution, the better the picture

run: a sequence of repeated characters, for example: aaaa

S

sampling: making physical measurements of the amplitude of an electronic representation of the sound wave at set time intervals and then converting the measurements to digital values

searching: looking through a file to see if particular data are there

secondary storage devices: devices that store information but which do not lose the data when they are switched off; usually not on the main circuit board (motherboard)

selection: a question is asked, and depending on the answer, the algorithm takes one of two courses of action

sequence: the order in which tasks are carried out

sequential: starts at the beginning and moves through the list one-by-one

social engineering: psychologically tricking people into divulging their secret information or doing things that they would not otherwise do

sorting: putting items of data into a precise order, for example alphabetical or numerical

static array: an array that is of a set size

storage location: a place in RAM where a single piece of data can be kept until it is needed

string traversal: moving through a string, one piece of data at a time; sometimes this might just mean counting

subroutine: a self-contained piece of code that can be 'called' by the main program when it is needed

substring: a smaller string which is part of the main string that you are using

sub-tasks: small steps making up a larger task

syntax: the rules of spelling, punctuation and grammar of a language so that the meaning of what is being communicated is clear (humans can make allowances if the rules are broken, but computers can't!)

syntax error: a grammatical mistake in the code. For example, it could be caused by a misspelling, e.g. 'prnit' instead of 'print' or by missing colons, semi-colons or brackets

systems development cycle: a defined process of planning, designing, creating, testing and deploying an information system

system software: software that manages the operation of the computer, tells it what to do, tells it which programs to run, controls what the users see on screen etc.

T

table: a collection of rows and columns forming cells which is used to store data and user information in a structured and organised manner

test data: carefully planned sample data, used to try out programs to check that they give the correct outputs

testing plan: a plan for the way in which a program is to be tested

trace table: while a dry run is being worked through, a table is drawn up showing the values of each variable, input and output, and how they change as the program is running. A trace table has columns for each of the variables and rows for each of the steps in the algorithm

topology: the structure of the network

traverse: go through a loop item by item

Trojan horse: a phrase used to describe unintentionally accepting a hidden enemy attack; from an ancient Greek myth where, a large wooden horse (in which enemy soldiers were hidden) was left a a gift for the city of Troy, and the people took it into the city, sealing their fate

true or false: indicates whether a logical statement is correct or incorrect; this could be represented in a computer as 1s (true statements) and 0s (false statements)

truth table: a table that shows all the possible combinations of outputs which can occur with all of the different possible inputs; usually used with logic problems

U

user interface: the way in which a user interacts with a computer system

unambiguous: this means that the instruction cannot be misunderstood and the correct action will always be performed. All instructions given to a computer must be unambiguous or it won't do anything!

V

validation: the process through which the program checks that data are sensible and that they are suitable for use by the program

variable: a container which is used to store values such as an 'attempts' counter

volatile: data are permanently lost when power is switched off

W

wearable technology: includes clothing or electronic devices that can be carried or attached to the body

wide area network: a network connecting local area networks over a large geographical area

Wi-Fi: consists of the protocols needed for communication over a wireless network. It is the wireless version of a wired Ethernet protocols

write mode: the program can 'write' to the file or in other words it can change the data in the file

Index

Acknowledgements

The authors and publishers acknowledge the following sources of copyright material and are grateful for the permissions granted. While every effort has been made, it has not always been possible to identify the sources of all the material used, or to trace all copyright holders. If any omissions are brought to our notice, we will be happy to include the appropriate acknowledgements on reprinting.

p001t/© Andrey Esin/Shutterstock, p001cr/ © iurii/ Shutterstock, p002/ © Eric Gevaert/Shutterstock, p003tl/ © 5 second Studio/Shutterstock, p003tr/ © Andy Heyward/Shutterstock, p004tl and tr/ © claudiodivizia/ iStock/Thinkstock, p026t/ © Sooa/Shutterstock, p026b/ © Webitect/Shutterstock, p027/ © Marcio Silva/iStock/ Thinkstock, p046t/ © Mopic/Shutterstock, p046c/ © piotr_pabijan/Shutterstock, p50t/ © Michael Schoppe | 8mb.de/Shutterstock, p054/ © Pavlo Burdyak/ Shutterstock/ p060/ © katiejaney/Stockimo / Alamy stock photo, p068t/ © iStock/Thinkstock, p068c/ alice-photo/Shutterstock, p070/ © Only background/ Shutterstock, p078/ © Daniele Carotenuto/Shutterstock, p080cl/ © Georgia Barnett/Alamy Stock photo, p080t/ ©Jay Brousseau/Getty Images, p084/ © Andrey_Popov/ Shutterstock, p092t/ © 2/Medioimages/Ocean/ Corbis, p092cl/ © rinderart/Alamy stock photo, 095b/ © Leudej Rodjanapaitoon / Alamy stock photo, 095cr/ © Library of Congress Prints and Photographs Division Washington, D.C. 20540 USA. [LC-DIG-ds-00175], p101/ © Tetra Images/Corbis, p116t/ © Giuseppe Cesch/ Getty Images, p116cl/ © Shotshop GmbH / Alamy Stock Photo, p118/ © tarczas / Alamy stock photo, p124b/ © Decollage Toucan/ESA/epa/Corbis, p130t/ © Jan Bruggeman/Photographer's Choice/Getty Images, p130cl/ © Michelle O'Kane/Moment/Getty Images, p134cl,cr,bl,br/ © Courtesy of David Waller, p150tl, cl, bl, b/ © Courtesy of David Waller, p152t/ © Kelly Redinger/Design Pics/Corbis, p152cl/ © INTERFOTO / Alamy Stock Photo, p154bl/ © Roman Milert /

Alamy Stock Photo, p154 c/ © Route55/Thinkstock, p154cr/ © Brand X Pictures/ Getty Images, p155b/ © PhotoQuest/Archive Photos/Getty Images, p156b/ © Simon Belcher / Alamy Stock Photo,p162c/ © kubais/ Shutterstock , p166t/ © scanrail/Thinkstock, p165b/ © cogal/E+/Getty Images, p168t/ © Rafe Swan/Cultura/ Getty Images, p168cl/ © Timashov Sergiy/Shutterstock, p174t/ © wanpatsorn/Shutterstock, p174cl/ © OJO Images Ltd/Alamy Stock Photo, p177/ © Volodymyr Krasyuk/Shutterstock, p178b/ © Reload_Studio/ Thinkstock, p178c/ © Powerbee-Photo/Shutterstock, p184t/ © Michelle O'Kane/Moment/Getty Images, p190t/ © alexskopje/Thinkstock, p190c/ © LanKS/ Shutterstock.com, p199b/ © www.cablemap.info, p199c/© amasterphotographer/Shutterstock, p199t/ © Toria/Shutterstock, p206cl/ © Hannu Liivaar / Alamy Stock Photo, p206t/ © Nicolas Ayer/ EyeEm/ Getty Images, p208/ © Image Source/Getty Images, p209b/ Wavebreak Media ltd / Alamy Stock Photo, p212b/© Image Source/Getty Images, p214/ © YAY Media AS / Alamy stock photo, p218b/ © trekandshoot / Alamy Stock Photo, p218c/ © Brain Computer Interface Lab / University of California, Irvine, p218t/ © Pete Farrington / EyeEm/Getty Images, p219b/ © cybrain/ Shutterstock, P219t/ © Sergio Azenha/Alamy Stock Photo, p220/ © Huguette Roe/Shutterstock, p221b/ © OPD/LOOK AT SCIENCES/SCIENCE PHOTO LIBRARY, p221c/ © ER_09/Shutterstock, p221t/ © PhotoStock-Israel / Alamy Stock Photo, p222b/ © Alexander Tihonov/Shutterstock, p223bl/ © Dario Sabljak / Alamy Stock Photo, p223bc/ © RainerPlendl/ Thinkstock, p223t/ © Sean Pavone / Alamy Stock Photo, p224/ © SCIENCE PICTURE CO/SCIENCE PHOTO LIBRARY, p226tc/ © Cultura Creative (RF) / Alamy Stock Photo, p226tr/ © Kheng Ho Toh / Alamy Stock Photo, p227br/ © Adam Hester/Getty Images, p228tl/ © BSIP SA / Alamy Stock Photo, p230bl/ © eldeiv/Shutterstock.